FINDING THE
HIDDEN-BALL TRICK

FINDING THE HIDDEN-BALL TRICK

THE COLORFUL HISTORY OF BASEBALL'S OLDEST RUSE

Bill Deane

ROWMAN & LITTLEFIELD
Lanham • Boulder • New York • London

Published by Rowman & Littlefield
A wholly owned subsidiary of The Rowman & Littlefield Publishing Group,
Inc.
4501 Forbes Boulevard, Suite 200, Lanham, Maryland 20706
www.rowman.com

Unit A, Whitacre Mews, 26-34 Stannary Street, London SE11 4AB

British Library Cataloguing in Publication Information Available

Library of Congress Cataloging-in-Publication Data

Deane, Bill.
Finding the hidden-ball trick : the colorful history of baseball's oldest ruse / Bill Deane.
pages cm
Includes bibliographical references and index.
ISBN 978-1-4422-4433-7 (hardcover : alk. paper) -- ISBN 978-1-4422-4434-4 (ebook) 1. Hidden
ball trick (Baseball) 2. Baseball--Defense. 3. Deception. I. Title.
GV869.5.D43 2015
796.357'24--dc23
2014036326

∞™ The paper used in this publication meets the minimum requirements of
American National Standard for Information Sciences Permanence of Paper
for Printed Library Materials, ANSI/NISO Z39.48-1992.

Printed in the United States of America

For John Thorn, friend and mentor, who changed the direction of my life.

CONTENTS

INTRODUCTION

I first started "collecting" hidden-ball tricks in the 1980s. Employed as senior research associate for the National Baseball Library from 1986 to 1994, and working on my own projects after hours, I spent hundreds of hours a year doing research for myself and others. Inevitably I stumbled upon interesting tidbits that had little or nothing to do with what I was working on and kept various lists based on these findings. Many of these feats, like three-pitch innings and scoring from first base on a single, turned out to be more common than I thought. But the hidden-ball trick (HBT) remains a rare and remarkable event, roughly as uncommon as a no-hitter.

It took the better part of a decade for the number of entries in my HBT list to reach double digits. Then came my big breakthrough: contact with Retrosheet. A nonprofit organization with close ties to the Society for American Baseball Research (SABR), Retrosheet was founded in 1989, by David W. Smith, and is vitally assisted by dozens of other volunteers. Their mission: to collect and computerize the scoresheet of every game in major league history. This is a daunting task, to be sure, but thanks to their efforts, 90 percent of all games since 1901— and 100 percent of all games since 1949—have been documented. David Smith and David Vincent searched their files and added scores of HBTs (and possible ones) to my list. Other individuals who have been particularly helpful include, alphabetically, David Arcidiacono, Greg Beston, Charlie Bevis, Cliff Blau, Steve Boren, Jim Charlton, Clem Comly, Dan Desrochers, John Gecik, Mike Grahek, Billy Hitchcock,

Dick Hunt, Herm Krabbenhoft, Dave Lamoureaux, John Lewis, Joe McGillen, Peter Morris, Rod Nelson, Bill Nowlin, Marc Okkonen, Tom Ruane, Lyle Spatz, Joseph St. George, Steve Steinberg, Dick Thompson, Rich Thurston, Bob Timmermann, Wayne Townsend, and Frank Vaccaro. Pre–SABR historians Ernest J. Lanigan and Harold Kaese also provided much assistance with their own documentation of this play. To date, with considerable help from these individuals and others, I have documented more than 250 successful executions of the HBT in the major leagues (with dozens yet to be found).

Another source of help has been SABR's online listserve (SABR-L). Through periodic pleas on SABR-L, I have received information or leads on dozens more HBTs. One example illustrates what I think SABR is, or should be, all about. In December 1997, after one of my posts, Bob Caldwell wrote me with his recollection of Dave Bergman pulling a HBT while playing first base for the Tigers. Caldwell provided many interesting details but none that could narrow down the game candidates. I was left with 579 possible games (the number of games that Bergman played first base for Detroit) between 1984 and 1992, so I filed the incident on my "unsubstantiated possibilities" list. Months later, Jeffrey Turner recalled seeing Baltimore's Alan Wiggins fall victim to the trick, also providing interesting but inconsequential details. This could have occurred in practically any of the 232 games Wiggins played for Baltimore between 1985 and 1987, so it became merely another "possibility." Then in March 1998, Greg Beston recollected seeing Dave Bergman nab Alan Wiggins on the HBT. Eureka! I contacted Caldwell and Turner with the details offered by the other correspondents, and each agreed that it sounded like they were remembering the same incident.

Analysis of the official American League day-by-day sheets from 1985 through 1987 narrowed the possibilities down to five games: ones in which Wiggins batted or pinch-ran for Baltimore against Detroit, while Bergman had at least one putout at first base. A check of the five contests in the *Sporting News* nailed it down: "The Tigers used the hidden-ball trick and caught Alan Wiggins napping in the third inning of their 6–3 victory over Baltimore June 17 [, 1986. Pitcher Randy] O'Neal threw to first baseman Dave Bergman, who faked a throw back to the pitcher and tagged out Wiggins, who had wandered off the bag."[1]

Thirteen years later, when I bought the video *Super Duper Baseball Bloopers* at a garage sale, I finally got to see the play for myself.

I would like to be able to report that all my unsubstantiated possibilities get wrapped up this neatly, but that's not the case. I've still got more than 30 on my list, which is included here in hopes that someone can offer additional details, confirmation, or refutation on one of these incidents.

Along with my collection of tricks came a pile of stories about these plays, some of them hilarious. I shared some of these stories at a couple of local SABR chapter meetings, and it was the late Gene Carney who half-jokingly suggested I turn them into a book. I eventually realized that I indeed had enough material for a book, it was just a matter of pulling it all together.

I'll readily admit that some of my sourcing is haphazard or incomplete. Most of this research was carried out with no expectation of compiling a book based on it, and much of it was mailed or e-mailed to me from people listed this introduction, sometimes with footnote information, sometimes not. Rest assured that no incident made my list unless I had solid evidence that it belonged there.

I

WHAT IS THE HIDDEN-BALL TRICK?

The New Dickson Baseball Dictionary defines the hidden-ball trick (HBT) as a "time-honored legal ruse in which a baseman [I'd say 'in-fielder'] conceals the ball and hopes that the base runner believes it has been returned to the pitcher. When the runner steps off the base, he is summarily tagged out with the hidden ball."[1] Author Paul Dickson, who originally cited 1908 as the earliest known published reference, also notes that the term has been used in other areas, particularly football and politics. For example, a 1947 article quotes Representative Al Gore Sr. calling a proposed tax cut the "hidden-ball trick—a sham and a phony."[2] And a 1948 *San Francisco News* article about senatorial quick-fix solutions says, "Those are 'hidden-ball' plays—now you see it, now you don't." The term has also been used euphemistically in discussions of the military, entertainment, and finance.

Society for American Baseball Research (SABR) member Eric Sallee gives a good explanation of what is required for the play to be successful, saying, "[T]he sun, the moon, and the stars all have to be in alignment in order for it to work:

1. Play cannot be 'dead,' i.e., time is not 'out';
2. The pitcher cannot be touching or straddling the pitching rubber;
3. The umpire has to be alerted or paying attention;
4. A bonehead runner must be willing to take a lead off a bag before the pitcher toes the slab; and
5. The bonehead runner's teammates and base coaches all have to be asleep, as well."

How is the play done? It often follows a sacrifice bunt, where the second baseman covers first to retire the batter; he then keeps the ball and returns to his position, hoping to catch the advanced runner, whose back had been to the play. Many a base runner has been duped by the old "step off the base so I can kick the dirt off it" ploy. In the days before large gloves, the most common hiding place for the ball was the armpit. Frankie Crosetti, for one, would hide the ball in the *back* of his glove. According to a 1938 edition of the *Sporting News*, "He conceal[ed] the ball inside the heel of his glove, so that he seem[ed] to be standing out there at shortstop innocently empty-handed."[3] Crosetti turned the trick no fewer than seven times between 1936 and 1940.

Two decades later, infielder Clete Boyer joined the Yankees. While sitting on the bench one day, Boyer was practicing the art of hiding the ball. Crosetti, by then a Yankee coach, looked at him disdainfully, his Yankee pride offended. "We don't do that here," he told Boyer.[4]

As we might expect, since there is no coach at second base and two fielders with the potential of pulling it off, the play occurs there most often—almost half the time, in fact. Of the 264 documented instances, 61 were completed by a second baseman and 60 by a shortstop. First base was the site 81 times and third base 59 (plus three others that went third baseman to catcher). The pitcher has to be savvy, too, so as not to give the play away or be called for a balk. As Willie Kamm said, "The pitcher has to cooperate in the act or the whole show collapses. We had a few like Ted Lyons, Tommy Thomas, and Red Faber who were real good at it. They'd keep the glove closed and fool with the resin bag and even go to the mound without actually touching the rubber."[5] According to author Dan Gutman, "Lefty Gomez used to enhance the illusion (that the ball had been returned to him) by putting the rosin bag in his glove with the white showing."[6] Crosetti credited Lefty, along with Red Ruffing, with being his top coconspirators: "Gomez and Ruffing were two of the best I ever worked with in making this play. Lefty would move around as if he were holding a baby in his arms, pawing the dirt with his spikes, killing a little, but not too much, time. A long delay would give away the play. Red was nonchalant. His deadpan expression was most deceiving."[7]

George DeTore, a major and minor league player and coach, had a way to nip the process in the bud. He would call "time" whenever he wasn't sure where the ball was, noting that "nothing can happen then until the pitcher is on the mound with the ball." Nowadays, base runners are quick to call time, rendering the HBT almost impossible.

Bill Nowlin interviewed Red Sox coaches Bill Haselman and Lynn Jones about the play. Haselman said, "I look for it all the time. . . . That would be the first-base coach's responsibility. . . . That's more of a Little League play." Jones said he'd never seen the play, adding, "but I'm always looking for it. Any time a guy's off the mound and he's not in contact with that dirt, I'm looking for that ball."

Jay Feldman provides some additional insight into the play. In 1985–1986, he was among a group of North Americans who played a series of goodwill games in Nicaragua. In one game, the middle-aged Feldman, playing shortstop behind Nicaraguan pitcher Roger Lopez, pulled the trick, which he called an "unrealized ambition of [his] baseball career." In SABR's *National Pastime*, Feldman writes that he and Lopez overcame the language barrier to conspire on the trick, each thinking it was his own idea:

> And I understood then what the hidden-ball trick is all about and why we could never pull it off when we were kids: We were going about it backward; it has to arise not from intent, but from circumstances. The essence of the play is not trickery—that's simply . . . the part that shows on the outside. From the inside, the hidden-ball trick is dependent on wordless communication and cooperation, because even if you speak the same language, you can't very well yell over to the pitcher, "Now we're going to do the hidden-ball trick!" You have to be on the same wavelength. You have to read each other's minds. Each player has to know what he *and* the other man need to do to make it work.[8]

2

HISTORY OF THE TRICK

The hidden-ball trick is almost as old as baseball itself. It has been said to date back to Harry and George Wright of the 1869 Red Stockings. According to *Baseball: The Biographical Encyclopedia*, Harry "introduced . . . the original hidden-ball trick, in which players concealed an extra ball to be produced if the game ball escaped them at an inconvenient moment," and George "supposedly pulled off the first hidden-ball trick, starting a tradition of early players who tucked a baseball away in their uniforms or in tall grass for use as needed."[1] These are obviously describing different things, and nineteenth-century baseball expert Peter Morris scoffs at the notion of the Red Stockings resorting to such deceptive ruses. Another source credits National Association utility man Tom Barlow with the innovation. It was described as an "old trick" as early as 1876. In any case, it dates back more than 140 years and has taken place to end games and complete triple plays. It once resulted in two arrests, another time cost a Hall of Famer a managing job, and even happened during a World Series. Through the end of the twentieth century, with TV monitors in the clubhouses and professional coaches at the bases, the play was still pulled off about once a year.

The earliest HBT I have documented occurred on May 20, 1872, in a Philadelphia–Baltimore National Association game. It happened in the eighth inning, setting off a row. According to the *Cleveland Plain Dealer*, in a reprint of the previous day's *Herald*, Fred Treacey

of the Athletics, was put out at first, [Cap] Anson was given his first, [Mike McGeary] made his first, placing Anson at second, and [Denny] Mack was put to first on three called balls. This necessitated the giving of a base to each of the others. [Catcher Bill Craver] of the Baltimores, threw the ball to third, and inadvertently the umpire decided that Anson was out. In reality Anson was entitled to his base under the rule. . . . An animated discussion followed, in the midst of which the umpire reversed his decision and placed Anson back at third. The game had not been called, however, by the umpire, and [Lip] Pike, second baseman of the Baltimores, secreting the ball, watched for his opportunity and put McGeary out at second. Judgment being asked for, the umpire decided McGeary was out. Immediately there was an outcry on the part of the Athletics, and the captain of the nine refused to play the game out. The umpire then called the game in the seventh inning.[2]

With the game over and the score reverting to Baltimore's 7–4 margin after seven innings, the contest was ruled a forfeit to Baltimore. It is unclear whether this was an official game or, if so, whether the HBT counts as having actually occurred.

Until 1897, there were no restrictions on the pitcher with regard to taking his position without the ball; the 1897 rule was amended in 1911 and 1919. *Sporting News* explained the 1919 change, predicting that it would render the HBT extinct:

The new balk regulation is a broadening of Section 7 of the rule regarding balks, which reads as follows: "A balk shall be ° ° ° Making any motion to pitch while standing in his position without having the ball in his possession." Under the new rule, taking the slab without the ball is a balk. . . . Under the old interpretation, the pitcher could step on the rubber without the ball in his hand and there was no offense, so long as he started no pitching motion. . . . The runner on first, seeing the pitcher on the slab, would infer he had the ball, start his lead off first, and a variety of the hidden-ball trick would be worked on him. The new ruling practically does away with the hidden-ball trick, for no base runner is likely to step off the bag until the pitcher takes the slab.[3]

Contrary to predictions, there was no noticeable decline in instances of the play after 1918. The current applicable rule, #8.05(i), reads, "If there is a runner, or runners, it is a balk when the pitcher, without having the ball, stands on or astride the pitcher's plate."[4]

The HBT naturally occurs much more often in the minor leagues and amateur ball (including the first televised baseball game, between college teams, on May 17, 1939) than in the bigs and has been barred in some leagues. The Class C Inter-State League ruled the play legal in 1939, after several league umpires had taken it upon themselves to outlaw it. The Texas League also banned it prior to World War II. According to *Sporting News*, the South Atlantic League outlawed it in 1946,[5] and the Big State League did so in 1956, to "speed the game."[6] On the other hand, some leagues reversed the ban: The Inter-State League relegalized the play in 1948,[7] and the Western League followed suit in 1950.[8] The Texas League dropped their ban in 1955, with the league president saying, "I think the 'hidden ball' is a colorful play—one that causes continuing comment."[9]

From time to time there has been talk about banning the move in the majors. Both Ban Johnson, American League president from 1901 to 1927, and John Tener, National League president from 1913 to 1918, campaigned against the practice. In 1910, when a proposal to abolish the play surfaced, the *St. Louis Globe-Democrat* wrote,

> Tinkerers with the baseball rules would go against the very first principle of the game in their crusade against the "hidden-ball" trick. The first thing a major league ballplayer, or, for that matter, a minor league one, is told is, "Keep your eye on the ball." Just so long as the player follows this fundamental rule there is as much danger of the hidden-ball trick being worked on him as there is that the pitcher will walk over and tag him out. When he is not in a position to watch for himself, he has a coach who is supposed to do this for him. Hence a rule against hiding the ball would really be one in favor of "boneheaded" playing.[10]

Cub president Charles W. Murphy expressed similar sentiments in the *Washington Post*:

> According to the Cub boss, the player who is smart enough to fool another player with any sort of trick should be encouraged and not penalized. "Such a rule would work to the advantage of the 'boneheaded' players only," declared President Murphy. "It would be easy enough for a blind man to see that President Johnson, of the American League, who proposed the new rule, is aiming at some of our players. For instance, it is one of the specialties of Johnny Ev-

ers. . . . A player who can hide the ball on his person and fool a base runner is just as smart as one who makes a good throw or a timely hit. Of course, I have but one vote on the proposed rule, but I do not think that any of the club owners in our league will vote for it."[11]

The *Post* editorialized on the subject two months later:

A trick in baseball which is as old as the game itself has been brought into the limelight recently through a controversy over its merits. The ancient subterfuge known as the "hidden ball" is referred to. It consists of concealing the ball in play by some infielder until an unwary base runner has walked off his aisle of safety from force of habit, only to be confounded when pounced upon by the trickster and touched out. It is a trap usually sprung in an exciting moment when the players have a lot to think of simultaneously. Its chief merit lies in the fact that it tends to keep the players wide awake to every movement of an adversary. It ought to, but does not always, have the effect of compelling the managers to keep experienced and wary men in the coachers' boxes. Inexperienced substitutes and mere noisemakers or clowns too often are put there. It also tends to keep the wisest coachers alive to the location of the ball, for even the wariest have been caught asleep. It puts a premium on the brains and quick thinking to which baseball owes so much of its popularity. The demerits of the trick are that, if attempted often, it delays the progress of a game, particularly if unsuccessful, and that a great portion of the public regards it as stupidity on the part of the runner rather than brainy work by the fielder when successfully executed, and that only a small portion of the public sees it at all, as a rule. Frequently, when worked at its best, the trick deceives the umpires, as well as the opposing players, and that always entails delay and disputes. The remedy is to have a staff of umpires who never fail to watch the ball at all times. No trick can be successful unless the umpire sees it. . . . [T]he trick has gone awry because the umpire, who ought to have seen the play, was not expecting it. But if the umpire never took his eye off the ball the "hidden-ball" trick would inevitably fail. By the mere fact of watching the infielder, who had the ball concealed, the umpire would defeat the trick and warn the base runner of his danger. So what's the odds?[12]

Johnson was supposedly set to ban the trick in 1913, according to *Sporting Life*:

President Ban Johnson, of the American League, will issue an order forbidding the ancient "hidden-ball" trick, according to George Hildebrand, one of his umpires, hailing from the Pacific Coast. The latter says that President Johnson is opposed to it because of a tendency to delay the game.[13]

Nevertheless, the HBT was executed at least three times in the American League within two months of that announcement and dozens of times during the remainder of Johnson's reign.

In 1915, *Sporting Life* ran the following:

President Tener of the National League is against the hidden-ball trick, which caused the fight between Charley Herzog [manager of the Reds] and Umpire [Cy] Rigler [after the trick Miller Huggins pulled on the Reds on May 1 of that year], and he has evolved a plan whereby it can be partly prevented. Mr. Tener declares that the play is unsportsmanlike, and yet under the rules it is permissible. He says that he has told his umpires not only to watch the course of the ball from the time that it leaves the pitcher's hand, but if they suspect that an attempt is going to be made to work the hidden-ball trick, to look directly at the man who is holding the horsehide. In this way the runner or the coaches will be tipped off to what the opposition is trying to do, and the play may be prevented.[14]

Three months later, the same publication wrote, "Now John K. Tener, in his league, has barred the hidden-ball trick on the theory that it is a trick that should have no part in a contest of athletic skill. It was the pulling of the stunt by Miller Huggins too, if we remember correctly, that caused Mr. Tener to take action."[15] Nonetheless, the play was executed at least two more times under Tener's tenure and became relatively commonplace again in the 1920s. In 1919, Hall of Fame American League umpire Billy Evans recommended to Johnson that the play be abolished following a controversial execution by Jimmy Austin. Said Evans, "Hiding the ball has nothing of skill or cleverness attached to it and is really no part of the game as a sport. Most of the other umpires and practically all the players think along the same lines." In 1920, Senators owner Clark Griffith proposed more restrictions on pitchers to control the ruse.

In 1922, according to Hugh Fullerton,

There [was] a campaign to bar the old, bewhiskered hidden-ball trick from baseball. Jim O'Leary, the veteran Boston scribe, [was] the father of this reform, and he [worked] on it as ardently as if someone once worked it on him, which he deni[ed]. That ancient trick really should be ruled out of the game with all the other relics of trickery. It is not a play; its sole result is to make a boob out of a good ballplayer, and, worse than that, it seldom is seen by the spectators; in fact, after a player has been caught on that age-old wheeze, usually no one excepting the players and an unusually suspicious umpire sees it. It is quite as much out of place in baseball as the old hidden-ball trick was in football. [16]

Sporting News spoke out against the play in 1945:

Except for the general rule on balks, there is nothing in the playing code that forbids the hidden-ball trick. However, several minor leagues have ruled against the deception, and now comes the Cleveland Baseball Federation, which governs the play of sandlotters in that city, with similar action. In explanation, President Bill Duggan of the Cleveland organization makes the best argument that has thus far been advanced against the play. "We believe that trickery has no place in our national pastime," said Duggan. "Everything should be open and above-board in the great sport of baseball, and trickery should not be a part of the proceedings." As a sport for youngsters, one of baseball's strongest points is the spirit of sportsmanship, which it inculcates. . . . (The major leagues) should be showing the way to the younger generation. For that reason and for the sake of uniformity, a brief paragraph, specifically forbidding the hidden-ball trick, ought to be written into the rules. [17]

Noted writer Dan Daniel responded two weeks later with a transcript of a mock meeting of team magnates to discuss the abolition of the trick. One called the play "un-American," while another suggested that it violated the Atlantic Charter and the GI Bill of Rights. One complained, "It forces the base runners to be on the alert. They have trouble enough playing the game without being asked to burden their mentalities with little things like keeping alive and awake on the bases." [18]

Despite all the agitation, the hidden-ball trick was never formally banned in the majors.

3

MASTERS OF THE TRICK . . . AND THEIR VICTIMS

Who were the masters of the play? Babe Pinelli, who played only 774 major league games before becoming a famous umpire, was one. I've found five tricks where he got the putout or assist and another in which he distracted the runner, allowing a teammate the glory. A reporter from the *New York World-Telegram* writes, "Babe Pinelli, the umpire, was one of the smoothest manipulators of the hidden-ball trick baseball has ever known. . . . The Babe, with Cincinnati, used to work it three or four times a year . . . not infrequently leading to riots, as his victims flew into a rage."[1] A *Sporting News* article reads,

> Babe's specialty in the good old days when he was playing, was the hidden-ball trick. He would have the ball under his right armpit and engage the runner in conversation until the latter strayed off the bag, and then Pinelli would suddenly pounce on him like a puma. He got a bigger kick out of pulling that stunt than some fellows get from making a home run.[2]

In another *Sporting News*, article Babe is quoted as saying,

> I never worked it unless it meant something—an out we needed in a big game. I had a way in which I actually threw the ball with my right hand, apparently starting it on its way back to the pitcher—while, instead, I actually caught it in my glove, and waited for the unwary runner to stray off the base.[3]

Upon his being traded from the American League, Hall of Fame umpire Billy Evans wrote,

> The other day I read that Babe Pinelli, with Detroit last year, had been sent back to the Pacific Coast League, whence he came. While he was a well-liked youngster, many big leaguers will feel more at ease now that Pinelli has passed out of the American League. Pinelli was the "champion hidden-ball artist" of the world. Last year in the American League he pulled the hidden-ball trick four times that I know of. I would say he missed getting away with it a dozen times, because he umpire gave a hairline decision against him. Never did I see a fellow who could secrete the ball as cleverly as Pinelli. . . . Pinelli told me he had pulled it at least once every year since he has been playing pro ball.[4]

Bill Coughlin is the all-time leader, with eight documented tricks (at three different positions) in 1,049 big league games, plus another in the 1907 World Series. In fact, it was news when Coughlin *didn't* execute the play, as indicated by a 1908 *Sporting Life* article:

> Bill Coughlin has not pulled off his hidden-ball trick yet during this series. Comments from Boston on his doing it there were amusing. When one falls victim to that old gag, the less he says the better. It's sportsmanlike enough for the average baseball consumer and adds a lot to the gaiety of the occasion.[5]

Other noted practitioners include Dan Brouthers, Perry Werden, Jake Beckley, Ed Cartwright, George Stovall, Miller Huggins, Jimmy Austin, Willie Kamm, Tony Cuccinello, Frankie Crosetti, Johnny Pesky, Connie Ryan, Billy Hitchcock, Joe Adcock, Gene Michael, and Marty Barrett. Kamm, in his *Sporting News* obituary, was called a "master of the hidden-ball trick." Willie (quoted in the book *Rowdy Richard*) claims that he was the best:

> I only did it two or three times a year, but that was more than anybody else. It probably happened more than 30 times during my career [the credibility of this claim fades due to the fact that I have documented only four, matching a 1929 *New York Times* article that reports that he had done it three times in his first seven seasons]. I didn't hide the ball in my glove. I'd go over to the pitcher and talk to

him, tell him not to get on the rubber or it would be a balk, and I'd quickly sweep the ball under my armpit and walk back to third twirling the glove in my hands. The pitcher would stall around a little, and I'd watch the runner until he took a few steps off the base, then I'd tag him. [6]

A *Baseball Magazine* article says, "He hid the ball under his armpit with the aid of a wrinkled undershirt that formed sort of a pocket. So cleverly was the ball concealed that Kamm could even spread his arms. . . . Many an unwary runner was trapped by his unique deceit." [7] Table 3.1 is a listing of the all-time leaders.

I've also documented a pair of tricks apiece for Jack Burdock, Hunter Hill, Shad Barry, Honus Wagner, Germany Schaefer, Ed McDonald,

Number of HBTs Player Position(s)

Table 3.1.   All-Time Hidden-Ball Trick Leaders

9	Bill Coughlin	3B, 2B, SS
8	Miller Huggins	2B, 3B
7	Frankie Crosetti	SS
6	George Stovall	1B
5	Perry Werden	1B
5	Jimmy Austin	SS, 3B
5	Babe Pinelli	3B
5	Gene Michael	SS
4	Jake Beckley	1B
4	Del Pratt	2B
4	Willie Kamm	3B
4	Tony Cuccinello	3B, 2B
4	Billy Hitchcock	2B, 3B
4	Joe Adcock	1B
3	Dan Brouthers	1B
3	Jim Rogers	2B, 1B
3	Ed Cartwright	1B
3	Ivy Olson	3B, SS
3	Bobby Bragan	SS
3	Johnny Pesky	SS
3	Marty Barrett	2B

Bob Fisher, Bobby Jones, Joe Judge, Marty McManus, Leo Durocher, Joe Stripp, Lou Boudreau, Connie Ryan, Earl Torgeson, Bob Watson, Dave Bergman, Jeff Treadway, Delino DeShields, Matt Williams, and Mike Lowell.

Nine players—Jack Burdock, Johnny Evers, Frank Chance, Fred Merkle, Bucky Harris, Rabbit Maranville, Lou Boudreau, Orlando Cepeda, and Willie Randolph—have been the both perpetrator and victim. Then there are Ty Cobb and Leo Durocher, perps who later got embarrassed by the trick while on the coaching lines. And poor Roger Bresnahan and Rich Dauer were victimized as both players and coaches.

The victim is oftentimes a rookie, but many an immortal has been duped by the trick. Among the victims are Hall of Famers Cap Anson, Charles Comiskey, Buck Ewing, John Montgomery Ward (twice in the same season!), Joe Kelley, Elmer Flick, Roger Bresnahan, Willie Keeler, Fred Clarke, Joe Tinker, Johnny Evers, Frank Chance (yes, Tinker, Evers, and Chance!), Billy Southworth, Max Carey (who was also caught twice, one short of Jack Martin and Ozzie Guillen's record), Eddie Collins, Bucky Harris, Harry Heilmann, Mickey Cochrane, Sam Rice, Rabbit Maranville, Chick Hafey, Earl Averill, Goose Goslin, Joe Cronin, Lou Boudreau, Jimmie Foxx, Billy Herman, Billy Williams, Orlando Cepeda, Willie Mays, Gary Carter, and Rickey Henderson. And Ward and Heilmann can share the blame with other Hall of Famers. When Ward, considered the most intellectual player of the nineteenth century, was caught dozing at the hot corner on September 28, 1893, King Kelly was coaching third. Likewise, when Harry was nabbed at third base by the Browns' Marty McManus on June 30, 1926, Ty Cobb was coaching just a few feet away.

4

1876–1889: THE EARLY TRICKS

Although the play didn't yet have a name, there were at least 20 hidden-ball tricks in the first 14 years of what we consider Major League Baseball. Five were in the American Association and one in the Union Association, with the rest in the National League. Hall of Fame first baseman Dan Brouthers had three of them.

Date: May 1, 1876
Teams: Boston Red Stockings vs. Hartford Dark Blues (National League)
Perpetrators: Hartford second baseman Jack Burdock and first baseman Everett Mills
Victim: Joe Borden, Boston
  In the third inning, Boston pitcher Joe Borden (aka Joseph Josephs) led off with a single, according to one account, "but got no farther than first, being caught between the bases by Burdock and Mills when he thought [pitcher Tommy] Bond had the ball." Hartford won, 15–3. Although it remains a bit unclear what happened, this is almost certainly the first HBT in major league history, considering Burdock's prior and future history of using the trick. Both Borden and Mills were in their only National League season. The Boston team much later became known as the Braves, now headquartered in Atlanta.

Date: May 8, 1876

Teams: St. Louis Brown Stockings vs. Chicago White Stockings (National League)
Perpetrator: St. Louis second baseman Mike McGeary
Victim: John Peters, Chicago

According to the *Chicago Tribune*, with one out in the eighth, "Chicago's Deacon White followed with a nice hit and went to third on a wild pitch. He was, however, put out at home plate on Peters's hit to McGeary. Peters got to second on the play but was sent out by McGeary, who held the ball and deceived the little man, who thought it was in the pitcher's [George Bradley's] hands."[1] Chicago won anyway, 3–2.

Date: May 25, 1876
Teams: Louisville Grays vs. Philadelphia Athletics (National League)
Perpetrator: Louisville third baseman Bill Hague
Victim: George Zettlein, Philadelphia

According to one account, in the first inning, "Philadelphia's Lon Knight had led off with a safe single-baser, but, imprudently attempting to run home on [pitcher George] Zettlein's rattling hit down to the left field fence, was easily put out, the latter directly afterward being caught napping by a bit of sharp practice on the part of Hague, who concealed the ball about him until Zettlein walked off the base and then touched him."

The *Louisville Journal* says, "Zettlein corked a two-baser over [left fielder Jack] Chapman's head; Knight tried to score on it when Chapman threw to Hague and Hague to (the catcher) and was retired at home plate. Zettlein in meanwhile got to third. In the excitement, Hague managed to get the ball some way, put it under his left arm without being noticed, spit on his hand, and [Jim] Devlin took his position to pitch. Zettlein stepped off third. Hague let him get a good distance away and then touched (him out)."[2] It was a big play, as the game ended in a 14-inning, 2–2 tie.

Date: May 25, 1876
Teams: Hartford Dark Blues vs. Chicago White Stockings (National League)
Perpetrators: Hartford shortstop Tom Carey and third baseman Bob Ferguson

Victim: Cap Anson, Chicago

After a force out at second base in the seventh inning, Hartford shortstop Tom Carey "kept the ball in his hand and completely fooled Anson, who played off from third and was caught in a foolish manner," according to the *Chicago Tribune.*[3] Carey threw to third baseman Bob "Death to Flying Things" Ferguson, "putting (Anson) out to his intense astonishment and disgust," according to an article in a Henry Chadwick scrapbook. The *Hartford Times* describes the play as follows: "After Carey had put out [Cal] McVey he held the ball and walked to his position. [Pitcher Tommy] Bond took his place and appeared to make ready to pitch the ball, and Anson hopped off third to edge toward home, when Carey threw the ball to Ferguson, who touched the modern Hercules before he could realize what was up, and he was out. It was cleverly done, and on the man above all others most desired by the audience to be caught."[4]

The *Hartford Daily Courant* describes it differently: "Carey held the ball, walked slowly down to third base, apparently to speak to Ferguson but in reality to give him the ball, which he did, unobserved by the Chicagos. He then walked back to his position, and Bond took his place between the pitcher's points. As soon as he did this, Anson stepped from the base, and Ferguson very coolly touched him with the ball, putting him out. The play was the greatest surprise, probably, to Anson, who, for an instant, did not comprehend the play, but when Ferguson showed him the ball, as the boys say, 'he tumbled.' The play received round after round of applause and probably earned the game."[5]

Anson, Chicago's longtime player-manager who was destined for the Hall of Fame, was beloved in the Windy City, but not so much elsewhere. His team still exists today as the Cubs.

Date: June 29, 1876
Teams: Cincinnati Red Stockings vs. Hartford Dark Blues (National League)
Perpetrators: Cincinnati shortstop Cherokee Fisher and first baseman Charlie Gould
Victim: Jack Remsen, Hartford

According to a scrapbook of Cincinnati newspaper clippings, in the seventh inning, "Hartford's Jack Remsen took first on [Cincinnati second baseman Charlie] Sweasy's muff of his fly, but, prancing about the bag, was neatly caught out by Fisher, who had the ball under his arm while the monkey shines were proceeding. This little stratagem of the 'Big Cherokee' was warmly applauded by the spectators." Fisher, normally a pitcher, pegged the ball to first baseman Charlie Gould for the putout. Hartford won, 13–6.

Date: August 9, 1876
Teams: Hartford Dark Blues vs. Philadelphia Athletics (National League)
Perpetrator: Hartford second baseman Jack Burdock
Victim: William Coon, Philadelphia

The Philadelphia Athletics were victimized by Hartford during a 9–1 loss. According to one account, the A's "came very near to getting one (run) in the fifth, but failed, thanks to Burdock's playing the old trick of holding the ball and touching (Philadelphia's William Coon) out on second base, when the ball was supposed to be in the hands of the pitcher." Note that this was called an "old trick" even in the first year of National League play. Coon, a 21-year-old rookie, never played in the majors after 1876.

Date: September 5, 1876
Teams: Philadelphia Athletics vs. Chicago White Stockings (National League)
Perpetrator: Philadelphia shortstop Davey Force
Victim: Ross Barnes, Chicago

According to the *Philadelphia Press*, "The strangest thing was that [Chicago star Ross] Barnes struck out twice and was once the victim of a trick that made him feel badly. He was on second, when Force and [pitcher Lon] Knight left their positions, as if to confer with each other. Knight gave the ball to Force, who put it under his arm and walked back. Barnes left second and walked up beside Force, who threw his arms around him and touched him."[6] Chicago still won, 11–5.

Date: June 28, 1877
Teams: Louisville Grays vs. Boston Red Stockings (National League)
Perpetrator: Louisville shortstop Bill Craver
Victim: Tim Murnane, Boston

Boston's Tim Murnane, later a noted sportswriter who railed against the ruse, "was nicely touched out at second by Craver, who caught him off the base by concealing the ball under his arm," according to the *Boston Globe*.[7] It was in the seventh inning of Boston's 3–1 victory.

Date: May 20, 1881
Teams: Chicago White Stockings vs. Boston Red Stockings (National League)
Perpetrators: Chicago third baseman Ed Williamson and second baseman Joe Quest
Victim: Jack Burdock, Boston

According to the *Chicago Times*, "A very clever play was made in the last half of the ninth inning by which a final tie was, doubtless, prevented. Burdock had opened with a clean two-baser, and the ball had been returned by [Chicago left fielder Abner] Dalrymple to Williamson. That wily third baseman concealed it, and [pitcher Larry] Corcoran helped on the ruse by pretending to have it. The consequence was that Burdock was caught napping off his base by a very clever play, which he couldn't understand for some time. [Boston rookie pitcher Jim] Whitney was nearly caught at first in the same way by [Chicago shortstop Tom] Burns and [first baseman Cap] Anson."[8]

The *Chicago Tribune* reveals more, saying, "Burdock, first at bat, hit for two bases, and while [Ezra] Sutton was at bat, was caught by Williamson to Quest, Williamson having in some mysterious manner got the ball and hidden it under his arm, while everybody supposed the pitcher had it. Burdock's discomfiture at falling into the trap was enormously amusing, and the crowd laughed and cheered at a great rate."[9] Chicago held on to win, 5–4. It's hard to believe that Burdock "couldn't understand" the play, since he was one of its earliest practitioners.

Date: May 23, 1884
Teams: Columbus Colts vs. St. Louis Brown Stockings (American Association)
Perpetrator: Columbus first baseman Jim Field
Victim: Charles Comiskey, St. Louis

According to *Sporting Life*, "The celebrated first baseman [Comiskey] had made a hit and was on first. He led off and [pitcher Frank] Mountain let the ball go to Field, but not in time to catch the runner.

Field then made a feint to return the ball to Mountain, but instead of doing so shoved it under his arm. Jimmie's compatriots felt grieved that the lengthy youth should endeavor to catch such a man as Comiskey on a chestnut like that, and those of them who had not lost the art blushed for fear that the audience might think their first baseman was 'new.' Already the cry of 'rats' was beginning to be heard when, to the surprise of the spectators and the consternation of Comiskey's confreres, that gentleman deliberately walked off the base with his eyes intently fixed on Mountain. Field yelled 'Mr. Umpire,' touched Comiskey, and that useful member of the St. Louis team sought a secluded seat, muttering to himself."[10] Comiskey would later earn Hall of Fame selection due to his role as Chicago White Sox president. The American Association played as a major league from 1882 to 1891; the St. Louis team would later move to the National League, where they still exist as the Cardinals.

Date: June 17, 1884
Teams: Buffalo Bisons vs. Chicago White Stockings (National League)
Perpetrator: Buffalo first baseman Dan Brouthers
Victim: Billy Sunday, Chicago

According to *Sporting Life*, "Brouthers, in one of the games with Chicago last week, worked a very old trick on Sunday. The latter had made a good base hit and was safe on first. The guileless Daniel had thrown the ball back to [pitcher Billy] Serad (in his mind), when Sunday slipped off the bag. Dan jerked the ball from under his arm and touched him out before the Chicago right fielder knew what happened. Any player stupid enough to be caught in that manner deserves a fine."[11] Buffalo won the game, 8–7, in ten innings. Brouthers was on his way to the Hall of Fame; Sunday was on his way to a lengthy career as an evangelist.

Date: July 4, 1884 (second game)
Teams: Louisville Colonels vs. Brooklyn Bridegrooms (American Association)
Perpetrator: Louisville third baseman Pete Browning
Victim: Adonis Terry, Brooklyn

According to the *Louisville Courier-Journal*, Louisville pitcher Guy "Hecker and Browning caught Terry napping at third yesterday in a very slick way. A ball was hit to center field, on which Terry ran from second to third. The ball was then thrown to Hecker, who walked over to third and said something to Terry, at the same time slipping Browning the ball. Hecker then returned to his box, with his hands closed as if he had the ball in them. Terry swallowed the bait and pranced off the bag a few feet, when Browning quietly produced the ball from under his arm and put him out."[12] This occurred in the second game of an American Association doubleheader, in which Hecker hurled two complete-game victories. Browning was the original Louisville Slugger, after whom the famous bat is named. The Brooklyn team later moved to the National League and then to Los Angeles, where they still play as the Dodgers.

Date: July 10, 1884
Teams: Boston Unions vs. Chicago Browns (Union Association)
Perpetrator: Boston third baseman John Irwin
Victim: Charlie Householder, Chicago

In the Union Association's lone season of play, Boston's John Irwin caught Chicago's Charlie Householder, playing in his only major league season. According to the *Boston Morning Journal*, "Householder was neatly trapped in the game at the Union Grounds yesterday." He had taken third on pitcher Hugh "One Arm" Daily's hit to left. Left fielder Patrick Scanlan threw the ball to Irwin, who was backed up by pitcher James Burke. "The latter returned to his box as if to pitch and Householder started to play wide of the base, when he was greatly surprised by being touched with the ball in Irwin's hands, the latter having held it after it was fielded in."[13]

Date: September 27, 1884
Teams: Buffalo Bisons vs. New York Gothams (National League)
Perpetrator: Buffalo first baseman Dan Brouthers
Victim: Buck Ewing, New York

In a play involving two future Hall of Famers and a novice umpire, Dan Brouthers apparently caught Buck Ewing on the trick. According to the *Boston Herald*, New York's John Montgomery "Ward protested because Ewing was put out by Brouthers for leaving his base on a call of time after a foul hit, when the ball had not been returned to the pitcher." One "Dr. Howard, a local enthusiast," was umpiring in place of

John Gaffney, who had gone home for the winter; Howard would be replaced by Bill Furlong for the rest of the season. New York won, 12–10. It is not clear exactly what happened on the play, but Brouthers's record as a perpetrator tips the scales in listing this as another HBT. The Gothams later became known as the Giants, and even later moved to San Francisco.

Date: June 23, 1886
Teams: Detroit Wolverines vs. Philadelphia Phillies (National League)
Perpetrator: Detroit first baseman Dan Brouthers
Victim: Ed Andrews, Philadelphia

According to the *Boston Globe*, in a game at Detroit, "Brouthers played a schoolboy trick on Andrews. The latter made a hit, which Brouthers tried to get, while [pitcher Lady] Baldwin covered first. Andrews reached the base safely, and Baldwin returned to his position in the box. Brouthers had the ball under his arm. Andrews left the base, and Brouthers put the side out by touching him with the ball." [14] The play ended the game, according to the *Chicago Daily Tribune*: "In the ninth . . . Andrews reached first base on a scratch. Brouthers got the ball and hid it under his arm until Andrews left his base and then touched him, making the last man out." [15]

Date: May 17, 1887
Teams: Louisville Colonels vs. Baltimore Orioles (American Association)
Perpetrator: Louisville third baseman Joe Werrick
Victim: Chris Fulmer, Baltimore

According to the *New York Sun*, Louisville pitcher Guy Hecker and third baseman Joe Werrick "played a clever trick. It was in the second inning when [Jumbo] Davis was on first base and Fulmer on second. Fulmer made a questionable steal to third base by going slightly out of the line and touching the bag with his hand. The decision provoked a wrangle, during which Werrick hid the ball up his sleeve. [Umpire Ned] Cuthbert finally called play, and Hecker returned to the pitcher's box, striking a superb attitude as if to deliver the ball. Fulmer, who thought Guy had the ball, stole off the base at least ten feet, when Werrick laughingly walked up to him and touched him out. Everybody was taken by surprise, and the trick provoked merriment." [16] The only game that fits these details was played on this date, although nothing was found in *Sporting Life*. Louisville was leading, 10–0, when Werrick pulled the trick, but Baltimore later had the tying run on deck when the game was called due to rain.

Date: June 17, 1888
Teams: Baltimore Orioles vs. Brooklyn Bridegrooms (American Association)
Perpetrator: Baltimore second baseman Jack Farrell
Victim: Bob Caruthers, Brooklyn
  According to the *Brooklyn Eagle*, "In (Brooklyn's) ninth inning, after two men were out, Caruthers hit a high ball close to the fence at right field, which [Blondie] Purcell made a fine effort to catch, but he could not hold the ball, and Caruthers got second base on the hit. The ball was thrown in to Farrell, who held it while making a feint to throw to [pitcher Phenomenal] Smith, who took his position in the box as if to pitch. Caruthers did not wait to see where the ball was, and getting off the base, was touched by Farrell, the trick ending the game, Baltimore winning by 9 to 8 runs."[17]

Date: May 4, 1889
Teams: New York Giants vs. Philadelphia Phillies (National League)
Perpetrators: New York shortstop John Montgomery Ward and first baseman Roger Connor
Victim: Sam Thompson, Philadelphia
  This play involved three future Hall of Famers. With two out in the top of the third inning (with the home team batting first), Thompson singled to left field. Ward took the throw in from the outfield and kept the ball. When Thompson led off the bag, Ward fired to Connor to catch him, and the inning was over.

Date: May 26, 1889
Teams: Baltimore Orioles vs. Philadelphia Athletics (American Association)
Perpetrators: Baltimore third baseman Bill Shindle and second baseman Reddy Mack
Victim: Curt Welch, Philadelphia

According to the *Philadelphia Inquirer*, Shindle held the ball after a force-out in the ninth inning, "and then Welch was caught napping at second by Shindle holding the ball under his arm and throwing it to Mack."[18] The A's won anyway, 6–2.

Date: July 2, 1889
Teams: Cleveland Spiders vs. Washington Senators (National League)
Perpetrator: Cleveland third baseman Patsy Tebeau
Victim: Walt Wilmot, Washington

According to *Sporting Life*, "The game was marked by a desperate finish. [Cleveland pitcher Jersey] Bakely weakened in the ninth, and Washington had earned three runs, with one out and Wilmot on third base, when [rookie third sacker Patsy] Tebeau hid the ball and caught Wilmot out."[19] Instead of one out and the tying run on third, Washington was down to its final out with none on base, and Cleveland won, 5–4.

According to Charles Mears of *Sporting News*, "Tricky little 'Patsy' Tebeau is again on time with one of his neat 'hide the ball' acts, and they count every time, too. He saved the last game in the Senatorial series from being a defeat. Thus, Wilmot had hit Bakely into right field for a three bagger, and the ball was returned to [shortstop Ed] McKean, who quickly handed it to Tebeau, and it was under his arm in an instant. The score was 5–4 in favor of Cleveland, but with a man on third and the heavy-hitting [Jack] Carney at the bat, we must confess the game looked like it belonged to the Senators. But [Washington manager Art] Irwin's men are too anxious! The whole home infield is onto the trick, and the Senators appeal to [umpire Wes] Curry to hustle the game on, thinking that the home team wants to delay. Bakely is getting shaky. He gets into the box but makes no motion to pitch, and Wilmot leads off third. He is at once touched out and of course it had to be given. And now drink to the health of Oliver Tebeau, Bart."[20]

5

1890–1899: GAIETY IN THE '90S

The Gay '90s featured 16 hidden-ball tricks (HBT), 13 of them by first basemen. Perry Werden led the way with five tricks. This decade featured the earliest-found references to the term *hidden-ball trick*, invariably accompanied by adjectives like "ancient." One trick was in the American Association and the rest in the National League.

Date: August 9, 1890
Teams: Columbus Colts vs. Rochesters (American Association)
Perpetrator: Columbus third baseman Charlie Reilly
Victim: Dave McKeough, Rochester

Date: September 18, 1892 (second game)
Teams: Baltimore Orioles vs. Cleveland Spiders (National League)
Perpetrator: Baltimore first baseman Sy Sutcliffe
Victim: Chief Zimmer, Cleveland
    In the fourth inning, Sutcliffe hid the ball under his arm and caught Zimmer leading off the bag.[1]

Date: May 22, 1893
Teams: Pittsburgh Pirates vs. St. Louis Browns (National League)
Perpetrator: Pittsburgh first baseman Jake Beckley
Victim: Kid Gleason, St. Louis
    According to *Sporting Life*, "Gleason, who was not watching the ball, got on first base. Beckley had the ball under his arm and touched him

out."[2] Pittsburgh won, 14–6. Gleason became better known as manager of the 1919 Chicago "Black Sox."

Date: May 30, 1893 (first game)
Teams: Pittsburgh Pirates vs. Baltimore Orioles (National League)
Perpetrator: Pittsburgh first baseman Jake Beckley
Victim: Joe Kelley, Baltimore

Beckley pulled the "ancient" HBT trick on Kelley, helping Pittsburgh to a 9–1 win in the morning game. According to the *Baltimore Sun*, "Kelley, in the visitors' half of the third, gave Beckley a chance to play that time-worn trick on him of hiding the ball. He made a single . . . but he failed to see [second baseman Lou] Bierbauer return the ball to Beckley. [Adonis] Terry assumed his pitching position, and Kelley took a lead for second. Then Beckley touched him out, and the youngster and the coachers looked sheepish."[3] Kelley, 21, was on his way to a Hall of Fame career, as was Beckley.

According to *Baseball: The Biographical Encyclopedia*, Beckley "developed a hidden-ball trick that was all his own: He hid the ball under a corner of the base, and when the runner took a lead, Beckley quickly reached under the base, grabbed the ball, and tagged the runner out. One day he reportedly lifted the wrong corner of the bag, and Honus Wagner zipped down to second, laughing all the way."[4] On another occasion, he supposedly duped Wagner by faking a hidden-ball trick. Wagner grabbed and threw the ball away and took off for second, only to be thrown out by the pitcher, who had the actual game ball. Still another time, Beckley's attempted trick supposedly resulted in a free ride around the bases. According to journalist A. H. Tarvin, "A Pittsburgh player—Billy Kuehne, if memory serves—is the only player, so far as we know, to make a home run on a bunt without an error being made on the play. Playing at Cincinnati . . . Kuehne bunted, the ball rolling very slowly toward the pitcher, who rushed in, picked it up, and threw with tremendous force to 'Old Eagle Eye' Jake Beckley, but Kuehne beat the throw. Beckley pretended to throw the ball back to the pitcher but decided to work the hidden-ball trick. He slipped the ball into his sleeve, one of those elbow-length affairs, and Kuehne, unaware of the concealment, edged off the bag a number of feet. That was the time for Beckley to go into action . . . but somehow the ball had become stuck in the sleeve, and he was unable to budge it. After a moment's

Figure 5.1.   Among Jake Beckley's victims were fellow Hall of Famers Joe Kelley, John Montgomery Ward, and Frank Chance. He tried for another, but Honus Wagner wasn't fooled. Courtesy of the Library of Congress.

survey of the frantic Red first sacker, Kuehne figured out the facts for himself and went tearing around the bases. He crossed the plate just as 'Noodles' Hahn, Red pitcher who had rushed over to first, ripped the sleeve from Beckley's shirt, the ball dropping to the ground. Never again did Beckley try the hidden ball."[5] However, Kuehne last played in 1892, and Beckley (1898) and Hahn (1899) didn't join the Reds until several years later.

Date: June 5, 1893
Teams: St. Louis Browns vs. New York Giants (National League)
Perpetrator: St. Louis first baseman Perry Werden
Victim: John Montgomery Ward, New York

According to the *Brooklyn Eagle*, "Werden worked a neat trick on [Giants future Hall of Famer John Montgomery] Ward in the seventh inning. John had beaten [second baseman Joe] Quinn's throw to Werden and stood upon the base. Werden walked over to [pitcher Kid] Gleason and apparently gave him the ball but really concealed it under his arm. Then Gleason assumed his pitching attitude, and Ward stepped off first only to be promptly put out by Werden. New York's captain, for once, was outwitted."[6]

Date: June 7, 1893
Teams: St. Louis Browns vs. Brooklyn Bridegrooms (National League)
Perpetrator: St. Louis first baseman Perry Werden
Victim: Tommy Burns, Brooklyn

According to the *Brooklyn Eagle*, Werden struck again two days later, nabbing Brooklyn's Tommy Burns in the seventh inning.[7]

Date: September 28, 1893
Teams: Pittsburgh Pirates vs. New York Giants (National League)
Perpetrator: Pittsburgh first baseman Jake Beckley
Victim: John Montgomery Ward, New York

According to the *New York Sun*, "It was in the ninth inning, and Ward had made a single. Of course John was tickled to death and did not observe that the ball was passed to Beckley. [Mike "King"] Kelly was coaching at first, and he, of course, did not see the renowned [pitcher Ad] Gumbert make an effort to get in a position to pitch, and Ward stepped from the bag. The instant he did so Beckley touched him out, and there were roars of laughter all around. John kicked, but he was out, and the umpire told him so. It was somewhat humiliating for the little manager, but it had to go."[8] For Ward, considered the most intelligent man in baseball in the nineteenth century, it was the second time in four months he had been caught with the trick. Kelly—like Ward and Beckley, a future Hall of Famer—was in the closing days of his colorful career; a year later, he would be dead.

Date: June 19, 1894
Teams: Washington Senators vs. Brooklyn Bridegrooms (National League)
Perpetrator: Washington second baseman Piggy Ward
Victim: Tommy Corcoran, Brooklyn

Date: July 4, 1894 (first game)
Teams: Washington Senators vs. St. Louis Browns (National League)
Perpetrator: Washington first baseman Ed Cartwright
Victim: Joe Quinn, St. Louis
According to the *St. Louis Post-Dispatch*, the Cardinals' "Joe Quinn was 'guyed' when Cartwright caught him napping on the old ball-under-the-arm racket."[9] This was in the morning game of a doubleheader.

Date: April 28, 1896
Teams: Washington Senators vs. Baltimore Orioles (National League)
Perpetrator: Washington first baseman Ed Cartwright
Victim: Willie Keeler, Baltimore
Future Hall of Famer Wee Willie Keeler was victimized by Cartwright in the second inning. According to the *Washington Post*, "Masterly work in the field resulted in teamwork for the Senators that made the Orioles appear as a lot of the veriest amateurs, the hidden-ball trick . . . being among the clever points gained. . . . The Orioles faced Jake Boyd for their turn at bat in the second. Jake celebrated his entry by hitting Jimmy Donnelly in the ribs. [Pitcher Arlie] Pond scratched out a single. Keeler hit to [shortstop Gene] DeMontreville, who assisted Pond out at second with [second baseman Bill] Joyce's help. Joyce stole over to Cartwright with the ball, slipping it in Ed's mitt. Ed tucked the spheroid under his arm, and Jake Boyd looked wise. Keeler was knocked off his guard by this little bunco game of pantomime and

played off the bag. Cartwright slipped the ball from its nesting place under the arm and tagged Keeler. A cynical smirk darkened the brow of Keeler, who asked Cartwright if he would do him a favor. 'What is it?' queried Ed. 'Take a kick out of me.' 'Come 'round to the hotel after the game is over, Keeler, and I'll see how good you are at blowing out the gas,' said Ed."[10] Washington won, 9–5.

Date: August 19, 1896 (first game)
Teams: Washington Senators vs. Cleveland Spiders (National League)
Perpetrator: Washington shortstop Gene DeMontreville
Victim: Cupid Childs, Cleveland

According to the *Washington Post*, "DeMontreville sprung the old gag of the hidden ball in the first on Cupid Childs, and it worked. [Cleveland's Jesse] Burkett beat out a bunt and was forced at second by [Ed] McKean. Childs singled to center, pushing McKean to second. [Jimmy] McAleer drove a hard grounder that [third baseman Harvey] Smith picked up neatly, tagging McKean. [Pitcher Carney] Flynn almost caught Childs napping on a throw to DeMontreville; Montey held the ball and turned the old trick on Childs."[11] Cleveland won this first game of a twin bill, 13–6. Childs almost got DeMontreville back two years later, as described in chapter 17, "Tricks Gone Awry."

Date: August 27, 1896 (first game)
Teams: Louisville Colonels vs. Brooklyn Bridegrooms (National League)
Perpetrator: Louisville first baseman Jim Rogers
Victim: Fielder Jones, Brooklyn

Date: April 22, 1897
Teams: Louisville Colonels vs. Cleveland Spiders (National League)
Perpetrator: Louisville first baseman Perry Werden
Victim: Chief Zimmer, Cleveland

According to *Sporting News*, "Werden turned an ancient trick during the opening game [of the season]. After Zimmer had reached first base on a safe hit to right, [right fielder Tom] McCreery threw the ball to Werden, and while everybody was looking in another direction, Perry tucked it under his arm. (Pitcher Chick Fraser) took his place on the rubber and Zimmer walked off the base, only to find himself out. . . .

Werden caught Zimmer off first base by that old trick of hiding the ball. The old chief felt quite small."[12]

Date: May 26, 1897
Teams: Louisville Colonels vs. Boston Beaneaters (National League)
Perpetrators: Louisville second baseman Jim Rogers and first baseman Perry Werden
Victim: Herman Long, Boston

According to *Sporting News*, "The same old trick was worked in by Louisville against Boston yesterday. This time it was on Herman Long. Rogers tucked the ball under his arm, and when Long walked off of the base he threw it to first and Werden tagged him out. It was simple enough, but [Boston pitcher Fred] Klobedanz, who was on the coach line, had very hard work explaining to Long how he thought that [Louisville pitcher Bert] Cunningham had the ball all the time."[13] This was the only 1897 date that Cunningham pitched against Boston before the date of the article. Rogers and Werden worked the same trick against Washington the next day; Rogers had at least three HBTs in his 152-game career.

Date: May 27, 1897
Teams: Louisville Colonels vs. Washington Senators (National League)
Perpetrators: Louisville second baseman Jim Rogers and first baseman Perry Werden
Victim: John O'Brien, Washington

According to the *Washington Post*, "Rogers and Werden worked the bewhiskered hidden ball trick on O'Brien in the second inning. Rogers smuggled the ball to Werden after [Deacon] McGuire was forced on O'Brien's grounder to Rogers. . . . O'Brien . . . was caught dreaming off first by Rogers and Werden."[14] Louisville won, 5–0.

Date: June 2, 1897
Teams: Washington Senators vs. Chicago Colts (National League)
Perpetrator: Washington first baseman Ed Cartwright
Victim: Tim Donahue, Chicago

According to the *Chicago Tribune*, "Donahue led the seventh with a clean hit and then was caught off first on the old hidden-ball gag."[15]

6

1900–1909: COUGHLIN CORNER TRICKS

Led by all-time leader Bill Coughlin's nine, major leaguers completed
35 hidden-balls tricks from 1900 to 1909. Seventeen were pulled by
National League players and 18 by American League glovemen, including one in a World Series game.

Date: July 9, 1900
Teams: Cincinnati Reds vs. Philadelphia Phillies (National League)
Perpetrator: Cincinnati third baseman Bob Wood
Victim: Elmer Flick, Philadelphia

    Sporting News cites an article from the *Cincinnati Enquirer* on July
8, 1900, but the details actually fit the game played on July 9. It concerns a trick played by Cincinnati's Bob Wood, normally a catcher:
"Robert Burn Woods [*sic*] covered third base yesterday in the absence
of Harry Steinfeldt. . . . In his young days, when Bob was the champion
cornhusker within a radius of ten miles of Girard, he played baseball
with the Blue Birds, a strong amateur team that eschewed socks and
shoes. Wood had not played long until the people of the neighborhood
looked upon him as a trickster. He played some 'ding-fudged' good
ones on visiting players and was once the recipient of three gallons of
cider and two pounds of ginger snaps by admirers when one of his
Herrmann tricks resulted in a victory for the 'Girard fellers.' . . . In the
fifth inning of yesterday's game, Bob thought of that trick. He chuckled
to himself and muttered: 'By gosh, I'll try it.' [Philadelphia's Ed]
McFarland had been given a base on balls, and Wood ran up to the

plate ostensibly to put in a kick. . . . When Wood came in to protect against the umpire's decision [catcher Heinie] Peitz met him near home plate. Peitz held the ball concealed in his right 'lunch hook.' Heinie pushed Wood back, at the same time releasing the ball unnoticed to the Girard man. Robert quickly transferred the ball to a snug place under his arm. Then Peitz, remembering that the Quakers were guests of the Reds, said, 'Get thee back to thy position. Mr. Terry [William "Adonis" Terry, the umpire, who as a player in 1884 had been victimized by the trick] has enough trouble from the other fellows.' This bunch of salves was not sidestepped by the umpire, who nodded approval. Then play was resumed. Elmer Flick was satisfied with himself and the world at large because he had stolen third base. Dr. Eustace Newton [a rookie pitcher known as "Doc"] squared off in position to pitch with nothing in his gloved hand save the ambient atmosphere. 'Watch third base,' said Peitz to the umpire in sub rosa terms. Mr. Flick took a nice lead, and then Wood walked out and touched him with the ball. 'You're out!' shouted the umpire, as he threw off his mask and walked back toward the grandstand. The antebellum jag, which is no older than the one that Charley Farrell worked on Tommy Corcoran the other day by bluffing at throwing to second and whipping the ball to third, had worked as smoothly as could be asked. Flick felt cheaper than a piece of soiled goods on a bargain counter at a fire sale. Acting 'Capting' Napoleon Bonaparte Lajoie let out an awful belch, but it availed him not. The other members of the Phillies kicked and looked at Flick compassionately. People in the stands laughed. Some roared. "Twas such a fine choke,' said Johann Schwab, the groundkeeper, as he kicked at a stray dog that had walked past the gate tender, who had been overcome with laughter. The Reds won in the eleventh inning by a score of 5–4, and Wood's trick and Flick's foolishness were factors."[1]

The *Brooklyn Eagle* reported the following: "An obsolete trick sprung by Wood at third cut off a probable victory for Philadelphia in the fifth; Flick had stolen third, and in the excitement, Wood put the ball under his arm, a la Piggy Ward, and when Flick walked off the bases, he was touched out."[2] Frank "Piggy" Ward was a major league player in 1883 and 1894, but he played only 105 games in the infield, 83 of them with the 1894 Washington Senators. He did have at least one HBT that year.

Date: May 8, 1901
Teams: New York Giants vs. Philadelphia Phillies (National League)
Perpetrator: New York first baseman John Ganzel
Victim: Harry Wolverton, Philadelphia

In the ninth inning, New York first baseman John Ganzel tagged out Philadelphia's Harry Wolverton—at *third* base—to end the game. New York won, 9–8.

Date: September 24, 1901
Teams: Washington Senators vs. Detroit Tigers (American League)
Perpetrator: Washington third baseman Bill Coughlin
Victim: Jack Cronin, Detroit

According to the *Washington Post*, Coughlin duped Detroit pitcher Jack Cronin in the second inning.[3] According to Coughlin's obituary 42 years later, "When only three years old, he picked up a revolver and pulled the trigger, the discharge tearing off the finger next to the thumb on his left hand. He attributed that accident to making it possible for him to execute the hidden-ball trick, as he had a special mitt made for his hand."

Date: April 17, 1902
Teams: Cincinnati Reds vs. Chicago Cubs (National League)
Perpetrator: Cincinnati first baseman Jake Beckley
Victim: Frank Chance, Chicago

On Opening Day at Cincinnati, Cincinnati's Buck Congalton reached first base to start the second inning, and Chance followed with a bunt single. Beckley held on to the ball and then nabbed Chance. *Sporting News* says, "Jake Beckley turned the hide-the-ball trick on Frank Chance in the opening game."[4]

Date: May 2, 1902
Teams: Boston Pilgrims vs. Baltimore Orioles (American League)
Perpetrator: Boston first baseman Candy LaChance
Victim: Billy Gilbert, Baltimore

According to the *Detroit Free Press*, "The old concealed-ball trick is having a new lease of life. LaChance is the latest to work it, catching Gilbert, of Baltimore, napping the other day."[5] Tim Murnane of the *Boston Globe* writes, "LaChance deserves a medal for hiding the ball

Figure 6.1.   Bill Coughlin is the all-time leader, with nine successful executions of the trick, including one in the 1907 World Series. Due to a childhood finger accident, Coughlin wore a special glove that he used to help conceal the ball. Courtesy of the National Baseball Hall of Fame Library, Cooperstown, New York.

and getting Gilbert off first. This is one of those old plays found in oil paintings but not considered good sport in up-to-date ball."[6] Baltimore won, 14–6. The Pilgrims would eventually become known as the Red Sox, while the Orioles would move to New York, becoming the Highlanders and then the Yankees.

Date: May 11, 1902
Teams: Chicago Cubs vs. Brooklyn Superbas (National League)
Perpetrator: Chicago first baseman Hal O'Hagan
Victim: Doc Newton, Brooklyn

According to the *Brooklyn Eagle*, O'Hagan caught Brooklyn pitcher Doc Newton in the fifth inning.[7] O'Hagan played only 63 games in his career. The Superbas later became known as the Robins and, finally, the Dodgers, moving to Los Angeles in 1958.

Date: May 13, 1902
Teams: Chicago Cubs vs. Brooklyn Superbas (National League)
Perpetrator: Chicago third baseman Charlie Dexter
Victim: Bill Dahlen, Brooklyn

For the second time in three days, the Cubs caught the Superbas napping. Dexter—normally an outfielder or catcher—nabbed the veteran Dahlen in the seventh inning. The *Chicago Tribune* remarks, "The frequency with which the hidden-ball trick is being worked this year leads to the supposition that the old-timers still left in the National League have forgotten it and the youngsters never heard of it before."[8]

Date: May 15, 1902
Teams: Washington Senators vs. Baltimore Orioles (American League)
Perpetrator: Washington second baseman Bill Coughlin
Victim: Kip Selbach, Baltimore

According to the *Washington Post*, Selbach became a victim after doubling to the scoreboard in the first inning: "Selbach was caught on the old hide-the-ball trick by Coughlin. . . . Some tricks will never grow old, and some players will never learn to keep awake, as witness Selbach's out at second. . . . [Center fielder Jimmy] Ryan returned the ball to Bill Coughlin, who hid it and waited for 'Dutchy' to walk off. He was properly rewarded."[9]

Date: June 3, 1902
Teams: Washington Senators vs. Detroit Tigers (American League)
Perpetrator: Washington shortstop Bill Coughlin
Victim: Ducky Holmes, Detroit

According to the *Washington Post*, Holmes doubled in the fourth inning. Coughlin concealed the ball and tagged Holmes when he stepped off the base.[10] It was Coughlin's third trick in less than a year, each at a different position. Washington won, 2–0.

Date: June 25, 1902
Teams: Washington Senators vs. Boston Pilgrims (American League)
Perpetrator: Washington shortstop Bill Coughlin
Victim: Patsy Dougherty, Boston

Coughlin strikes again! According to the *Washington Post*, he took a throw from outfielder Jimmy Ryan, after Boston put runners on first and second with none out in the first inning. Coughlin then pulled the "concealed-ball trick" when Dougherty wandered off second base. Washington won, 4–3. According to *Sporting Life*, the "second game was lost through the failure of Dougherty to keep his eyes open for the moth-eaten hide-the-ball trick."[11]

Date: June 25, 1902
Teams: Philadelphia Phillies vs. New York Giants (National League)
Perpetrator: Philadelphia shortstop Rudy Hulswitt
Victim: Steve Brodie, New York

Rookie Hulswitt got Brodie—in the final season of a 12-year career—in the eighth inning of a 3–1 Phils' win.

Date: May 30, 1903 (first game)
Teams: Brooklyn Superbas vs. Philadelphia Phillies (National League)
Perpetrator: Brooklyn third baseman Dutch Jordan
Victim: Bill Hallman, Philadelphia

In the first game of a Decoration Day doubleheader, the rookie Jordan nailed the veteran Hallman in the sixth inning. Hallman was in the final season of his 14-year career.

Date: June 3, 1904
Teams: Brooklyn Superbas vs. Pittsburgh Pirates (National League)

Perpetrator: Brooklyn first baseman Fred Jacklitsch
Victim: Ed Phelps, Pittsburgh

With the game tied at four in the top of the ninth inning, Phelps reached first on an error by Brooklyn shortstop Charlie Babb. Jacklitsch, normally a catcher, was playing first base for one of only 19 times in his career. According to the *New York Evening Telegram*, "Jacklitsch had the ball at first and touched Phelps as he stepped off the bag."[12] Brooklyn went on to win, 5–4, in 12 innings.

Date: June 13, 1904
Teams: New York Highlanders vs. Chicago White Sox (American League)
Perpetrator: New York shortstop Wid Conroy
Victim: Doc White, Chicago

With one out in the bottom of the eighth and White Sox pitcher Doc White on second base, Fielder Jones flied out to left fielder John Anderson. Conroy took the throw from Anderson, held the ball, and tagged out White when he wandered off the bag.

Date: June 24, 1904
Teams: Washington Senators vs. New York Highlanders (American League)
Perpetrator: Washington third baseman Bill Coughlin
Victim: Deacon McGuire, New York

In the top of the tenth inning, McGuire was on first when Champ Osteen's only double of the season sent him to third. Coughlin took the throw, hid the ball, and tagged McGuire when he stepped off the base. It was too little, too late, however, as the Highlanders had already scored twice to earn a 5–3 victory.

Date: August 26, 1904
Teams: Washington Senators vs. Cleveland Blues (American League)
Perpetrators: Washington third baseman Hunter Hill and catcher Mal Kittridge
Victim: Charlie Carr, Cleveland

Carr—acquired along with Fritz Buelow from Detroit by Cleveland less than three weeks earlier—was nabbed by Hill, who threw to Kittridge for the out. According to the *Washington Post*, "Carr ripped off a beautiful triple in the second but wasted it by walking off the base while Hill had the ball under his arm. As soon as Carr saw he was tricked, he started for home, but Hill chased him and then chucked the ball to Kittredge [*sic*] for the out. Carr snarled at Buelow, who was coaching, for not keeping his eye on the ball, but this function belongs to base runners as well."[13] Cleveland won, 1–0, in 12 innings. The Blues later became known as the Naps and finally the Indians.

Date: April 22, 1905
Teams: Detroit Tigers vs. Chicago White Sox (American League)
Perpetrator: Detroit second baseman Germany Schaefer
Victim: Lee Tannehill, Chicago

According to the *Chicago Tribune*, "Schaefer pulled the concealed-ball trick out of moth powder in the sixth when he and [shortstop Charley] O'Leary nipped Tannehill at second."[14] O'Leary's role in the scam remains unclear. According to the *Detroit News*, "Schaefer even worked the old hidden-ball trick on Tannehill and put him out."[15] A cartoon in that paper depicts Tannehill standing off the bag, eyes closed, saying, "Please go 'way and let me sleep."[16] Detroit won, 3–2.

Date: April 29, 1905
Teams: Washington Senators vs. Boston Pilgrims (American League)
Perpetrator: Washington third baseman Hunter Hill
Victim: Freddy Parent, Boston

Hill—in the final season of his 325-game career—tricked Parent, with Chick Stahl serving as third base coach. With one out in the third inning, Jesse Burkett walked and Parent followed with a single. Kip Selbach doubled to center, scoring Burkett and sending Parent to third. Freddy, thinking pitcher Benny Jacobson had the ball, walked off the bag and was tagged out by Hill.

Sporting Life reprinted an item from the *Boston Journal* that reads as follows: "Chick Stahl felt like crawling into a hole yesterday when he allowed Parent to get caught napping off third base. That was all Chick had before him, and he might have kept his eyes open. As the Boston team never tries hiding the ball, they are naturally likely to get caught off their guard. It was the late Harry Wright who insisted that the trick was unprofessional, and he would not allow his players to attempt it on opponents. Mr. Wright argued that the spectators were entitled to see how each man went out and could not be expected to follow the ball when it was juggled by the players; therefore, few, outside the brush [*sic*] leagues, attempt the old trick, and it should be cut out for good."[17]

According to the *Washington Post*, "Fred Parent, to make matters worse, was put out at third base on a play that should make him ashamed to ask any salary for a week. Years ago, when Jim O'Rourke was in his prime and when Henry Chadwick began to write, baseball players were frequently put out by walking off a base when the baseman had the ball tucked up his sleeve. Boston fans yesterday, however, found out that the play is not entirely obsolete, and when Parent walked off third in the third inning, Hill walked over to him and tagged him out, Parent, of course, thinking Jacobsen [*sic*] had the ball. . . . Jacobsen seemed to be 'going up,' but Parent's 'asleep at the switch' specialty gave Jacobsen enough courage to stop the Boston stampede."[18] It was a big play, as Washington won, 4–2.

Date: May 6, 1905
Teams: Philadelphia Phillies vs. Brooklyn Superbas (National League)
Perpetrator: Philadelphia first baseman Fred Abbott
Victim: Fred Mitchell, Brooklyn

Fred fools Fred! According to the *New York Evening World*, Brooklyn all-purpose player Fred Mitchell led off the seventh inning with a single. Then, Fred "Abbott hid the ball and caught Mitchell napping."[19] Abbott, normally a catcher, played only 15 games at first in his career, which was in its final year.

Date: May 12, 1905
Teams: Detroit Tigers vs. Boston Pilgrims (American League)
Perpetrator: Detroit third baseman Bill Coughlin
Victim: Hobe Ferris, Brooklyn

According to the *Detroit Free Press*, "Ferris hit towards the club house for a triple. This so tickled Cy Young, who was coaching, that he forgot about the ball. As a result, Coughlin got the hidden-ball trick out of camphor and tagged Hobe when he stepped off the bag, making the triple valueless."[20] The *Boston Herald* had "HIDE-THE-BALL GAG WORKED ON FERRIS" in headlines,[21] also naming Young as the coach. The Tattersall box score scrapbook notes that "Detroit worked both the hidden and trapped ball on them."

The *Boston Globe* gave a quite different version, including a different coach: "There was a bit of comedy injected into the game. In the second inning Ferris, the third man up, smashed the ball to the clubhouse for three bases. Coughlin got the throw then booted the ball, and Big Bill Dineen, who was coaching off third, urged Ferris to start for home. Meantime Coughlin had tucked the ball under his left arm, and [John] Sullivan behind the plate made a pass to return the ball, which he did not have. . . . Coughlin tagged Ferris with the ball, while Hobe stood stock still ten feet from third. . . . Coughlin got Ferris with the hoary old trick of hiding the ball."[22]

The *Free Press* also remarked that, "The 'History of Early Baseball' [Mills] commission . . . will devote a special chapter of its report to the origin of this play." As baseball historian Peter Morris says, "That would certainly have made better reading than the report they actually produced!"

Date: July 23, 1905
Teams: Chicago White Sox vs. Philadelphia Athletics (American League)
Perpetrator: Chicago shortstop George Davis
Victim: Topsy Hartsel, Philadelphia

According to the *Chicago Tribune*, in the first inning, "George Davis worked the moss-grown hidden-ball trick on (Hartsel) and caught him dead to rights when he stepped off second, saving [pitcher Frank] Owen much trouble. . . . Hartsel hadn't the nerve to hold his head up after George Davis pulled the ball in play out of his sleeve and tagged him out at second in the opener."[23] Philadelphia managed to win, 1–0.

Date: August 3, 1905
Teams: Cincinnati Reds vs. Brooklyn Superbas (National League)
Perpetrator: Cincinnati first baseman Shad Barry
Victim: Charlie Malay, Brooklyn

In the top of the ninth inning, Malay—in his only season in the majors—led off with a bunt single to third base. Barry hid the ball under his arm and touched Malay when he stepped off the base.

Date: May 12, 1906
Teams: Cincinnati Reds vs. New York Giants (National League)

Perpetrators: Cincinnati first baseman Shad Barry and shortstop Tommy Corcoran
Victim: Roger Bresnahan, New York
Future Hall of Famer Bresnahan led off the game with a walk and advanced to second on George Browne's grounder. Barry kept the ball in his glove, then threw to Corcoran. Bresnahan spiked Corcoran but was out. The Reds went on to win, 3–2.

Date: May 18, 1906
Teams: Pittsburgh Pirates vs. New York Giants (National League)
Perpetrator: Pittsburgh shortstop Honus Wagner
Victim: Bill Dahlen, New York
Dahlen became a two-time victim, being tricked by Wagner in the eighth (or possibly the sixth) inning. "Wagner caught Bill Dahlen on the moss-covered trick of hiding the ball and touching him as he stepped off the bag," reports *Sporting Life*.[24] Dahlen was fined $100, but the fine was later rescinded.

Date: September 3, 1906 (second game)
Teams: Detroit Tigers vs. St. Louis Browns (American League)
Perpetrator: Detroit third baseman Bill Coughlin
Victim: George Stone, St. Louis

Date: April 13, 1907
Teams: Washington Senators vs. New York Highlanders (American League)
Perpetrator: Washington third baseman Lave Cross and shortstop Nig Perrine
Victim: Wid Conroy, New York
According to the *Washington Post*, "'Nig' Perrine has not had much experience in the major league, but that did not prevent him from pulling off a rather clever trick in the sixth inning, which put the laugh on Win [*sic*] Conroy and incidentally prevented trouble for the Nationals [an alternate nickname for the Senators]. A base on balls and a sacrifice had placed Conroy on second. (Highlanders' pitcher Lew Brockett) fouled out to [Washington catcher Mike] Heydon, and the latter rolled the ball to [third baseman] Lave Cross, who, without changing his position, rolled it through his legs (and their construction

allows this) to [shortstop] Perrine. The youngster placed the ball under his arm and took his position. [Pitcher Frank] Kitson and Heydon saw the scheme and took their positions. Conroy ventured off the bag and, quick as a flash, Perrine had the ball on him and he was out."[25]

Date: August 19, 1907
Teams: Detroit Tigers vs. Boston Red Sox (American League)
Perpetrator: Detroit third baseman Charley O'Leary
Victim: John Knight, Boston

According to the *Detroit Journal*, the Red Sox had the go-ahead run—in the person of 21-year-old John "Schoolboy" Knight—at third base with two out in the 12th inning. At this point the "beans of [Detroit pitcher Ed] Killian and O'Leary, when they got to working in harmony to consummate a diabolical plot, afforded another feature, over which the bugs are not through laughing yet. The Knight kid was the victim, and the plot was nothing more than the frazzled concealed ball. It is usually worked once a season. . . . (Knight) went to sleep and was jammed in the soft spot with the ball in the hands of O'Leary, the prestidigitator."[26] Detroit scored in the bottom of the inning to win, 4–3. According to the Society for American Baseball Research's (SABR) *Deadball Stars of the American League*, "Killian was especially fond of the hidden-ball trick, which he and teammate Charley O'Leary successfully performed on several occasions."[27]

Date: September 22, 1907 (second game)
Teams: Boston Doves vs. Chicago Cubs (National League)
Perpetrator: Boston first baseman Fred Tenney
Victim: Joe Tinker, Chicago

According to the *Chicago Daily Tribune*, Tenney ended the second game of a doubleheader by duping Hall of Famer Tinker: "Tinker gave the fans one last hope in the seventh by singling after two were out. Just as [pitcher Kid] Durbin came up to try to win his own battle, Manager Tenney grabbed the ball from under his own arm and touched Joe as he led off first, ending the game with the moss-grown trick."[28] Boston won, 4–2, beating Durbin in his only major league start.

Date: October 9, 1907

Teams: Detroit Tigers (American League) vs. Chicago Cubs (National League)

Perpetrators: Detroit second baseman Germany Schaefer and third baseman Bill Coughlin

Victim: Jimmy Slagle, Chicago

The HBT has even been executed in the World Series, although most sources don't account for it (*The World Series* lists it as a pickoff, Tigers' pitcher George Mullin to Coughlin).[29] In the first inning of Game 2 of the 1907 Fall Classic, according to *Sporting Life*, "Slagle was passed, stole second, and got to third on [catcher Freddie] Payne's wild throw, but was caught napping on the 'hide-the-ball' trick, Schaefer to Coughlin."[30] The 1908 edition of *Spalding's Official Base Ball Guide* says, "Coughlin, working that ancient and decrepit trick of the 'hidden ball,' got 'Rabbit' Slagle as he stepped off the third sack." According to author Stephen D. Boren, Schaefer caught a pop fly and then joined Coughlin in a conference with Mullin, during which Coughlin secreted the ball under his arm. After the tag, umpire Hank O'Day yelled, "You're out. Where did the ball come from?"[31] SABR's *Deadball Stars of the American League* gives Schaefer credit for the ruse: "Schaefer was also a master of the hidden-ball trick, which he performed in the 1907 World Series."[32]

Date: May 13, 1908

Teams: Detroit Tigers vs. Boston Red Sox (American League)

Perpetrator: Detroit third baseman Bill Coughlin

Victim: Amby McConnell, Boston

In the third inning, rookie McConnell hit a bases-clearing triple. As Tim Murnane writes in the *Boston Globe*, "About the meanest thing known to baseball occurred at this point. With Cy Young coaching, the ball was fielded to Coughlin, who tucked it away under his arm, and McConnell, supposing the pitcher had it, moved off the base and was touched out. This is one trick as old as the game that should never be allowed to go in baseball. . . . Hiding the ball is an ancient trick and long since barred from the game by custom. No Boston player has been allowed to attempt the trick since Harry Wright declared it was unsportsmanlike and an insult to the spectators."[33]

The *Detroit Times* says, "News of the barring of the play is fresh out this way. It has always been understood heretofore that the base runner was supposed, with the assistance of his coaches, to take reasonable care of himself and not be caught napping against any such transparent stratagem."[34] It's interesting that Murnane would take such umbrage at the play: On September 20, 1875, he pulled it on Cincinnati's Emmanuel Snyder to end a National Association exhibition game. Then again, Murnane was the victim of the play in an 1877 game. The 1908 trick had no bearing on the result of this game: Boston 10, Detroit 3.

By 1913, Murnane had become president of a minor league and acted on his opinion of the play. According to *Sporting Life*, "President Murnane of the New England League has followed the example of President Ban Johnson of the American League and has ordered his umpires not to give an out on the 'hidden-ball' trick."[35]

Murnane was hardly the first person to express disdain with the HBT. An anonymous *Sporting Life* writer devoted an article to such "infantile" and "amateurish" plays: "It is noticed that [Dodgers' president] Charley Byrne sets his face against such stupid tricks on the field as hiding the ball under the arm to catch a man off his base. He is a whole heap right about such things. Fine points of play and new, snappy tricks are admired by most all spectators, but the loggy calf play of the ball under the arm was born when the game was played in a cow pasture and is the practice of a country lout and not of an up-to-date brainy ballplayer. Of all the stupid and disgust-breeding things among professional players, this ball-hiding custom is among the worst. The man who does it should be disciplined, and the base runner who is caught by it should suffer more of a penalty than the usual disgust of spectators at his stupidity. Why, it is not playing ball. It is simply horseplay."[36]

Date: May 24, 1908
Teams: Cincinnati Reds vs. Brooklyn Superbas (National League)
Perpetrator: Cincinnati second baseman Miller Huggins
Victim: Tim Jordan, Brooklyn

Huggins worked the trick on Jordan in the ninth inning. Jordan had beaten out a grounder to Red third baseman Hans Lobert. Tommy Sheehan sacrificed him to second, with first baseman John Ganzel fielding the ball and Huggins covering the bag. Hug never returned the ball to pitcher Andy Coakley but played close to second, and when Jordan ventured off, Huggins caught him by several feet.[37] Brooklyn won anyway, 2–0.

Date: August 29, 1908
Teams: Boston Red Sox vs. St. Louis Browns (American League)
Perpetrator: Boston third baseman Harry Lord
Victim: Tom Jones, St. Louis
   Jones was caught by Boston rookie Lord to end the second inning.

Date: April 15, 1909
Teams: Cincinnati Reds vs. Pittsburgh Pirates (National League)
Perpetrators: Cincinnati second baseman Miller Huggins and first baseman Dick Hoblitzel
Victim: Fred Clarke, Pittsburgh
   In a play involving two future Hall of Famers on Opening Day, Huggins nabbed the speedy Clarke. According to the *Cincinnati Commercial Tribune*, "To Miller Huggins belongs the credit of pulling off the play that pleased the audience most. It was in the third inning, and Fred Clarke had singled and was on first base. [Pitcher Bob] Ewing appeared to take his position in the box, and Clarke immediately stepped off of first base a short distance, when to the surprise of not only Clarke, but about 3,999 fans out of the 4,000, Huggins got busy, tossed the ball to (first baseman Dick Hoblitzel), and Clarke was nipped. It was the old hidden-ball trick, and it nailed the veteran of Pittsburg [*sic*], showing very plainly that any of them can be fooled. . . . Clarke certainly felt like taking a walk around the block when Miller Huggins played the old hidden-ball racket on him yesterday. The play was worked in such a neat manner and so quickly that it took a few minutes for the joke to soak in on Clarke, as well as the spectators."[38]

Date: July 22, 1909
Teams: Chicago Cubs vs. New York Giants (National League)
Perpetrators: Chicago second baseman Johnny Evers and first baseman Frank Chance
Victim: Josh Devore, New York
   Score it Evers to Chance. According to the *Chicago Record-Herald*, reprinted in *Sporting News*, "Johnny Evers fathered the joke play of the Cubs game at the Polo Grounds on July 22 and put one over on [the

Figure 6.2.   Miller Huggins ranks number two on the all-time list, with eight tricks, the last of which led to two arrests. The "Mighty Mite" went on to become a Hall of Fame manager. Courtesy of the Library of Congress.

Giants'] John McGraw that had the whole populace laughing at the doughty little manager. It was an old barnacled trick, at that, which makes the fact that John of Troy got away with it all the more humorous. That bit of humor was perpetrated in the eighth inning. Larry Doyle, batting for [pitcher Hooks] Wiltse, had singled, and, as Larry has a hesitating leg when he runs nowadays, John ["Josh"] Devore took his place on the sack; John is rated as some base runner. 'Devore running for Doyle,' announced [umpire Bill] Klem. In the excitement attendant on the liberation of this silver-plated Klem oratory, Chance slipped the ball slyly to Evers. 'Take a big lead,' says [Fred] Snodgrass, coaching on first and watching [pitcher Ed] Reulbach. Devore obeyed instructions, and Evers threw the ball to Chance and Devore was nipped by a mile. Johnny nearly worked himself into hiccoughs laughing, and 'Muggsy' McGraw tried to make a kick. But even the populace was laughing at him and not with him. That took all the heart out of the Polo Ground athletes, and they were lambs for the slaughter thereafter, never making another bid to score."[39] The Cubs won, 3–1, and Devore wasn't even listed in the box score or official sheets as playing in the game.

Sporting News adds that, "Evers worked the moth-eaten trick of hiding the ball after a single had been made, so that when Josh Devore, innocent as the day is long, stepped off first base, the aggressive little second baseman, by a quick throw to Chance, made him a foolish victim. It was a trick that caused much laughter, and Evers was applauded. But not so with one of the owl-like persons who can never take a joke. There was a painful wail the next day about a violation of the rule as to the calling of 'time!' and the umpires got an old-fashioned tanning. In fact, the squeak about this rule continued for two days, Evers coming in for some old-ladyish censure for the mean advantage he had taken of the innocent Devore. But did you ever stop to think what would have happened if a Giant had pulled off this stunt? Why, man alive, the Boosters would have had pictures of it! Their pens would have reeked with nauseating praise, and the Cubs would have received the horse-laugh. It all depends on how the shoe pinches, you know."[40]

The play is reviewed in *Baseball Magazine*: "Last summer at the Polo Grounds in New York, the Cubs and Giants were doing battle. In the last of the ninth, with the visitors leading by a run, McGraw sent Doyle, his second baseman, who was on the bench with a bad ankle, up as a pinch hitter. 'Larry' made good, slamming a single out to center. As he was just able to limp about, Devore, a substitute, was put on first to run for him. The ball had been relayed into second, and Evers had received and secreted it, the excitement of the moment permitting him to do so unnoted. [Cub ace Mordecai "Three Finger"] Brown stepped into the pitchers' box. Devore took a lead off first and, like a bullet, the ball flashed from Evers to Chance, and a rally had been nipped in the bud."[41]

Sporting Life correspondent John B. Foster had much to say about the incident and the HBT in general: "That instance where Klem passed a rule up to make a decision which was wrong gives a general idea of the way in which all the staff has been wabbling [*sic*]. Evers pulled a hide-the-ball trick in New York under Klem's nose, and he was wrong on that. He had turned his back from the field to make an announcement to the grandstand. If he did not call time the inference was that he called time, and if he suspended play without calling time he was not living up to the rules. If he did call time he should have seen that the ball was in the possession of the pitcher, and if the ball had been where it belonged it would not have been possible for the Chicago players to work an old trick, which may be considered cute, but which is dishonest and should be legislated out of the game. . . . There are some persons in the world whose sense of fairness and honesty is so dulled that they consider the hidden-ball trick a bright play. No play is bright when it is unsportsmanlike, and no play that is unsportsmanlike is strictly honest. . . . [H]iding the ball and other similar practices are all a part of one side of our professional sport, which puts winning above everything and which does not add greatly to the reputation of American sport in general. It is the small greed to win, whether on a technicality or by good sportsmanship, which has dulled so much of the real manly spirit which should be the dominating force in all outdoor pastimes."[42]

According to a 1971 article by Bob Addie, "There is a favorite story about the old, old days when one of John McGraw's Giants was caught with the hidden-ball trick by the master, Johnny Evers, Cub second baseman. McGraw, instead of stripping the hide off the culprit, was the model of compassion. The guilty player had a fondness for cantaloupe a la mode. That night the player ordered his favorite dessert, and instead of ice cream, he found a baseball in his cantaloupe—presumably the same one that had nailed him earlier."[43] This sounds suspiciously like the July 15, 1931, Rabbit Maranville story you will read about later.

Date: July 31, 1909
Teams: Cincinnati Reds vs. Brooklyn Superbas (National League)
Perpetrator: Cincinnati third baseman Miller Huggins
Victim: Wally Clement, Brooklyn

"Huggins stopped a rally in the fourth by working the hidden-ball brick [*sic*] on Clement at third," according to the *New York Times*.[44] In the first game of what was to be a doubleheader, the Reds won, 1–0, with the game called by rain after eight innings. This was Clement's only full season in the majors.

7

1910–1919: BAN TRIES TO BAN IT

Despite American League president Ban Johnson's intentions of banning the hidden-ball trick, no decade saw more executions than the 1910s. There were 49 in all, including 25 in the American League, 21 in the National League, and 3 in the Federal League. First sacker George Stovall was the leader, with six.

Date: May 18, 1910
Teams: Cleveland Naps vs. Washington Senators (American League)
Perpetrator: Cleveland first baseman George Stovall
Victim: Gabby Street, Washington
According to the *Washington Post*, "'Gabby' Street was caught off first by the mossy hidden-ball trick. A throw had been made to the plate and [Cleveland catcher Harry] Bemis had tossed to Stovall, who neatly tucked his hand and the ball behind his back. Dr. [pitcher Frank 'Doc'] Reisling was coaching at first, at least he was standing nearby. Street walked off the base, and Stovall planted the leather in the small of Gabby's back. Street doubled up in horror—so did the fans. Umpire [Jack] Sheridan was dazed by the play, but umpire [John] Kerin was on duty, too, and he upheld the move. . . . It cost Gabby Street several packages of fine cut, some cheroots, and a dictionary load of adjectives to square himself for being caught by the moth-eaten hidden-ball trick. Dr. Reisling was his accomplice, such coaching being too suggestive of a man asleep standing up to be appreciated."[1] Ironically, earlier in the game, Cleveland's George "Perring tried to work the 'hide-the-ball'

trick on Killefer in the third, but 'Red' refused to move from the base. The lesson did not get Street's attention."[2] Washington held on to win, 4–3.

Date: May 19, 1910
Teams: Cleveland Naps vs. New York Highlanders (American League)
Perpetrator: Cleveland first baseman George Stovall
Victim: Hal Chase, New York
    In the bottom of the tenth, with the score tied, 3–3, between the visiting Naps and the Highlanders, Chase loaded the bases with none out on what was described in the *New York Telegram* as a "bunt." At this point, "Chase walked off first when Stovall held the ball and was touched out."[3] It was the second day in a row that Stovall had duped someone. New York still won, 4–3.

Date: June 28, 1910
Teams: Philadelphia Phillies vs. New York Giants (National League)
Perpetrator: Philadelphia first baseman Joe Ward
Victim: Josh Devore, New York
    According to the *New York Telegram*, Ward nabbed Devore in the fourth inning.[4] It was the second time in less than a year that he had been caught.

Date: July 13, 1910
Teams: New York Highlanders vs. Cleveland Naps (American League)
Perpetrator: New York first baseman Hal Chase
Victim: George Stovall, Cleveland
    Fifty-five days after being nabbed by George Stovall, Hal Chase exacted his revenge. According to this date's *New York Evening Telegram*, in the ninth inning of the New York–Cleveland game, Chase caught Stovall at first base on the same trick. It didn't affect the outcome of the game: Cleveland won, 9–2.

Date: August 6, 1910
Teams: Detroit Tigers vs. New York Highlanders (American League)
Perpetrators: Detroit third baseman George Moriarty and second baseman Jim Delahanty
Victim: Birdie Cree, New York

Figure 7.1. **First baseman George Stovall pulled off the trick six times in a little more than three years. Courtesy of the Library of Congress.**

Moriarty nailed Cree in the fifth inning of a 5–0 Tiger win, tossing to Delahanty for the out. According to the *New York Times*, "The time-honored hidden-ball trick perhaps prevented the Yankees from scoring in the fifth. . . . (Frank LaPorte) sent [center fielder Ty] Cobb so far into the offing for his fly that Cree essayed to travel along after the catch. Cobb's good throw, however, turned him back (to second). Moriarty tucked the ball under his arm, when [pitcher George] Mullin sauntered back to the box. Cree watched him instead of Moriarty, and his out was easy."[5] The *Detroit Free Press* called the play a "mossy one," adding, "Right here Moriarty and Delahanty pulled off a play that was ruled out of the Ark for being too ancient to be of further service. Evidently Cree hadn't heard of it, for he fell like a Rube for a gold brick. Moriarty carelessly concealed the ball under his left arm and when Cree focused his attention on Mullin, tossed to Delahanty, who plunked the man from Gotham in the ribs, much to his surprise, not to say chagrin."[6] Moriarty later witnessed the HBT as both an umpire a and manager/coach.

Date: September 22, 1910 (first game)
Teams: New York Giants vs. Chicago Cubs (National League)
Perpetrator: New York first baseman Fred Merkle
Victim: Johnny Evers, Chicago

The Giants' Fred Merkle has forever been remembered for his September 23, 1908, "boner," when he failed to advance to second base on an apparent game-winning hit and was called out when Cub second baseman Johnny Evers retrieved a ball and touched the base, forcing Merkle for the third out and nullifying the run. The game wound up a tie, replayed at the end of the season and resulting in a Cub victory to win the pennant by one game over the Giants.

Merkle could never live down this humiliation, but he did gain a measure of revenge. It happened in New York in the first game of a doubleheader against the Cubs. According to I. E. Sanborn of the *Chicago Tribune*, "A feature of the day not indicated in the tabulated summary occurred in the first game, when J. Evers was made the victim of a moth-ball-scented trick by none other than Fred 'Bone' Merkle. Everyone has seen first basemen try to trick runners into stepping off first base by bluffing to throw the ball back to the pitcher after receiving a quick throw to drive the runner back. Few ever were fortunate enough to see the play pulled off. We have been watching for it since early in the '90s, but without being rewarded until today. Evers was on first with none out in the fifth inning, having just accepted his third straight pass from [Louis] Drucke. The hurler pegged across to first to drive him back. Merkle went through the time-worn motion of bluffing to return the throw but holding the ball. Evers yanked his foot off the bag. Merkle stabbed him, and the umpire saw it. There was great joy among the bugs who dearly love the Trojan, we don't think so. What made it all the more noteworthy is that tomorrow is the anniversary of 'Merkle day' at the Polo Grounds. Just two years ago tomorrow, Merkle gave Chicago it's [sic] third pennant by forgetting to touch second."[7]

Date: June 1, 1911 (second game)
Teams: St. Louis Cardinals vs. Cincinnati Reds (National League)
Perpetrator: St. Louis second baseman Miller Huggins
Victim: Bob Bescher, Cincinnati

Huggins nabbed the speedy Bescher in the second game of a doubleheader. The *Atlantic Constitution*, reprinted from the *Philadelphia Times*, gave a detailed account of Bescher's day's work, including "First Inning—singled; fell victim to hidden-ball trick, worked by Huggins."[8]

Date: June 30, 1911
Teams: St. Louis Cardinals vs. Pittsburgh Pirates (National League)
Perpetrator: St. Louis second baseman Miller Huggins
Victim: Max Carey, Pittsburgh

A Hall of Famer got a Hall of Famer, as Miller Huggins caught Pirate rookie Carey in the ninth inning. Carey is regarded as the best base runner of his era. According to Huggins's obituary in the *Brooklyn Daily Eagle*, "Before Huggins's day [the HBT] was unknown. It was Hug who introduced it into the big league."[9] That would be news to those who were practicing the play before Huggins was even introduced to the world.

Date: July 9, 1911
Teams: Detroit Tigers vs. Washington Senators (American League)
Perpetrator: Detroit second baseman Charley O'Leary
Victim: Jack Lelivelt, Washington

According to the *Washington Post*, "In the second inning, after [Doc] Gessler and Lelivelt had hit and [George] McBride had sacrificed, O'Leary worked the old 1812 hidden-ball trick on Lelivelt. Charlie took a throw at first, and instead of throwing the ball back to the pitcher, O'Leary darted over and pinned him."[10]

Date: September 1, 1911
Teams: Cleveland Naps vs. Chicago White Sox (American League)

Perpetrator: Cleveland shortstop Ivy Olson
Victim: Felix Chouinard, Chicago

Cleveland rookie Olson caught Chicago rookie pinch-runner Chouinard at second base in the ninth inning. According to the *Chicago Tribune*, the White Sox coaches were watching the scoreboard to see how the crosstown Cubs were doing.

Date: April 14, 1912
Teams: St. Louis Cardinals vs. Chicago Cubs (National League)
Perpetrator: St. Louis shortstop Arnold Hauser
Victim: Jimmy Sheckard, Chicago

The day the *Titanic* hit the iceberg, Arnold "Pee Wee" Hauser sunk 16-year veteran Jimmy Sheckard on a HBT in the eighth.

Date: May 11, 1912
Teams: St. Louis Browns vs. Boston Red Sox (American League)
Perpetrator: St. Louis first baseman George Stovall
Victim: Les Nunamaker, Boston

Date: June 15, 1912
Teams: St. Louis Browns vs. New York Highlanders (American League)
Perpetrators: St. Louis second baseman Del Pratt and first baseman George Stovall
Victim: Bert Daniels, New York

"Two hits went for naught in the sixth as Daniels was nailed on the hidden-ball trick by Pratt and Stovall," according to the *New York Times*.[11] St. Louis won, 2–1.

Date: June 17, 1912 (first game)
Teams: Boston Braves vs. Cincinnati Reds (National League)
Perpetrators: Boston third baseman Ed McDonald and catcher Johnny Kling
Victim: Armando Marsans, Cincinnati

According to the *Boston Herald*, "Eddie McDonald pulled Boston out of a hole when he worked the 'hide-the-ball' trick on Marsans. Marsans was on third, and after McDonald had caught [Dick] Egan's foul over by the third base bleachers, instead of throwing the ball to [pitcher Hub] Perdue, 'Mac' stuck it under his arm. Perdue walked over behind the box, and when Marsans took a lead off third, McDonald ran him in and tossed the ball to Kling, who tagged the Cuban for the third out of the inning."[12] Boston won, 4–3.

Date: July 3, 1912 (first game)
Teams: Washington Senators vs. New York Highlanders (American League)
Perpetrator: Washington first baseman Chick Gandil
Victim: Jack Martin, New York
Gandil—later to be implicated in the "Black Sox Scandal"—scandalized Martin on the HBT in the second inning.[13] It was the first of a record three times Martin would be duped on the trick—in a career spanning just 187 games.

Date: July 14, 1912 (first game)
Teams: St. Louis Cardinals vs. New York Giants (National League)
Perpetrator: St. Louis third baseman Wally Smith
Victim: Fred Snodgrass, New York
According to the *New York Times*, "Wally Smith pulled 'the hidden-ball trick' at the expense of Fred Snodgrass in the sixth inning, and it probably saved the game for [pitcher] Bob Harmon. . . . [Beals] Becker hit with Snodgrass on the 'hit-and-run,' whacking a single to right field, Snodgrass taking third base. . . . However Snodgrass forgot to follow the ball, Smith hiding it in his glove, and when Fred stepped off the bag, Wally tagged him. Umpire Bob Emslie, who was making base decisions, said that he did not see the play, but umpire [Mal] Eason, who was working behind the bat, saw it and waved Snodgrass out."[14] It was a crucial play, as the Cards won, 3–2. Interestingly, Snodgrass—who would become infamous for a fatal World Series error later that same year—had been similarly tricked by the Cardinals two years before, with Emslie calling him out but Cy Rigler overruling his fellow arbiter, nullifying the play.

Date: August 29, 1912
Teams: Boston Braves vs. Philadelphia Phillies (National League)
Perpetrator: Boston third baseman Ed McDonald
Victim: Doc Miller, Philadelphia

With two out in the seventh inning, Miller tripled in a run but was promptly caught napping by McDonald.[15] McDonald pulled the trick at least twice in his 176-game career.

Date: September 2, 1912 (second game)
Teams: Cincinnati Reds vs. St. Louis Cardinals (National League)
Perpetrator: Cincinnati second baseman Dick Egan
Victim: Bob Harmon, St. Louis

In the seventh inning, Egan nabbed Harmon, pinch-running for player-manager Roger Bresnahan after Bresnahan doubled. After the inning's second out was made on a fly ball to center fielder Armando Marsans, "Egan caught Harmon . . . on the hidden-ball trick at second base," according to the *Cincinnati Enquirer*.[16]

Date: September 3, 1912
Teams: Washington Senators vs. Philadelphia Athletics (American League)
Perpetrator: Washington shortstop George McBride
Victim: Eddie Murphy, Philadelphia

McBride caught Murphy in the seventh inning. According to the *Washington Post*, with teammate Ben Egan on third, "Murphy hit to [first baseman Chick] Gandil, who threw to [catcher John] Henry. The latter ran his man back, and he was retired near third base. Murphy took second on the play. This was followed by the comedy incident of the contest. In the rundown, Henry chased Egan back, and [third baseman Eddie] Foster and McBride protected third, [pitcher Bob] Groom covering the plate. The play, of course, was right under the eyes of the men on the Athletics' bench. As the three Nationals dispersed, McBride had the ball slipped to him and went over to his position, playing rather close to the bag. Groom stood on the hill, but not on the slab. Murphy moved off second, and the instant he did so McBride pounced on him, pinned him to the ground, and tagged him out."[17] Washington won, 4–2.

Date: September 25, 1912 (first game)
Teams: St. Louis Browns vs. Chicago White Sox (American League)
Perpetrators: St. Louis second baseman Del Pratt and third baseman Jimmy Austin

Victim: Rollie Zeider, Chicago

According to the *Chicago Evening American* and the *Chicago Tribune*, Pratt and Austin worked the trick on Zeider in the fourth inning. After Zeider tripled, Brown shortstop/manager Bobby Wallace went to the mound to confer with pitcher George Baumgardner. When Zeider tried to sneak home, Austin put the tag on him.

Date: September 30, 1912
Teams: St. Louis Cardinals vs. Cincinnati Reds (National League)
Perpetrator: St. Louis second baseman Miller Huggins
Victim: Hank Severeid, Cincinnati

According to the *Cincinnati Enquirer*, Huggins tricked Severeid after Hank had doubled in the sixth inning.[18]

Date: April 13, 1913
Teams: St. Louis Browns vs. Chicago White Sox (American League)
Perpetrator: Browns' first baseman–manager George Stovall
Victim: Frank Lange, White Sox

April 13, 1913 was an unlucky day for White Sox pitcher Frank Lange. According to *Sporting News*, "Someone had circulated a story that [American League president] Ban Johnson had barred the hidden-ball trick, but George Stovall pulled it on . . . Lange in the first game of the Browns–White Sox series and got away with it in great shape. It upset Lange so that he went to pieces in the next inning, and Ed Walsh had to be called to his rescue."[19] Lange walked the bases loaded to start the bottom of the ninth, but Walsh struck out the next three and the White Sox won, 7–2.

Date: May 14, 1913
Teams: Cleveland Naps vs. New York Yankees (American League)
Perpetrator: Cleveland third baseman Ivy Olson
Victim: Birdie Cree, New York

Olson worked the ruse on the Yankees, who had nine runners retired on the bases during the game—so much for old-time ballplayers having better fundamentals! According to the *New York Times*, "Three more [New York runners] were put out at third base at critical moments. One of the latter trio was Birdie Cree, who fell victim to the old hidden-ball trick, worked by Olson."[20] The game ended in a 15-inning, 2–2 tie, called by darkness.

Date: May 28, 1913
Teams: St. Louis Browns vs. Detroit Tigers (American League)
Perpetrator: St. Louis first baseman–manager George Stovall
Victim: Donie Bush, Detroit

Stovall executed the trick for the sixth time in a little more than three years. According to the *Frederick Post*, "In the third inning Stovall played the old hidden-ball trick on Bush after that gentleman had turned first safely on a hit to left. The joke of the play was that Hughey Jennings was on first base line coaching at the time."[21]

Date: May 31, 1913 (second game)
Teams: St. Louis Cardinals vs. Cincinnati Reds (National League)
Perpetrators: St. Louis second baseman Lee Magee and first baseman Ed Konetchy
Victim: Johnny Bates, Cincinnati

According to the *Cincinnati Enquirer*, "Johnny Bates was much chagrined when the hidden-ball trick, musty with age, was pulled on him in the first inning of the second game. Johnny had singled and was comfortably ensconced near first base, fanning himself with his cap and viewing the scenery. Magee had the ball under his arm and shot it quickly to (Konetchy), who touched Johnny before he could scramble back to the base."[22]

Date: July 13, 1913
Teams: St. Louis Browns vs. New York Yankees (American League)
Perpetrators: St. Louis second baseman Del Pratt and first baseman Bunny Brief
Victim: Ezra Midkiff, New York

According to the *New York Times*, Midkiff undid the goodwill of an earlier fine fielding play: "Midkiff made up for it in the ninth, when he was caught on the old-time hidden-ball trick after he had reached first on a single. Pratt nipped him with a throw to Brief."[23] New York won anyway, 3–2.

Date: July 28, 1913

Figure 7.2.   Second baseman Del Pratt, better known for his bat, executed the hidden-ball trick on four occasions. Courtesy of the Library of Congress.

Teams: Chicago Cubs vs. Boston Braves (National League)
Perpetrator: Chicago third baseman Art Phelan
Victim: Wilson Collins, Boston

According to *Sporting Life*, "As a conclusion to the game, Phelan played the famous hidden-ball trick on [rookie Wilson] Collins, a pinch runner, and the game was over. In this inning the visitors scored two men and had a man on second and third. There was much confusion while [Rabbit] Maranville was coming up to bat, and Phelan calmly held the ball and stood a few feet from third. [Bert] Humphries then walked into the pitchers' box, and Collins stepped off third and was tagged out."[24] The Cubs won, 9–4. Ernest Lanigan recalled the play six years later, when another game was ended on a HBT by Jimmy Austin on Wally Schang: "On July 28, 1913, the Braves, rallying in the ninth against the Cubs, saw the last gent retired in the same manner as Austin retired Schang—by concealing the ball from the runner and the coacher and then plastering it on the runner when he stepped off the bag. (It was Wilson) Collins, graduate of a Southern college, and he was doing a pinch-running stunt for John Titus."[25]

Date: May 26, 1914
Teams: St. Louis Browns vs. Philadelphia Athletics (American League)
Perpetrator: St. Louis shortstop Buzzy Wares
Victim: Amos Strunk, Philadelphia

According to *Sporting Life*, the rookie "Wares worked the hidden-ball trick on Strunk in the second inning, it being the first time this play had been seen locally [in Philadelphia] in years."[26] It was a big play, as St. Louis went on to win, 6–5.

Date: May 26, 1914
Teams: Cleveland Naps vs. Boston Red Sox (American League)
Perpetrator: Cleveland second baseman–manager Nap Lajoie
Victim: Del Gainer, Boston

Lajoie pulled one of the three tricks on this date. He covered first on a sacrifice by Boston's Bill Carrigan and then returned to his customary position with the ball still in hand. When Gainer (playing his first game for the Red Sox) left the sack, Lajoie tagged him. "The second out in the fifth inning produced one grand row," writes Tim Murnane of the *Boston Globe*. "Gainor [sic] was on first base and went to second on a sacrifice by Bill Carrigan. The first baseman tossed the ball to Lajoie, who stole over to second, where he caught Gainor in a trance, starting off his base before he knew where the ball was. There was quite a mix-up at the base, and when umpire Jack Sheridan looked, he saw Lajoie holding the Boston runner off the base and declared him out. This caused a sharp cry of protest from the Boston players, who argued that Lajoie pushed Gainor off the base, and as Sheridan had been caught looking anywhere but where the ball was, he turned to the umpire at the plate for advice. [Rookie umpire Ollie] Chill waved his hand, as much as to say that the man was safe. Then Sheridan turned and waved Gainor safe. At this stage, nearly the whole Cleveland outfit, headed by the irate Frenchman from Woonsocket, headed for the umpire at the plate. Chill evidently saw them coming, for he immediately changed his mind and commenced to wave the player out. Umpire Sheridan then made his third decision and this time was in full accord with the umpire in charge of the game, the pair of them having made five decisions on the one play. . . . The Boston players then crowded around the umpire and spent five or six minutes protesting. Then the game went on. The great Lajoie had stooped to one of the long-since-discarded by-plays of the game—the old hidden-ball trick—and a play not allowed by a Boston club."[27] Cleveland won, 3–2.

Date: May 26, 1914
Teams: St. Louis Cardinals vs. Boston Braves (National League)
Perpetrators: St. Louis second baseman–manager Miller Huggins and first baseman Dots Miller
Victim: Jack Martin, Boston

  One of two St. Louis tricks (and two Boston victimizations) on the day went Miller to Miller: Miller Huggins to Dots Miller. According to Ernest Lanigan in 1919, "Another youngster . . . who was careless about following the course of the ball was Jack Martin, a young shortstop tried by Charlie Dooin and George Stallings five years ago. While (Martin) was a Brave, Miller Huggins worked the hidden-ball trick on him."[28] The event was found in the *Boston Herald*: "The hidden-ball trick reappeared here after a long absence. Huggins pulled it at the expense of Martin in the seventh inning and nipped a Boston rally in its incipiency. [Jim] Murray, batting for [catcher Bert] Whaling, had opened this round with a line single. He was forced by Martin on a great play, [third baseman Cozy] Dolan to Huggins, who retained possession of the ball after [Bill] Doak went to the hill. Martin wandered away from his moorings and was tagged out when Huggins handed the pill to Miller."[29]

According to the *St. Louis Star*, "The hidden-ball trick was again brought back to earth Tuesday when Manager Huggins pulled the ancient trick on Youngster Martin in the seventh inning. Martin was but two feet off first base when Huggins shot the ball to Miller. Martin was caught flatfooted and made little effort to get back to the bag. The same trick was pulled by the Browns in Philadelphia by Clyde Wares."[30]

Date: May 30, 1914 (second game)
Teams: Baltimore Terrapins vs. Pittsburgh Rebels (Federal League)
Perpetrator: Baltimore second baseman Otto Knabe
Victim: Tex McDonald, Pittsburgh
     In the second game of a Decoration Day twin bill, Knabe made a play at third base to get McDonald in the 11th inning.

Date: June 9, 1914
Teams: Pittsburgh Pirates vs. Philadelphia Phillies (National League)
Perpetrator: Pittsburgh shortstop Honus Wagner
Victim: Beals Becker, Philadelphia
     In the eighth inning, Wagner pulled the ruse on Becker, who had singled and been sacrificed to second. Wagner also pulled a decoy earlier in the same game, but it doesn't quite qualify as a HBT. After Hans Lobert stole second in the first inning, according to the *Pittsburgh Gazette Times*, "Wagner tricked him into starting for third. Wagner then picked up the ball behind the bag and tagged Lobert trying to get back."[31] Despite Wagner's theatrics—including his 3,000th career hit— the Phillies won, 3–1.

Date: June 23, 1914
Teams: Cleveland Naps vs. Detroit Tigers (American League)
Perpetrator: Cleveland third baseman Ivy Olson
Victim: Bobby Veach, Detroit
     According to *Sporting News*, discussing a later event, "This is the second time this season that Detroit has been involved in the stunt. The first time it was the victim, when Olson of the Naps caught Bob Veach off third base with it while Jennings was coaching there. It cost the Tigers a game with Cleveland."[32] The *Cleveland Plain Dealer* reports the following: "It was not until Mr. Ivan Olson, the Nap third sacker, had reintroduced Hugh Ambrose Jennings to the hidden-ball trick,

which he had not seen since he worked for Ned Hanlon, that victory was finally chased away by the Tigers. Mr. Olson's revival of the dead was staged in the eighth inning, right in the midst of a ferocious Tiger rally which apparently destined to give the game to Detroit. Lots of credit must be given to Ivan for the neat manner in which he conducted the resurrection, but more belongs to the aforesaid Mr. Jennings, who was coaching at third. . . . (With nobody out, Marty Kavanaugh) bumped a nice single into right, putting Veach on third with the tying run. [Right fielder Roy] Wood made a fine throw and all but got Bobbie sliding into third, though Olson made no attempt to tag him, merely bluffing Kavanagh [sic] back from second. Olson walked over toward [pitcher Fred] Blanding and then back to third. Veach was about three feet off the bag waiting for Blanding to get back on the mound when Ivan suddenly produced the ball from under his arm and made a dive for him. At that, he barely got him, for Bobbie dropped as he saw the ball coming but couldn't quite make the bag with a standing hop. That took the heart out of the rally, making the Tigers look foolish."[33] Detroit lost, 5–4.

Date: July 4, 1914 (first game)
Teams: Pittsburgh Rebels vs. Baltimore Terrapins (Federal League)
Perpetrator: Pittsburgh shortstop Eddie Holly
Victim: Harvey Russell, Baltimore
It was the first game of an Independence Day doubleheader. With the bases loaded and none out in the eighth, Baltimore got a sacrifice fly to center field. The Pittsburgh outfielder threw in to Holly, who tagged rookie Russell soon thereafter.

Date: July 10, 1914
Teams: Detroit Tigers vs. Philadelphia Athletics (American League)
Perpetrators: Detroit third baseman Billy Purtell and second baseman Marty Kavanaugh
Victim: Eddie Collins, Philadelphia
"Probably the most mortified person after the Tigers' series at Philadelphia was Eddie Collins, who had the hidden-ball trick played on him to catch him off second with one out and a run needed to win in the (ninth inning) of the final game," writes *Sporting News*. "Billy Purtell was the man who pulled the stunt, and Harry Davis was the coacher on

third who overlooked Billy's trick. Collins had walked and stolen when [Frank] Baker flied to [Bobby] Veach. Veach returned the ball to Purtell at third. Billy hid it until the proper time had come, when he threw to Kavanaugh and Collins was caught off the bag. Both Collins and Davis were to blame for the trick, and Purtell deserved the greater part of the credit for it."[34] Purtell was in the waning days of his brief career. As Ernest Lanigan wrote five years later, "There is no smarter athlete in captivity than Edward Trowbridge Collins of the White Sox, yet Eddie, when he was a Mack man, was a victim of the hidden-ball trick, Bill Purtell . . . tucking the sphere under his arm."[35]

Date: July 14, 1914 (first game)
Teams: Baltimore Terrapins vs. Buffalo BufFeds (Federal League)
Perpetrator: Baltimore first baseman Harry Swacina
Victim: Everett Booe, Buffalo

In the top of the fourth inning, Booe reached first base to lead off the inning. He was picked off first by Baltimore pitcher George Suggs and broke for second base. Swacina threw to shortstop Mickey Doolan, who dropped the ball for an error, enabling Booe to scamper back to first ahead of Doolan's return throw. But Swacina held the ball and tagged out Booe when he took another lead off first.

Date: September 9, 1914 (first game)
Teams: Boston Braves vs. Philadelphia Phillies (National League)
Perpetrators: Boston shortstop Rabbit Maranville and third baseman Red Smith
Victim: Jack Martin, Philadelphia

According to Ernest Lanigan, Martin was caught twice in 1914 alone, with Maranville effecting the second trick.[36] The event was found in the *Boston Post*: "At this point [of the first inning] little Jack Martin, the former Brave, was so thoughtless as to drive a high one to center, which Herbie Moran lost in the sun. . . . Martin reached third when the ball was missed and [Dode] Paskert scored. A second later Martin was caught napping on the moss-grown hidden-ball trick, Maranville having the sphere in his possession and throwing to Smith for the putout."[37]

Date: May 1, 1915

Teams: St. Louis Cardinals vs. Cincinnati Reds (National League)
Perpetrator: St. Louis second baseman–manager Miller Huggins
Victim: Tommy Leach, Cincinnati

In a play involving two stars near the end of their playing careers, Huggins nailed Leach, precipitating a fistfight between Red manager Buck Herzog and umpire Cy Rigler that landed both of them in jail. According to the *St. Louis Post-Dispatch*, "The fracas which eventuated in the arrest of the umpire and manager was imposed suddenly upon some 6,000 fans in the seventh inning of a game which the Cardinals won from the Reds, 9–5. . . . Manager Herzog exploded when Tommy Leach, his veteran outfielder, was victimized on the hidden-ball trick, a moth-eaten affair, by Manager Huggins. This play took place at second base. Hug held the ball until Leach wandered off second and then dove for his prey and landed him. Umpire [Bill] Hart, officiating on the bases, didn't see the play. He appealed to Rigler, who was behind the plate. Rigler called Leach out. Then Herzog rushed at the umpire. Rigler promptly ordered Herzog out of the game. The Cincinnati manager went to the bench but returned and renewed his argument with Rigler. He tapped Rigler on the chest with his index finger. . . . Rigler hit Herzog with his mask and then followed with blows from his fist. The pair clinched and fists were flying freely."[38] After the game, both men were arrested on peace disturbance charges and fined five dollars. Ernest Lanigan recalled the play four years later, saying, "Herzie got set down indefinitely by John Tener for mixing things up with the arbitrator, and the row all came from the hidden-ball trick."[39]

This event also supposedly precipitated the National League president's outlawing of the play. According to *Sporting News*, "Now John K. Tener in his league has barred the hidden-ball trick on the theory that it is a trick that should have no part in a contest of athletic skill. It was the pulling of the stunt by Miller Huggins, too, if we remember correctly, that caused Mr. Tener to take action."[40] Nonetheless, there were at least three National League executions of the play between this one and Tener's resignation on June 17, 1918.

An article in the *St. Louis Times* belies the notion that Tener even had the authority to outlaw it: Tener "said he would eliminate the hidden ball (and similar trick plays). Tener expressed himself then as being opposed to such petty tricks of the diamond and hinted that they bordered on foul tactics. Such is the opinion of President Tener, but it is not supported by Manager Huggins. . . . 'If a base runner takes a nap on the bases, and if there's a wide awake guy on the infield to put over the hidden-ball trick, he should be permitted to win the play. That's part of baseball. It puts spice into the game, and when they attempt to remove the pep from the game, they're crimping it for the fan. . . . I don't know if they're going to discuss these plays, but if they do I'm going to dip in my oar. You bet I will.' And Huggins can dip in his oar, too, because he is a member of the Rules Committee. The Big Chief only can make the suggestion, and then it will be up to Huggins and the other two members to pass their OK. And there will be one vote opposing the bill."[41]

Decades later, *Sporting News* reminisced that "Huggins . . . was the greatest artist of them all in pulling the hidden-ball trick, which is very seldom seen these days. Hug would work it five or six times in a season. In fact, he pulled it so often there was some agitation in the press to make it illegal."[42]

Date: May 10, 1915
Teams: Chicago Cubs vs. Pittsburgh Pirates (National League)
Perpetrator: Chicago shortstop Bob Fisher
Victim: Doug Baird, Pittsburgh
   In the second inning, Pirate rookie Baird tapped to the Cub pitcher but reached second on a fielder's choice when the pitcher ran down the base runner between second and third. Baird was then caught on the HBT by Fisher. The Pirates won anyway.

Date: June 17, 1915
Teams: Pittsburgh Pirates vs. New York Giants (National League)
Perpetrator: Pittsburgh shortstop Alex McCarthy
Victim: Dave Robertson, New York
   According to the *New York Times*, in the ninth inning of a game at Pittsburgh, the "old hidden-ball trick was worked on Robertson, and it saved the home team from being further scored upon. Robertson had beaten out an infield [hit] and went to second when [Fred] Merkle singled to center. [Zip] Collins returned the ball to McCarthy, and as Robertson stepped off the bag, he was tagged and called out. That stopped the rally, but the Giants had enough,"[43] winning 3–1.

Date: August 29, 1915

Teams: St. Louis Browns vs. Washington Senators (American League)
Perpetrator: St. Louis second baseman Del Pratt
Victim: Horace Milan, Washington

In the eighth, pinch runner Horace Milan was caught by Pratt. Horace, brother of Senator star Clyde Milan, was making his major league debut. St. Louis won, 2–1, with George Sisler outdueling Walter Johnson. According to the *Washington Post*, "Griffmen Fall for Hidden-Ball Trick. . . . When the hidden-ball trick, so ancient that it is not used by pennant ball clubs, comes along to beat you, then it is time to wake up. The Nationals [Senators] fell into a clever trap laid by second baseman Derrill Pratt this afternoon, and a rally in the eighth inning was nipped at second base and the Browns won the final game of the series, 2–1. Whom would you blame for having the hidden ball catch a base runner? Eph Milan was the victim, but then the boss on the field was the coacher, and even Griff [Washington owner-manager Clark Griffith] failed to see Pratt tuck the ball under his arm. It all came about in this fashion: [Ray] Morgan opened the eighth. He shot a slow bounder to [shortstop Doc] Lavan, which the fielder booted long enough to put Ray on first. In hiking down the path, though, Morgan sprung a leak in his right leg, and the game was stopped a few moments. Griff looked to the bench for a substitute base runner and picked out Eph. With proper announcement, Milan became the base runner. [Danny] Moeller followed with a perfect bunt down the first base line. [First baseman Ivan] Howard ran for the ball, and when he saw Milan was running a safe race for second, he played for Dan and tossed to Pratt, who was on the bag for the putout. Griff was right there on first and saw Pratt glove the ball, but like Milan and others, he did not see Del hide it under the right arm. Pratt leisurely returned to his fielding territory. Catcher [Hank] Severeid gave a signal to Sisler, who was moving around the hill in the pretense of being ready to pitch to Foster. On the coaching line Griff shrieked, 'Hey, there, you get up just as far as the shortstop,' and Milan obeyed the order. Step-by-step he walked away from the bag, and then Pratt ran and took a dive. Milan saw the play, but it was too late. Pratt tagged Milan sliding back to the bag, and umpire [Billy] Evans ruled the out. The 6,500 fans gave Griff and Milan the laugh."[44]

Date: August 9, 1916 (second game)
Teams: St. Louis Cardinals vs. New York Giants (National League)

Perpetrator: St. Louis second baseman Bruno Betzel
Victim: Fred Merkle, New York

According to *Sporting News*, "Fred Merkle always has to be the goat for something. In the second game of the doubleheader between the Giants and Cardinals on August 9, the Cardinals pulled the hidden-ball trick on Fred at second base, catching him sound asleep."[45] Betzel turned the trick in the second inning. Fred, of course, was famed as the goat of "Merkle's Boner," a crucial baserunning blunder during the 1908 pennant race.

Date: July 3, 1918
Teams: St. Louis Cardinals vs. Chicago Cubs (National League)
Perpetrator: St. Louis second baseman Bob Fisher
Victim: Dode Paskert, Chicago

Date: July 4, 1918 (second game)
Teams: Detroit Tigers vs. Chicago White Sox (American League)
Perpetrator: Detroit first baseman Ty Cobb
Victim: Joe Benz, Chicago

In the second game of a holiday doubleheader, Cobb (in one of his 14 career games at first base) was inspired by Bob Fisher's trick the day before. According to the *Detroit Free Press*, "Cobb, having read in the papers of the old hidden-ball trick used on Dode Paskert in St. Louis Wednesday, thought he'd try it, and he made good, too. In the sixth inning [Chicago's Fred] McMullin was on third and [Otto] Jacobs on first with one out when Benz tapped to the pitcher. McMullin was run down, and the ball was thrown to second later for a play on Jacobs. It got away from [Pep] Young and was recovered by Cobb, who tucked it under his arm, walked back to first base . . . and when Benz stepped off the bag, Ty stung him with the ball."[46] The Sox won anyway, 2–1.

Date: July 26, 1918
Teams: St. Louis Browns vs. Washington Senators (American League)
Perpetrator: St. Louis shortstop Jimmy Austin
Victim: Wildfire Schulte, Washington

According to the *Washington Post*, "Nationals Fall for the Hidden-Ball Trick and Still Score Over Browns: The Nationals had a terrible time in the fourth. Among other things, they fell victims of the moss-covered hidden-ball trick. [Washington's Clyde] Milan opened with an infield single, and Schulte walked. [Howard] Shanks's best was a pop to Austin. Then [Doc] Lavan singled to left. Milan rounded third and attempted to get back, only to find [Fritz] Maisel waiting with the ball. A moment later Schulte wandered off second and was tagged out by Austin. He had taken the ball from Maisel after Milan's putout at third. Umpire [Brick] Owens, working on the bases, had his back turned and didn't see the hidden-ball trick pulled. The Browns appealed to [plate umpire Silk] O'Loughlin, who allowed the putout."[47] Schulte was winding down a 15-year big league career. Washington still won, 3–2.

Date: September 2, 1918 (second game)
Teams: Chicago White Sox vs. Detroit Tigers (American League)
Perpetrator: Chicago third baseman Babe Pinelli
Victim: George Harper, Detroit

According to the *Toledo Blade*, rookie Pinelli caught Harper with manager Hughie Jennings coaching.[48] It was during the second game of a season-ending doubleheader at Detroit, and there was a feeling that this could be the last regular-season baseball game of the foreseeable future. The campaign was being cut short by World War I, and the game featured a squad of military airplanes exhibiting maneuvers above the field. According to the *Detroit Free Press*, "George Harper helped to make this game historic by allowing Pinelli, the Sox recruit third sacker, to pull the hidden-ball trick on him. It made Harper look bad. . . . In the inning in which Harper was nailed, it looked like the Tigers must have a bat on their opponents, a double, two singles, and a long fly that enabled two runners to advance a base, being bunched without a run resulting and with only one man left."[49] The *Detroit News* writes, "George also fell victim to the hidden-ball trick in the second game. Harper watched the airplanes after getting as far as third base, and Pinelli shoved the ball into his ribs."[50] Detroit still won, 7–3, but Harper announced afterward that he was thinking of enlisting in the navy.

Date: June 18, 1919
Teams: St. Louis Browns vs. Boston Red Sox (American League)
Perpetrator: St. Louis third baseman Jimmy Austin
Victim: Wally Schang, Boston

According to the *Boston Globe*, "Once in about every ten years, the age-old 'hidden-ball' trick is worked successfully. The world's champions [Red Sox] were the victims yesterday. This particular trick has no place in the game, and there has been considerable agitation in favor of prohibiting it, but it has not been barred, and so, of course, it is always the business of the player to protect himself against it. . . . (Brown first baseman George Sisler) leaped into the air, extended his gloved hand to the limit, and came down with (a line-drive hit by Ray Caldwell). He threw over to third to double up Schang, but the whole thing was over so quickly, Wally had no chance to get far from the bag and was back before the ball got there. The Red Sox were so stunned by Sisler's great catch . . . that they did not notice that Austin had tucked the ball under his arm and waited until Schang, who assumed that the pitcher had it, walked off the bag. Then, fishing the ball from his armpit, Jimmy made a dive for Schang and touched him out. It may have been difficult for Schang and Jack Barry—the latter was coaching at third—to explain how they were imposed on by Austin . . . but they can come back with the alibi that there was a coach at first, [Frank] Gilhooley at bat, and a whole dugout full of Red Sox players, not to mention several thousand spectators, every one in the whole collection in just as much of a fog, mentally, as were Schang and Barry, which proves that Austin had the psychology of the situation OK and knew when the hoary hidden-ball trick was workable."[51] The play ended the game by nipping the potential tying run in the ninth inning, giving St. Louis a 3–2 victory.

The *St. Louis Times* added a bit to the account: "Schang dusted himself, stood on the bag, and paused while Frank Gilhooley appeared at the plate as pinsh [*sic*] hitter for Pitcher [George] Dumont. Austin at third was tightening his cap and giving some sort of signal to [pitcher Allan] Sothoron. 'Don't let this bird hit, Al!' shouted Pepper Jim to his pitcher. Schang moved away from third base, and the moment he took his foot off the safety zone, Austin made a dive for the runner. He applied the ball on Schang, and the Red Sox runner was caught before he could get back to the bag."[52] The *Boston Herald* summarizes the game, saying that it "became ancient history, a sad chapter for the Sox."[53]

Sporting News editorialized against the hidden-ball trick in the wake of this play: "The rules should prohibit the 'hidden-ball trick.' It has no place in the game. One of the beauties of baseball which appeals to

most of its devotees is that the play is wide open, dignified, and grace-
ful, and none of these features can be associated with a trick that comes
pretty near to being a blow below the belt, if it were not so childish in
its nature."[54]

Date: July 25, 1919
Teams: Chicago White Sox vs. St. Louis Browns (American League)
Perpetrator: Chicago third baseman Fred McMullin
Victim: Joe Gedeon, St. Louis
    According to *Sporting News*, "The hidden-ball trick worked on
Gedeon in the first inning and saved the Chicago pitcher [Lefty
Williams] . . . and with an old-timer like Jimmy Burke on the coaching
lines, too."[55] McMullin pulled the trick as the White Sox won, 6–4.
McMullin and Williams were just a few months away from pulling tricks
of a more dastardly nature, in the "Black Sox Scandal."

Date: September 11, 1919 (second game)
Teams: Philadelphia Phillies vs. Pittsburgh Pirates (National League)
Perpetrators: Philadelphia second baseman Gene Paulette and third
baseman Lena Blackburne
Victim: Billy Southworth, Pittsburgh
    In the third inning, Pirate Possum Whitted doubled, moving South-
worth to third base. Paulette hid the ball and then threw to Blackburne
to catch Southworth. The play cost the Bucs at least one run, as Walter
Barbare followed with a home run, but Pittsburgh won anyway, 7–2.
Southworth would later make the Hall of Fame as a manager, while
Blackburne would become famous for the mud used to rub down base-
balls before a game.

8

1920–1929: A DECADE DOMINATED BY BABE WHO?

Baseball in the Roaring '20s was dominated by Babe Ruth, but the leader in trick plays was another Babe. Of the 24 hidden-ball tricks in the decade, Babe Pinelli participated in four and abetted in another. American League players continued to thumb their noses at Ban Johnson, pulling off the play 19 times.

Date: June 19, 1920
Teams: Detroit Tigers vs. Boston Red Sox (American League)
Perpetrator: Detroit third baseman Babe Pinelli
Victim: Stuffy McInnis, Boston

According to *The Ballplayers*, Pinelli "once caught veterans Sam Rice and Stuffy McGinnis [*sic*] with the 'hidden-ball trick' on consecutive days."[1] Not quite, but close: The plays were three days apart. On this day, McInnis opened the sixth inning with a single and advanced to third on Eddie Foster's double. There Stuffy "fell asleep, and Pinelli, who hid the ball, tagged him out,"[2] according to the *Detroit Free Press*. The play cost the Sox at least one run, as Tiger pitcher Howard Ehmke promptly balked. Per the *Toledo Blade*, Ossie Vitt was coaching third base.[3] Umpire Billy Evans recalled the play as follows: "McInnis fell victim on the final day of Boston's stay in Detroit. . . . The pitcher developed a wild streak, and the next two balls were high. Pinelli walked over to say a few words of encouragement and, while talking, got the ball. As play was resumed, McInnis took the usual lead off third base and was an easy victim for Pinelli. I never saw a player look so crestfallen as did McInnis. . . . If looks were injurious, Pinelli would have passed away on the spot."[4]

Date: June 22, 1920
Teams: Detroit Tigers vs. Washington Senators (American League)
Perpetrator: Detroit third baseman Babe Pinelli
Victim: Sam Rice, Washington

Pinelli notched his second trick of a star player in four days on future Hall of Famer Rice. According to the *Washington Post*, in the first inning, Braggo "Roth doubled off the top of the scoreboard. . . . [Joe] Judge scored on the smash, and Rice pulled up at third. Rice was trapped by Pinelli on the old hidden-ball trick."[5] The *Detroit Free Press* blamed third base coach George McBride and Roth as much as Rice: "Roth, McBride, and Rice went fast asleep, however, and 'Babe' Pinelli, hiding the ball from the gaze of those worthy gentlemen, applied it to Rice."[6] Decades later, in an article in *Baseball Digest*, Pinelli reflects, "It was an awful thing to do, making the manager look bad like that. But could I help it if they were both in a trance?"[7] The play cost the Senators at least one run, but they still won, 6–1. Umpire Billy Evans recalled this trick as well: "Kindly remember that in getting Rice on the old 1776 stunt, he pulled it on the champion base runner of the American League. . . . Washington came to Detroit to open a series of four games. Of course Pinelli's exploit [the recent HBT on McInnis] was played up in the papers. The Washington players laughed about it before the game. During the game. Sam Rice reached third. The game was halted for some reason, such as slipping the pitcher some advice, and when resumed. Pinelli had the ball and Rice was an easy out."[8]

Date: August 8, 1920
Teams: Detroit Tigers vs. New York Yankees (American League)
Perpetrator: Detroit second baseman Ralph Young
Victim: Ping Bodie, New York

Young, with some help from teammate Babe Pinelli, caught Bodie in the fifth inning of a 1–0 Detroit win. Pinelli recalled the trick years later, stating, "Another time, when I was with Detroit, Pep Young, an infielder with us at the time, had the ball, I knew. It was a tight game, and Ping Bodie, the Yankee outfielder, was on second. I thought I would lure Ping off so Young could apply the ball. 'You are not the only Italian player in the game, or even the best Italian player,' I taunted. Bodie took the bait. 'Go on, you are not a real wop,' Ping answered, glaring at me, a busher, while he strayed off the base. When Young put the ball on Bodie, I thought they would have to put Ping in a cage, he was that mad."

According to *Baseball Magazine*, Bodie evened the score with Pinelli years later in the minor leagues, although the story sounds like a corruption of this one: "Paul Waner relates a humorous incident which concerns Babe Pinelli, when the former Red player arrived on the coast after leaving the majors. Playing in one of his early games in the Coast League, Pinelli bumped into an old friend of his in Ping Bodie, former Yank, who played with a rival team. In Bodie's first at bat, he fanned ingloriously, while Pinelli, in his first time at bat, hit a hard single. Trotting up to first base, where Bodie played, Pinelli started to josh Bodie saying, 'Yes, there's only one good ballplayer in this game. Just one good ballplayer.' Pinelli kept repeating this remark in an endeavor to get a rise out of the former Yankee. In the later innings, he again hit safely, and when he reached first, he revived his chatter muttering, 'Yes sir, just one.' But he couldn't finish his sentence, for Bodie, working the ancient hidden-ball trick, tagged Pinelli out as he started to take his lead off first base, at the same time innocently remarking, 'Yes sir, there's just one good ballplayer in this ball game.'"[9] Waner played in the Pacific Coast League from 1923 to 1925; however, Pinelli was a regular with the Reds during those years.

This wasn't the first time Bodie had been victimized. On July 8, 1913, while playing in an exhibition game for the White Sox, he was caught by the Princeton team.

Date: September 18, 1920
Teams: Washington Senators vs. Cleveland Indians (American League)
Perpetrator: Washington second baseman Bucky Harris
Victim: Doc Johnston, Cleveland

Date: July 4, 1921 (second game)
Teams: St. Louis Browns vs. Detroit Tigers (American League)
Perpetrator: St. Louis shortstop Jimmy Austin
Victim: Joe Sargent, Detroit

The *St. Louis Post-Dispatch*, describing Jimmy Austin's July 9, 1921, HBT, mentions that it was the second time within a week Austin had pulled it off: "Austin's other victim was Sargent of the Tigers in the afternoon contest, July 4."[10] Austin had just returned the day before, after recovering from a broken arm. Sargent was a rookie.

Date: July 9, 1921
Teams: St. Louis Browns vs. Washington Senators (American League)
Perpetrator: St. Louis shortstop Jimmy Austin
Victim: Patsy Gharrity, Washington

The Browns beat the Senators, 12–3. Writes the *St. Louis Globe-Democrat*, "The game ended when Austin worked the hidden-ball trick for the second time within a week and tagged Gharrity at second."[11] *Sporting News* confirms it, saying, "Austin worked the hidden-ball trick, and the game ended when Gharrity was tagged after walking off second for the third out of the ninth inning."[12] The *St. Louis Post-Dispatch* has the best description: "For the second time since he has been in the game regularly, in fact, in the space of a week, the ancient Jimmy Austin worked the hidden-ball trick. Yesterday it came in the ninth, and Gharrity, the Washington catcher, was the victim. Gharrity was on the pivot station by virtue of his single and another by [Frank] Brower. [Joe] Judge popped up to [first baseman George] Sisler in short right. Sis tossed to [pitcher Urban] Shocker. Austin walked over, took the ball out of Shocker's hands, walked leisurely toward second, and the moment Gharrity stepped off the base tagged him, ending the game."[13] Interestingly, three days later, Fred Lieb mentioned in the *New York Telegram* that the "trapped-ball and the hidden-ball tricks have practically disappeared from baseball."[14]

Date: August 2, 1921
Teams: Detroit Tigers vs. Washington Senators (American League)
Perpetrator: Detroit third baseman Bobby Jones
Victim: Bing Miller, Washington

According to the *Washington Post*, in the fifth inning, Washington's Clyde Milan "was run down between home and third on Miller's tap to Jones. Miller reached third while Milan was being run down, but he would have fared better had he stopped at first base, as he fell a victim

Figure 8.1. Jimmy "Pepper" Austin worked the trick five times, including twice in six days. Courtesy of the Library of Congress.

to the ancient hidden-ball trick by Bobby Jones."[15] Washington still won, 5–4.

Date: April 22, 1922
Teams: St. Louis Cardinals vs. Pittsburgh Pirates (National League)
Perpetrator: St. Louis first baseman Jack Fournier
Victim: Max Carey, Pittsburgh

With two out in the bottom of the seventh inning, Pirate future Hall of Famer Carey was on first base. Fournier caught Carey on the HBT, unassisted. It was the second time Carey had been bamboozled.

Date: April 24, 1922
Teams: Washington Senators vs. Boston Red Sox (American League)
Perpetrator: Senators' first baseman Joe Judge
Victim: Shano Collins, Red Sox

Judge nailed Collins in the first inning. Writes the *Washington Post*, "Collins started with a scratch hit to [Bobby] LaMotte. [Elmer] Smith popped to [pitcher George] Mogridge in attempting a sacrifice. Mogridge's throw in attempting to complete the double play was too late, but Judge doubled up Collins on the hidden-ball trick."[16] Washington won, 11–3. Judge pulled another HBT less than three months later.

Date: June 24, 1922 (second game)
Teams: Boston Red Sox vs. New York Yankees (American League)
Perpetrator: Boston first baseman George Burns
Victim: Chick Fewster, New York

In the first inning, Tioga George Burns held outfielder Elmer Smith's return throw and then nabbed Fewster.

Date: July 11, 1922
Teams: Washington Senators vs. Chicago White Sox (American League)
Perpetrator: Washington first baseman Joe Judge
Victim: Johnny Mostil, Chicago

Date: August 20, 1922 (second game)
Teams: Cincinnati Reds vs. Brooklyn Robins (National League)

Perpetrators: Cincinnati third baseman Babe Pinelli and shortstop Ike Caveney
Victim: Ray Schmandt, Brooklyn

It was the fourth inning of the second game of a doubleheader. After Pinelli caught a pop-up hit by the Robins' Andy High, Babe held the ball. Pinelli recalled the trick years later: "One day in Brooklyn I worked the trick on Ray Schmandt. Ray was watching the pitcher, but Caveney sneaked into second behind Schmandt. I threw the ball, and when it landed with a 'pop' in Caveney's glove, Schmandt thought he'd been shot from behind. He jumped a foot." According to the *Toledo Blade*, manager Wilbert Robinson was coaching third base.[17]

Date: September 21, 1922
Teams: Detroit Tigers vs. New York Yankees (American League)
Perpetrators: Detroit third baseman Bobby Jones and catcher Johnny Bassler
Victim: Everett Scott, New York

In the eighth inning, Frank Baker flied to Detroit's Ty Cobb in left, scoring what proved to be the Yankees' winning run in a 9–8 victory over the Tigers. Moments later, Jones caught Scott off third base with the HBT and ran him down, throwing to Bassler for the putout.

Date: May 26, 1923
Teams: Boston Red Sox vs. Washington Senators (American League)
Perpetrator: Boston shortstop Johnny Mitchell
Victim: Bucky Harris, Washington

According to the *Washington Post*, "Stan Harris, captain of the Nationals [Senators], was at once the goat and the hero of the last game of the series (in Boston). . . . It was largely due to his hitting in the pinches that the Capital Clan won from the Red Sox, 3–2, but he was the target of the old, venerable, and mossy hidden-ball trick in the fifth inning, and was caught flatfooted off second, spoiling what had all the earmarks of being a big inning for the Nationals. . . . (With one out and Ossie Bluege on first, Stan 'Bucky') Harris lifted a fly to center, but Joe Harris muffed it and Bluege went to third, and Stan to second. But here Mitchell managed to work the hidden-ball stunt at the expense of the usually alert Nat captain, and he was caught off second and retired. [Umpire George] Moriarty made the final ruling on this play, as it escaped the notice of Clarence ['Pants'] Rowland. The Bush clan kicked, but Stan was guilty and was out a mile."[18]

Date: May 17, 1924
Teams: Boston Red Sox vs. Chicago White Sox (American League)
Perpetrator: Boston third baseman Danny Clark
Victim: Roy Elsh, Chicago

With White Sox manager Johnny Evers hospitalized following an emergency appendectomy, Ed Walsh finally got his dream job of managing his former team—but thanks to this incident, it lasted only three days. On May 17, Walsh was coaching third base when Elsh was nabbed on the HBT by Clark. Per the *Chicago Sunday Tribune*, "[Harry] Hooper singled to score [Roy] Schalk and to plant Elsh on the far corner. There was a lull in the proceedings. Suddenly Clark fell on Elsh and tagged him with the ball, which he had concealed about his person, after it was returned from right field. Ed Walsh, acting as manager in place of Johnny Evers, was the coach involved. The revival of this ancient trick cut the rally short and left the Sox in such shape that they never did tie the score."[19] A Ford Sawyer article the next day reads, "Probably there were a number of spectators who were quite as surprised as Roy Elsh when Danny Clark pulled the hidden ball on him in the seventh." Chicago lost, 5–4, and within two days, Walsh was replaced by Eddie Collins as interim manager. According to the *Chicago Tribune*, "Ed Walsh and Tom Needham will assist Collins in running the team. Among other things they can be on the watch for the hidden-ball trick."[20]

Date: June 30, 1926
Teams: St. Louis Browns vs. Detroit Tigers (American League)
Perpetrator: St. Louis third baseman Marty McManus
Victim: Harry Heilmann, Detroit

McManus bamboozled two Tiger Hall of Famers in one play. According to an Associated Press wire, "In the fourth inning, McManus worked the hidden-ball trick on Heilmann, tagging him when he took a lead off third. Ty Cobb was coaching at third base at the time." The Tigers won nevertheless, 4–1.

Date: July 20, 1926

Teams: Cincinnati Reds vs. Brooklyn Robins (National League)
Perpetrators: Cincinnati shortstop Frank Emmer and third baseman Babe Pinelli
Victim: Johnny Butler, Brooklyn

Emmer and Pinelli combined to nab Robin rookie Butler in the fourth inning. According to the *New York Times,* "Johnny Butler fell the victim of sunstroke or something and was caught on such a childish prank as the hidden-ball trick."[21]

Date: May 17, 1927
Teams: Cincinnati Reds vs. New York Giants (National League)
Perpetrator: Cincinnati third baseman Chuck Dressen
Victim: George Harper, New York

According to the *New York Evening Journal,* the Giants' Jim Hamby forced out Bill Terry at the plate after Reds first baseman Wally Pipp threw to catcher Bubbles Hargrave. Hargrave threw to Dressen, and Harper (a previous victim of the trick), who didn't know that Dressen had the ball, stepped off the bag and was tagged out by the third sacker. This doesn't necessarily sound like a genuine trick, but a recollection made 21 years later certifies it. According to writer Clifford Bloodgood, "A most brazen bit of sleight of hand was engineered by wily Charley Dressen when the present Yankee traffic cop was third-basing for the Reds, back in the Roaring Twenties. On the day of our tale, Cincinnati was playing the Giants, managed by the fiery John J. McGraw. Coaching at third for the New Yorkers was Roger Bresnahan, former catcher. . . . The Giants had a runner on second base, an outfielder by the name of George Harper, and one on first. The batter hit a line single to left field. The (Red) pitcher, submarine-baller Carl Mays, watched the drive but made no attempt to back up home plate, so Dressen took it upon himself to do so. Sure enough, the throw-in escaped catcher Eugene 'Bubbles' Hargrave, and Dressen grabbed it. The speed with which all this action took place prompted Bresnahan to hold Harper up at third. Charley walked over, handed the ball to Mays, and then lifted it out of his glove, telling the pitcher to make like he had it and fool around for a minute near the mound. The third baseman returned to his position with his arms at his side and the ball in one hand. It was not visible to the Giants' coach, but there were folks in the stands who were in a position to spot it. Chuck took his place and put his hands on his

Figure 8.2.   Although he played in just 774 games before becoming a famous umpire, Babe Pinelli executed five tricks and aided in another. He later passed his knowledge on to Frankie Crosetti. Courtesy of the National Baseball Hall of Fame Library, Cooperstown, New York.

knees, a natural pose for an infielder before the pitcher throws to the batter. He began a conversation with Bresnahan. 'It's a good thing you didn't send Harper in. I would have nailed him.' The unsuspecting coach answered by letting Harper edge off the bag. Dressen nonchalantly eased toward his prey and put his foot down on George's tootsies. They were off the base when he made his tag. . . . The Giants lost that battle of wits, 3–2."[22]

Date: April 23, 1928
Teams: Chicago White Sox vs. Detroit Tigers (American League)
Perpetrator: Chicago third baseman Willie Kamm
Victim: Jackie Tavener, Detroit

Kamm, quoted in the book *Rowdy Richard*, says, "One time I pulled it, and George Moriarty was the umpire. He said to me, 'If I was the manager of a team and that happened to one of my baserunners, I'd fine the coach $500.' Well, a couple years later, George was managing Detroit and coaching at third. One day I saw a chance and pulled the trick on one of his players. When the umpire called the runner out, I turned to George and said, 'Who are you going to fine the $500 this time?'"[23] This matches up with another story involving Detroit's Jackie Tavener. In a 1956 *Baseball Digest* article by Edgar Munzel of the *Chicago Sun-Times*, Kamm is quoted as saying the following about the play: "Biggest kick I ever got out of it was when I pulled it on Detroit one day. George Moriarty was an American League umpire who had called five or six guys out on me when I pulled the hidden ball on runners at third base. One day after he had called a guy out, he blurted, 'How stupid can these guys get? If I were a manager and you pulled that on a runner, I'd fine the third base coach $500. It's his job to keep an eye on the ball.' The following year, Moriarty became manager of the Tigers. The White Sox were playing Detroit one day, and Moriarty was doing his own job coaching at third base. Jackie Tavener laced out a triple and just beat the throw to third base. He dusted himself off and felt pretty proud of himself. Moriarty yelled at Tavener, 'All right, Jackie, get a good lead now.' Jackie took a few steps off the bag, and I walked up behind him with the ball. As I tagged Tavener, I turned around to Moriarty and shouted, 'Who you going to fine now, George?' He was so mad he couldn't talk."[24]

Another *Baseball Digest* article, by Gordon Cobbledick of the *Cleveland Plain Dealer*, repeats the story, saying Tavener triple plated two runners and tied the game. Kamm is quoted as saying, "The play was fairly close at third, and I kicked up a fuss with the umpire just to create a diversion. Then I stuck the ball under my arm. I heard Moriarty say, 'Find the ball, Jackie,' and I thought, 'Well, this isn't going to work.' Then I heard him say, 'All right, Jackie, take a good lead.' So I put the ball on Tavener, and I said to Morry, 'Now who you gonna fine 500 bucks?'"[25]

Despite these accounts, it took a long time to find the incident, which occurred the day Shirley Temple was born. According to the *Chicago Tribune*, "For fans under 40 years of age, who never have seen the hidden-ball trick worked in baseball, we shall pause to tell how it was performed. Tavener opened the inning with a triple to right. [Right fielder Johnny] Mostil relayed the ball to third through [second baseman Bill] Barrett to Kamm. Moriarty was coaching at third base, which is directly in front of the Tiger bench. [Pitcher Sarge] Connally took his place in the box, and Tavener took a lead toward home. Kamm flashed the ball out of the recesses of his glove and tagged Jackie."[26] This occurred in the fifth inning, with Bill McGowan umpiring. Detroit won anyway, 3–0.

Date: July 27, 1928
Teams: Chicago White Sox vs. Philadelphia Athletics (American League)
Perpetrator: Chicago third baseman Willie Kamm
Victim: Mickey Cochrane, Philadelphia

Per a 1951 article in *Baseball Digest*, "Back in the days when Willie Kamm played third for the White Sox, Mickey Cochrane tripled home two Philadelphia Athletic runs at Comiskey Park. He began dancing up and down, shouting. . . . Kamm let him kick his heels a couple of times and then met him on the way down with the ball. 'Lookee, lookee,' chortled Willie, 'now dance over to the bench.' And with the umpire watching, Cochrane had no choice."[27]

Francis Powers of the *Chicago Daily News* quotes Jimmy Dykes about the same play: "I remember once, back when I was with the Athletics, we were playing the White Sox, and as I recall it, we were having a big inning in which we got five or six runs. In the rally, Mickey

Cochrane hit one and came hustling into third base. At that time we used to have a sort of battle cry. When we were in a rally or doing well, we'd yell, 'Give 'em a touch of high life.' Well, Cochrane is standing on third, and we yell from the bench, 'Give 'em a touch of high life, Mike!' So he starts dancing off the bag. No sooner does Mike get off the bag than Bill Kamm, the Sox third baseman, walks over and says, in a voice that we can hear on the bench, 'Here's a touch of high life for you, Mickey,' and tags him with the ball. Cochrane could have killed Kamm right then and there."[28]

The details don't quite match up, but the play was found on this date, as described by the *Chicago Tribune*: "The big eighth might be going yet but for the fact that Mickey Cochrane fell for the hidden-ball trick. In this inning . . . Cochrane singled, and so did [Al] Simmons. The net result was six runs when Kamm ended it with the hidden-ball maneuver."[29] The A's won, 7–4.

Date: September 13, 1928
Teams: St. Louis Browns vs. Chicago White Sox (American League)
Perpetrator: St. Louis first baseman Lu Blue
Victim: Art Shires, Chicago

According to the *New York Times*, "Lu Blue, Browns' first baseman, resurrected the ancient hidden-ball trick to touch out [Art 'The Great'] Shires, Sox rookie first baseman, in the seventh."[30] The Browns won, 6–4.

Date: April 21, 1929
Teams: St. Louis Browns vs. Detroit Tigers (American League)
Perpetrator: St. Louis third baseman Frank O'Rourke
Victim: Nolen Richardson, Detroit

Says the *New York Times*, O'Rourke "used the hidden-ball trick on Richardson, Detroit's rookie shortstop. This came in the second, after [Roy] Johnson, who walked, scored on singles by [Eddie] Phillips and Richardson. On [pitcher Earl] Whitehill's single, Phillips was retired at third. O'Rourke held the ball after tagging the catcher. [General] Crowder feinted a pitch, and Richardson was caught napping."[31] The box score lists this as a double play, right field to shortstop to catcher to second base to third base. It sounds as if Phillips was caught between third and home and retired by O'Rourke in a rundown, before the trick completed the double play. Richardson had made his major league debut just five days earlier.

Date: April 30, 1929
Teams: Chicago White Sox vs. Cleveland Indians (American League)
Perpetrator: Chicago third baseman Willie Kamm
Victim: Charlie Jamieson, Cleveland

The White Sox were clinging to a 5–3 lead in the seventh inning, but the Indians had the tying runs in scoring position with none out. The rally was killed by a triple play, concluding with a hidden-ball trick. It started with White Sox shortstop Bill Cissell throwing to first baseman Bud Clancy to retire batter Carl Lind and Clancy tossing to catcher Buck Crouse to head off any scoring attempt by lead runner Johnny Hodapp. Hodapp retreated to third but found trail runner Jamieson there. Crouse fired to Kamm, who tagged both Cleveland runners. Hodapp was out number two, but Jamieson, a 15-year veteran, was entitled to the base. According to *Baseball Digest*, "Jamieson was properly and understandably irate. After blistering Hodapp's ears with some pertinent observations upon his intelligence and ancestry, he continued in similar vein with only Kamm for an audience. 'Can you imagine a dumb Dutch so-and-so like that?' he asked. Kamm clucked sympathetically. 'A tough break,' he agreed. 'What I like is a heads-up ballplayer like you, Jamie.' Jamieson snorted and, as the pitcher moved to the box, took a short lead off third. The voice he heard behind him was Kamm's. 'Look what I've got, Charlie,' it was saying, as Willie removed the ball from under his arm and touched Jamieson gently on the chest for the third out."[32]

The *Elyria Chronicle Telegram* adds, "A weird but fatal triple play killed the Indians' chances of victory in the seventh inning of the farce today. Hodapp started off the inning as a pinch hitter for [pitcher Willis] Hudlin and singled. Jamieson singled to center, sending Hodapp to third and taking second on the throw in. Cissell threw out Lind, Hodapp holding third, and when Jamieson ran up from second, Hodapp was put out. . . . The Sox third baseman kept the ball pocketed in his glove, and when Jamieson strayed off third, he was tagged out. This completed the triple play that goes on records as Cissell to Clancy to Crouse to Kamm [say *that* five times fast], as well as enlightening the fans as to what kind of baseball the Indians have been playing the last few days."[33] Kamm was hit in the back by a pitch during his next plate appearance. The White Sox won, 8–4.

Date: July 18, 1929
Teams: Brooklyn Robins vs. Chicago Cubs (National League)
Perpetrators: Brooklyn second baseman Billy Rhiel and shortstop Dave Bancroft
Victim: Riggs Stephenson, Chicago

In the ninth inning, Robin rookie Rhiel held the ball and then flipped to Bancroft to put out Stephenson.

9

1930–1939: THE CROW FLIES HIGH

Even hidden-ball tricks were affected by the Great Depression, as once again they declined by about half from the previous decade, but the emergence of shortstop Frankie Crosetti in the second half of the 1930s breathed new life into the trick. "The Crow" performed the last six of the 15 successful tricks in the decade, leading the American League to a 9–6 edge.

Date: September 20, 1930
Teams: Cincinnati Reds vs. New York Giants (National League)
Perpetrators: Cincinnati shortstop Leo Durocher and third baseman Tony Cuccinello
Victim: Freddy Leach, New York
    Durocher and rookie Cuccinello conspired to nab Leach in the first inning; Durocher concealed the ball and threw it to Cuccinello for the putout. The play was recalled by Arthur Daley in the *New York Times* 15 years later: "Dave Bancroft was coaching at third. 'We need this run, Fred,' urged Banny. 'Get a big jump on anything that's hit and bring it in.' While he was talking, Tony was doing some talking of his own. 'Stay off the rubber,' he said to Pitcher Larry Benton. . . . Cuccinello innocently parked himself near the bag. . . . Leach walked away from the base. 'Ye're out!' bellowed the umpire. 'What happened?' screamed Banny. 'You dirty sneak!' howled Leach—or words to that effect."[1]

Date: June 25, 1931

Teams: Cleveland Indians vs. Boston Red Sox (American League)
Perpetrator: Cleveland third baseman Willie Kamm
Victim: Jack Rothrock, Boston

Date: July 15, 1931
Teams: Cincinnati Reds vs. Boston Braves (National League)
Perpetrators: Cincinnati third baseman Joe Stripp and second baseman Tony Cuccinello
Victim: Rabbit Maranville, Boston

This is the most written-about HBT in baseball history, although there are different versions of what happened. This much we know: The Braves trailed the Reds, 1–0, going into the ninth. Maranville, a colorful future Hall of Famer in his 20th season, led off the frame with a single and advanced to second on a wild pitch, representing the tying run with none out. Billy Urbanski then popped up to Stripp, who, according to the *Boston Globe*, "slipped the ball under his arms, and the Reds prepared as though [Jack] Ogden was going to pitch to [Wally] Berger. But as soon as Maranville took a lead off second, Stripp whipped the ball to Cuccinello, who slapped it on the Rabbit before the latter could slide back to second base."[2] Berger then flied out to end the game.

In his book *Run, Rabbit, Run*, culled from 1953 interviews, Maranville recalls the play and its aftermath in remarkable detail. Rabbit was distracted by an argument between the Red first baseman and the umpire. "Cuccinello was playing about two yards off second base when I noticed him. I said, 'What are you trying to do, pick me off?' Tony said, 'No.' I took another step away from second when, *bing*, I saw the ball go over my shoulder to Tony, and I was picked off second on that old hidden-ball trick. . . . When I reached the bench, I asked, 'Who threw the ball to Tony?' Not one of the twenty-three men could tell me."

Brave manager Bill McKechnie scolded Maranville, who recalled, "I was furious. I said, 'All right, you were coaching at third base. Just who did throw that ball to Tony?' He said, '[Shortstop Leo] Durocher.' I said 'You're as blind as the rest of your ball club; Durocher could never have thrown that ball from the angle at which it was thrown.'" After arguing with McKechnie for a while, Maranville went over to the Cincinnati clubhouse to solve the question. "Dan Howley, manager of the Reds, said, 'Looking for the ball, Rabbit?'" Maranville finally got Stripp to confess. Rabbit further describes what happened that night at his hotel: "The head waiter came over to me and, putting down a delicious melon à la mode, said, 'Compliments of Manager Howley.' I said, not very friendly, 'Tell him many thanks.' I started eating the ice cream and melon and had just about enough of it when I struck something hard in the ice cream. . . . (It) was a little ball about the size of a golf ball, and written on it was, 'Here is the hidden ball, Rabbit.'"[3]

Brave teammate Lance Richbourg, quoted by Sam Levy in the *Milwaukee Journal*, recalls that the ball was concealed in a cake given by the team hotel manager.[4] In a 1942 interview, Maranville said it was a real baseball (inscribed "Cuccinello to Maranville") in plain cantaloupe, and he fired the ball at the waiter. Shirley Povich's June 15, 1943, column says the dessert was chocolate ice cream.[5] *Sporting News* adds a contemporary account: "An incident of the Braves' visit to Redland Field was the falling for the old hidden-ball trick by Rabbit Maranville. It was the first time this had ever happened in his long and honorable career. Joe Stripp, who has been quite a player for Dan Howley, was the perpetrator of the trick. The Rabbit had doubled. When he failed to keep his eye on the ball and walked off the bag, Stripp snapped the ball to Cuccinello, and the Rabbit was forced to listen to the raucous razz of the Reds. The manager of the Sinton Hotel pulled another on him later in the evening, when he invited the Rabbit in to have a dish of ice cream. Maranville went to work on the mound of frozen cream but found another baseball hidden in the center. It looks as though they'll never let Maranville forget, especially in Cincy."[6]

Date: September 6, 1931 (second game)
Teams: Cincinnati Reds vs. St, Louis Cardinals (National League)
Perpetrators: Cincinnati shortstop Leo Durocher and second baseman Tony Cuccinello
Victim: Chick Hafey, St. Louis

In the sixth inning of the second game, the Reds got what appeared to be a double play against the Cardinals, going from left fielder Nick Cullop (catching Jimmie Wilson's fly ball) to catcher Lena Styles (nabbing Jim Bottomley at the plate). Styles threw to Durocher, but Hafey was safe—until a moment later, when Durocher slipped the hidden ball to Cuccinello and Tony tagged Hafey out. The next day, the official scorer ruled that it was a triple play.

Date: June 15, 1933
Teams: Chicago Cubs vs. Pittsburgh Pirates (National League)
Perpetrator: Chicago shortstop Billy Jurges
Victim: Hal Smith, Pittsburgh

Jurges caught Smith in the fifth inning of a 5–0 Chicago victory. According to the *Boston Globe*, "The faces of Manager George Gibson, Coach Grover Hartley, and pitcher Hal Smith of the Pittsburg Pirates were still red today—because of an experience with the old hidden-ball trick. Smith was the victim in yesterday's game with the Chicago Cubs, while Gibson, who lodged an official protest, and Hartley, felt responsible, as they were on the coaching lines. Smith opened the fifth with a double, and after Lloyd Waner had flied out, his brother Paul lined one at Babe Herman. Herman came in fast, snared the ball, and tossed it to Bill Jurges. Umpire [Cy] Pfirman ruled that Herman had trapped the ball, however. The Cubs rallied around to argue that Herman had caught the ball and of course lost the argument. Gibson and Hartley resumed their coaching positions, and Smith led off second. Jurges sneaked over and tagged him out. [Pirate coach] Honus Wagner thundered out and claimed that pitcher Bud Tinning had toed the rubber, but the Pirates lost that argument, and the hidden-ball trick had worked again."[7]

Sporting News added four separate mentions of the play, saying that Gibson announced he was playing the game under protest, but that "[n]o official protest was lodged."[8] The *Chicago Tribune* had this to say: "Smith led off the fifth with the first hit off Tinning, a line double to right center. Smith stayed on second while L. Waner flied to [Riggs] Stephenson and also lingered there while P. Waner lined the ball toward Babe Herman. Herman came up with the ball and thought he had made a fair catch, but Umpire Pfirman ruled that he had trapped the ball. After throwing the ball to Jurges, Babe ran in from right field to squawk, and members of both teams gathered around to listen to his oratory. After a spell the forum disbanded, and the players went back to their positions, Tinning taking a position near the pitching mound. With Mgr. Gibson hollering spirited encouragement, Smith took a lead off second, whereupon Jurges ran up and tagged him with the ball, which he had hidden in his glove (thus executing) the mossiest of all ancient baseball maneuvers—the hidden-ball trick."[9]

Date: August 21, 1933
Teams: Boston Red Sox vs. Cleveland Indians (American League)
Perpetrator: Boston third baseman Marty McManus
Victim: Earl Averill, Cleveland

In the sixth inning, Averill doubled to left and continued to third when Red Sox left fielder Smead Jolley's throw to second was wild. McManus hid the ball in his glove and returned to third base, tagging Averill when he stepped off, according to the *New York World-Telegram*.[10] McManus, who in 1926 had caught Harry Heilmann while Ty Cobb coached, had tricked yet another future Hall of Famer.

Date: July 15, 1934 (first game)
Teams: Brooklyn Dodgers vs. St. Louis Cardinals (National League)
Perpetrator: Brooklyn third baseman Joe Stripp
Victim: Bill DeLancey, St. Louis

DeLancey led off the Gas House Gang's seventh inning with a double and advanced to third on a fly out to center. According to the scoresheet kept by Edward T. Murphy, Stripp then caught DeLancey on a HBT in front of Coach Mike Gonzalez. The Cards managed to win, Dizzy Dean's 15th victory en route to a 30–7 season.

Date: August 22, 1935
Teams: Boston Red Sox vs. Detroit Tigers (American League)
Perpetrator: Boston second baseman Oscar Melillo
Victim: Billy Rogell, Detroit

Melillo tricked Rogell in the fifth inning, after Rogell had singled and been sacrificed to second. According to an unidentified scrapbook clipping, "Melillo handled [pitcher Jack] Wilson's throw and merely held onto the ball. 'Skee' returned to his second-base position, and Rogell pranced off the bag. Melillo raced over and planked the ball on him." It was a crucial play, as the Sox won, 10–9.

Thirteen years later, Melillo, by then an Indian scout, recalled the incident in *Sporting News*: "'I always used to try and let the umpire know I had the ball,' said Oscar, who then proceeded, under prompting, to tell the story of the time he worked the hidden-ball play on Billy

Rogell, when the latter was with Detroit and Oscar was with the Browns. 'Rogell used to deliver milk to me in Chicago during the winter,' explained Melillo, 'and he would rattle those bottles on the back porch about four every morning and yell, "Here's your milk, Mr. Melillo." I once threatened to take a shotgun to him, but I couldn't wait up all night for him to show up. Anyway, this day in Detroit, Rogell leads off the last half of the tenth with a two-bagger, sliding into second just ahead of the throw. I palmed the ball inside my glove while he was getting up and dusting himself off. I had to distract him, so I started talking about milk. "Remember when you used to wake me up every morning, yelling, 'Here's your milk, Mr. Melillo?'" I asked him. "Sure," says Bill, laughing, "I used to get your goat, didn't I?" And with that he steps off the bag. "Well, Mr. Rogell," I says stepping up to him real quick, "here is the ball!" and I plunked it in his ribs. He didn't speak to me for two years.'"[11] Thirteen years seem to have hazed some of the details for Oscar, like which team he was on, how Rogell got to second, and what inning it was, but this is clearly the same incident.

Another version, by Arthur Daley in the *New York Times*, reprinted in *Baseball Digest*, had Melillo responding, "That's a long time ago, and I've been waiting all these years for the chance to wake you up. The time has come, Billy, and revenge is sweet."[12] He then tagged Rogell between the shoulder blades. Still another account, in the July 1951 edition of *Baseball Digest*, has Melillo replying, "You sure did. But this makes us even."[13]

According to Rogell's version in *The Baseball Hall of Shame 4*, his reply to the milk question was, "Boy, do I. That sure made my day." Melillo retorted, "Well, this is going to make *my* day. Now you've got some explaining to do to your manager. Who knows, you may wind up delivering milk again sooner than you think."[14] Rogell later got his revenge by leaving a dead sparrow in Melillo's glove between innings.

Date: May 9, 1936
Teams: St. Louis Cardinals vs. Chicago Cubs (National League)
Perpetrator: St. Louis first baseman Johnny Mize
Victim: Frank Demaree, Chicago

According to the *St. Louis Post-Dispatch*, "To make the reverse more painful for the league champions, the Cardinals pulled the ancient hidden-ball trick out of moth balls to break up an eighth-inning

Chicago rally. Frank Demaree was on first base, with one out, and the stands were cheering for a run that would tie the score, when Phil Cavarretta hit a fly to right field. Pepper Martin charged after the ball and finally caught it and threw to Mize in an effort to double Demaree off first. Demaree reached first safely, but Mize held the ball in his big mitt and when [pitcher Roy] Parmelee walked over to get it, Mize gave him a wink and Parmelee returned to the mound as if he had received the ball. Demaree and all the other Cubs, including Coach Red Corriden, were too much concerned with the possibility of a score-tying rally to pay attention to the whereabouts of the ball, and when [Stan] Hack stepped into the batter's box, Demaree stepped off first, Mize tagged him, and everybody laughed, except the Cubs in general and Demaree in particular."[15] *Sporting News* adds that, "Inside baseball, as well as 'Gas House Gang' methods, still mark the play of the Cardinals. In the eighth inning of their game of May 9 at Wrigley Field, they worked the hidden-ball trick on Frank Demaree. The Bruin gardener had just hit safely in his 14th consecutive game and was standing grinning on first base after Phil Cavarretta had flied to Pepper Martin, who tossed the ball to first baseman Johnny Mize. Pitcher Roy Parmelee sauntered slowly over to first, then slowly walked to the mound—without the ball. When Demaree took a step off the bag, Mize tagged him out."[16]

Date: June 19, 1936
Teams: New York Yankees vs. Detroit Tigers (American League)
Perpetrator: New York shortstop Frank Crosetti
Victim: Goose Goslin, Detroit

According to *Sporting News*, "Goose Goslin, veteran of many campaigns, was fooled by the hidden-ball trick in the Yankee–Tiger game, June 19. In the eighth inning, Goslin advanced to second on a left field single by Al Simmons. Crosetti received the ball from Joe DiMaggio, and when Goslin thought Lefty Gomez had the pellet, he took a short lead off the bag. Crosetti lunged at him and tagged the Detroit flychaser and was the schnozzle on Goose's face red!"[17]

The play is recalled by Gomez in a 1950 issue of *Baseball Digest*: "I pick up the resin bag and walk over to Crosetti, who fakes handing me the ball and gives me the sign he's going to try and pull something. So I walk back toward the mound, that white resin bag in my glove—and to Goslin it looks like the ball. Under his breath, the umpire warns me not to step on the rubber, and I know it means he'll call a balk if I do, without the ball. I make a motion like I'm winding up, and Goslin prances off second base. Then he feels something hit him right between the shoulder blades as Crosetti tags him. 'Yer out!' bellows the umpire. 'Not me!' shrieks Goslin. 'Gomez has the ball.' I stopped laughing long enough to toss Goslin the resin bag. He gives it a dirty look and then throws it into the 20th row behind our dugout."[18] Shirley Povich tells the same story in a 1943 column.[19]

Sporting News scribe Harold Burr later credited Crosetti with reviving the play with a new twist: "Another old favorite brought forth from the mothballs is 'Frisco Frank Crosetti's hidden-ball trick. It is one of the most mortifying of tricks, yet one of the oldest, but Crosetti has smartly added an innovation. He conceals the ball inside the heel of his glove, so that he seems to be standing out there at shortstop innocently empty-handed."[20]

Date: May 29, 1937 (first game)
Teams: New York Yankees vs. Philadelphia Athletics (American League)
Perpetrator: New York shortstop Frank Crosetti
Victim: Billy Werber, Philadelphia

A 1948 article by Clifford Bloodgood discusses some HBTs pulled by Crosetti: "Bill Werber, a smart and intelligent player, was caught in the Crosetti trap. Fans who saw it happen may have thought he was telling Crosetti off when he staggered to his feet, but he was telling Frank that it was a damned good play. Bill Werber was big enough to recognize true genius when he came in contact with it."[21]

I phoned Werber 65 years after the fact, and he remembered the play quite clearly. He said it was when he was with Boston, playing at Yankee Stadium: "I hit a ball hard that curved a little inside the third base line for a double. George Selkirk was the left fielder, and Red Ruffing was the pitcher. Crosetti was talking to me, you know, giving me shit. Next thing you know he pulls out the ball. I run to third, but Crosetti throws to Red Rolfe and I'm out. Joe Cronin was the coach at third base. . . . Just a year ago, Frankie called me up and said, 'Hey Billy, seen any hidden-ball tricks lately?'"[22]

Some of Werber's recollections are off, but the play was found on this date, following a single by Werber for the Athletics. According to the *New York Times*, "The ancient hidden-ball trick was pulled by Frankie Crosetti in the eighth to save Ruffing further embarrassment. . . . Crosetti secreted the ball while Werber was on second, and when Werber unsuspectingly took the customary lead off the base in the belief Ruffing was going to pitch, Crosetti dived over and tagged him out, amid the guffaws of the crowd."[23] The Yanks won, 9–4.

Per *Sporting News*, "Billy Werber, Athletics' third baseman, was the victim of the ancient hidden-ball trick in the first game of the May 29 doubleheader in New York. He did not watch for a return throw when Wally Moses singled him to second, strayed off the bag, and was tagged out by Frank Crosetti."[24]

Date: July 16, 1937
Teams: New York Yankees vs. Detroit Tigers (American League)
Perpetrator: New York shortstop Frank Crosetti
Victim: Boots Poffenberger, Detroit

Date: August 29, 1937
Teams: New York Yankees vs. Detroit Tigers (American League)
Perpetrator: New York shortstop Frank Crosetti
Victim: Gee Walker, Detroit

Writes the *New York Times*, "When Crosetti sprang the hidden-ball trick on Gerald Walker in the fifth, an alert move, incidentally, which gummed a promising Tiger rally right in the middle, it marked the fourth time in two seasons that Frankie has caught somebody napping at second base. What hurt even more was that two of his previous victims were also Tigers."[25] *Sporting News* says, "Crosetti worked the hidden-ball trick on Walker in the fifth inning—the third time in two years that the New York shortstop had made such a play at Navin Field."[26] According to a 1948 *Baseball Magazine* article, "Walker was so infuriated that he said to a laughing Crosetti, 'If you ever pick me off again, I'll chase you right out of the park.'"[27] An earlier *Baseball Magazine* article quotes Crosetti as saying, "Boy, wasn't G. Walker angry when I pulled the trick on him? He exploded and threatened to run me out of town if I ever pulled the trick on him again. If I do get him again it might be a good idea for me to start running for the nearest exit as soon as I tag him. He was really upset."[28] The Yankees won, 7–4. Ironically, it was the first anniversary of a play in which Walker had badly spiked Crosetti.

Date: July 4, 1938 (first game)
Teams: New York Yankees vs. Washington Senators (American League)
Perpetrator: New York shortstop Frank Crosetti
Victim: George Case, Washington

A 1948 issue of *Baseball Magazine* discusses some HBTs pulled by Crosetti: "Among others Frank has disposed of in this manner are the flying George Case, base-stealer extraordinary."[29] The trick was found on this date. According to a Shirley Povich column, "Out of the moth balls the Yankees pulled the age-old hidden-ball trick yesterday to the great embarrassment of young George Case, who suddenly found himself taking the long walk from second base back to the dugout. . . . (T)o the ballplayer who has just been nipped off second by the moss-covered hidden-ball trick, it must be akin to the last mile. Because the guy who is caught off base by the shortstop or second baseman possessing a hidden ball is invariably shown up as something of a dunce who was made an awful chump of. It means he was asleep at the switch and not playing heads-up baseball. There is only one consolation for (rookie) Case. He was trapped in the fifth inning of that first game by the master of the (hidden)-ball trick, Frankie Crosetti. Except for Crosetti's contributions, the hidden-ball play is virtually a lost art. Attempts at it are made sporadically, but only Crosetti has been able to pull it with any consistency. . . . Crosetti, after walking to the pitcher's mound and faking a motion to hand the ball to the pitcher, took it back to second base, where Case was standing a few feet off the bag. Crosetti is a master of the art, as we were saying, and he did not walk bluntly to Case and tag him, for any motion of that sort might have scared Case back to the bag; instead, he took his regular place at short stop, with the ball still concealed in his glove, and motioned for second baseman Joe Gordon to move toward second base and scare Case back to the bag. That was done, and thus Case was lulled into a false sense of security, when Crosetti finally ambled over and put the ball on him."[30]

Baseball Magazine quotes Case as saying, "I wanted to find a hole and crawl into it. You made me feel sick." Crosetti replied, "I think I know exactly how you feel. It wasn't a nice trick to pull on a fellow,

especially before a big crowd." The article describes how the play un-
folded: "The mob cheered Case noisily when, with two down and the
bases empty, he slashed a two-bagger into right-center off Charley
Ruffing. . . . Case went into second base standing up. Within the next
ten seconds the crowd was silenced, and Case had become the most
dejected figure in Washington. The alert Crosetti had made the outfielder the latest victim of the ancient hidden-ball trick. Case had not
strayed more than three feet off the base when Frankie, with the ball
expertly concealed in his gloved hand, lunged toward the unsuspecting
base runner. Case, sensing what was up, made a desperate attempt to
return safely to the bag, but it was too late. Crosetti tagged him before
he could get back. 'You're out!' barked umpire Cal Hubbard, who
seemed to know what was coming off and was on top of the play when it
was executed. And so the utterly embarrassed Case felt like disappear-
ing from sight, but that was impossible. He had to remain in full view of
his manager and teammates and start the long trek back to the Senators'
bench. To make matters worse for the outfielder, the game was close.
When he reached second base, he represented the run the Senators
needed to tie the score. . . . Case's face turned crimson when Frankie
nipped him, but the young Washington outfielder can gain some satisfaction from the fact that more experienced players were thoroughly
embarrassed by the slick Italian before he suffered his humiliation."[31]

The article includes information on how Crosetti learned the trick
and how he pulls it off. "'It is more important to fool the coaches than
the fellow whom you set out to pull the trick on,' declares Crosetti. 'If
both of the coaches do not suspect you have the ball, the chances are
the runner doesn't and your chances of getting away with the trick are
good.' . . . He graduated from the San Francisco Seals, of the Pacific
Coast League. He learned how to conceal a baseball when he was the
Seals' shortstop and didn't forget the trick making the switch to the
Yankees. Babe Pinelli . . . instructed Frankie in the art of hiding base-
balls. Pinelli was the Seals' third baseman when Frankie was their shortstop [in 1928–1930]. . . . The fashion in which Babe worked the stunt
fascinated Frankie. Would Babe let Frankie in on the secret of how he
got possession of the ball when everyone thought the pitcher had it?
Babe did. . . . No attempt will be made to reveal how Crosetti, in
making the first step toward executing the trick play, comes into possession of the ball. To do so would be unfair; however, it can be said that

Frankie, in setting his trap, actually tosses the ball toward the pitcher. But the pitcher doesn't get it. Like a stroke of magic, the pellet gets back in Frankie's possession. Right there is where Crosetti must fool the coaches and the base runner. And how often he succeeds! Once he has the ball and is reasonably sure he has fooled the other fellows, Frankie hides it from view, shoving it between the back of his gloved hand and the mitt. With that done, Crosetti takes up his normal place in the short field, and frequently, by way of luring the base runner off second base, he makes sure that the prospective victim gets a full view of the face of his glove. . . . When Crosetti thinks the runner is far enough off second base to be nailed, he sprints into action and, at the same time, yanks the ball from its hiding place with his bare hand. When the attempt to perform the trick has gone that far it is, more often than not, carried to a successful conclusion. . . . Pulled successfully, the hidden-ball trick is a weapon which does more than break up a rally. It not only takes the pep out of the runner who has been caught in the trap but has a psychological effect on the entire team. . . . The victimized team is immediately put in the position of picking itself off the floor."[32]

Crosetti, quoted decades later in *Baseball Digest*, said, "Babe taught me to carry the ball to the pitcher, tossing it a couple of feet in the air with my bare hand and catching it in my glove. Then, as I pretended to hand the ball to the pitcher, I slipped it inside my glove—not in the pocket, but between my hand and the glove. When I walked back, I had my gloved hand down at my side and the runner knew or thought he knew that I didn't have the ball. Then if he wasn't careful, I had him."[33]

Date: July 2, 1939 (first game)
Teams: New York Yankees vs. Boston Red Sox (American League)
Perpetrator: New York shortstop Frank Crosetti
Victim: Joe Cronin, Boston

This one took nearly two decades to pin down. I had seen stories about Crosetti pulling a trick on player-manager Cronin in multiple sources, one saying Crosetti was at third base, others at shortstop. I narrowed down the hot-corner possibilities to three dates in 1941 but found nothing. If Crosetti was at short, it could have happened any time between 1935 and 1945, encompassing about 120 possible dates.

According to *A Rooter's Guide to the Red Sox*, "Joe Cronin's embarrassment was double-fold when Frank Crosetti of the Yankees caught him on the hidden-ball trick: 'It's humiliating. I taught it to him in San Francisco.'"[34] *Sporting News* writes, "General Manager Joe Cronin of the Bosox, seeing Frank Crosetti coaching third base for the New York Yankees, mused, 'Well, at least he can't pull the hidden-ball trick on us there.' Joe was thinking back to the day that Frankie pulled it on him when he was playing third base for the Bombers and embarrassed the Gold Sox boss before a packed house at Fenway Park."[35]

Crosetti, when asked about it at the age of 90 in 2001, answered with clear, strong handwriting, if imperfect spelling: "I do not remember to much about it. One thing, Cronin never taught it to me. Looking back now, it was a dirty trick and should have been abolished right away."[36] I was losing hope at ever finding this trick.

Finally, in 2013, Retrosheet's Dave Smith came through with the answer. He was working with Edward T. Murphy's July 2, 1939, scoresheet and found a handwritten notation: "hidden-ball trick: Cronin . . . ole razzle dazzle." It happened in the sixth inning of the first game. Ted Williams walked, and Cronin and Joe Vosmik followed with singles for the Sox, the latter scoring Williams and moving Cronin to second base. Jim Tabor then hit a ball caught by second baseman Joe Gordon. Somehow, Crosetti came into possession of the ball and tagged out Cronin, a future Hall of Famer. Of six newspapers checked, only the *New York Mirror* even mentioned the feat: "Cronin was picked off second on the hidden-ball trick by Crosetti."[37] The Red Sox won, 7–3.

10

1940–1949: PESKY HOLDING THE BALL

Johnny Pesky has been unfairly maligned for holding the ball too long while the Cardinals scored the winning run in the 1946 World Series, but Pesky did hold the ball a couple of times in the 1940s in executing the hidden-ball trick, one fewer than decade leader Bobby Bragan. There were 18 tricks during the decade: ten in the American League and eight in the National League.

Date: April 24, 1940
Teams: New York Yankees vs. Philadelphia Athletics (American League)
Perpetrator: New York shortstop Frank Crosetti
Victim: Al Brancato, Philadelphia

On February 24, 1990, Brancato was recalling his brief playing career during a symposium at the Historical Society of Pennsylvania. The Yankees' Red "Ruffing was pitching," the former Athletic infielder recalled. "I . . . get on base, I stole second base, a very young fellow I was, brush myself off, look around, and I thought to myself, 'This big league is not gonna be too tough.' . . . I got up like this, and I looked around to [second baseman] Joe Gordon. Over here was Crosetti, and I looked over there again, I had my foot on the base, I wanted to make sure, and . . . I looked at the coach. I went like this, that's as far as I went. . . . And I got back and turned around, and who's standing in front of me, but Crosetti. He said, 'Hey, Dad, look what I got.' He pulled the hidden-ball trick on me, another Italian, and I didn't even see it. I crawled right under the base."[1] According to the *New York World-Telegram*, "To Frankie Crosetti, Yankee shortstop, today went the accolade for performance of the classic hidden-ball trick. Frank may be counted on for one a season, but he usually works up to it in July or August. His victim in the stadium yesterday was rookie Brancato. It happened in the fifth inning, while Al was preening himself over having stolen second."[2] This was the seventh straight HBT in the majors recorded by Crosetti.

Date: July 28, 1940
Teams: Philadelphia Phillies vs. Cincinnati Reds (National League)
Perpetrator: Philadelphia shortstop Bobby Bragan
Victim: Billy Werber, Cincinnati

Per the *Helena Independent*, the rookie Bragan "pulled the hidden-ball trick on Bill Werber in the third inning. Werber was tagged when he stepped off second base."[3] For Werber, considered one of the headiest players of his era, it was the second time he had been caught with the trick.

Date: June 1, 1941 (second game)
Teams: Chicago White Sox vs. Washington Senators (American League)
Perpetrators: Chicago catcher Mike Tresh and first baseman Joe Kuhel
Victim: Doc Cramer, Washington

Discussing a game from the previous season, *Baseball Magazine* says, "Washington was trailing the Chicago White Sox by only one run in the seventh inning. There was one out, and George Case was on third base. Roger Cramer slapped a grounder to Luke Appling at short. Appling pegged out Case at the plate, and Cramer reached first. Catcher Mike Tresh simulated a gesture of handing the ball to pitcher Edgar Smith. Instead, he slipped it to first sacker Joe Kuhel. Cramer ventured off first and felt the unexpected jolt of a round, hard object in his ribs. The potential tying run was wiped out; Washington lost the game."[4] The event was found in the second game of a doubleheader on this date.

According to famed journalist Shirley Povich, "The full measure of ignominy befell the Nats in the tenth. That was when (Doc) Cramer, on first with the potential winning run, was the victim of the moth-eaten hidden-ball trick that snuffed him out. During a heated debate between George Case and umpire Curly Grieve at the plate, catcher Mike Tresh tossed the ball to first baseman Joe Kuhel, and when Cramer innocently stepped off the bag, he was surprised when Kuhel tagged him out with the equivalent of 'You're it, Skinny.' Cramer has only been in the big leagues for 12 years, and with Ossie Bluege coaching at first base for the Washington club, the Nats had a combined major league experience of only 30-odd years in the vicinity of the hidden-ball ruse of Kuhel. . . . Case was nipped at the plate when he tried to score on Cramer's grounder to Appling. Cramer, who reached first, learned about the hidden-ball trick from Kuhel at that point."[5] The play was fatal, as the White Sox won in the 11th, 4–3. Kuhel, incidentally, was an accredited member of the American Society of Magicians.[6]

Date: June 3, 1941
Teams: Philadelphia Phillies vs. Chicago Cubs (National League)
Perpetrator: Philadelphia shortstop Bobby Bragan
Victim: Augie Galan, Chicago
    According to *Baseball Magazine*, "Shortstop Bobby Bragan used the same legerdemain to nip Augie off second."[7] Writes *Sporting News*, the incident happened on this date: "[T]he hidden-ball trick, worked by shortstop Bob Bragan, kept the Chicagoans from reaching third base."[8] Elsewhere in the same issue, it says that the "Phillies worked the hidden-ball trick on Augie Galan after he had walked in the eighth to become the Cubs' first base occupant."[9] The Phillies won, 7–0.

Date: June 24, 1941
Teams: Cleveland Indians vs. Boston Red Sox (American League)
Perpetrator: Cleveland shortstop Lou Boudreau
Victim: Skeeter Newsome, Boston

Date: August 13, 1941
Teams: Philadelphia Phillies vs. Brooklyn Dodgers (National League)
Perpetrator: Philadelphia shortstop Bobby Bragan
Victim: Dixie Walker, Brooklyn
    According to the *Philadelphia Inquirer*, in the fourth inning, "Dixie Walker was victimized by the old hidden-ball trick. He had doubled. [Cookie] Lavagetto flied to [Philadelphia right fielder Stan] Benjamin.

Bragan got the ball on the throw-in, palmed it. When Walker wandered off second base, Bragan raced up from behind him and tagged him out."[10] Per *Sporting News*, "Leo Durocher, Dodgers' manager [and a two-time HBT perpetrator who was coaching third base], took full blame for a hidden-ball trick, which the Phillies pulled on Dixie Walker in the night game at Ebbets Field, August 13. Declared Durocher: '[Center fielder] Joe Marty threw the ball in to [third baseman Pinky] May at third. I saw that much, but when May slipped it to Bobby Bragan, I must have been asleep. I was thinking of the play we were putting on, looking around, and saw the Phils had Dixie caught off second. I was entirely to blame; I must have been dreaming.'"[11] The Dodgers still won, 7–2. It was the third trick Bragan had pulled in a little more than a year. Nearly seven decades later, he told me, "It's easy when you're at shortstop and the ball comes back in. You go to the mound, talk to the pitcher, and ostensibly put it in his hand. When the runner drifts off the bag, you tag him."[12]

Date: May 31, 1942 (second game)
Teams: Boston Red Sox vs. Washington Senators (American League)
Perpetrator: Boston shortstop Johnny Pesky
Victim: Bill Zuber, Washington

According to *Baseball Digest*, "Pesky worked the hidden-ball trick three times in his first season—on Bill Zuber of Washington, on [the Yankees' Tommy] Henrich, and on Glenn McQuillen of St. Louis."[13] The one on Zuber, a pitcher, occurred in the second game on this date, during a 4–3 loss to the Red Sox. According to the *Washington Post*, "Zuber was not only the losing pitcher, but he was the victim of the ancient hidden-ball trick that cost the Nats an important run in the fifth inning. After leading off with a two-bagger, Zuber was picked off second base by shortstop Johnny Pesky on the hidden-ball ruse. Zuber was tagged out as he wandered off the bag, unaware that Pesky was holding the ball. A bit later, [Stan] Spence singled to center, and there was nobody on base to drive home."[14] The game was called after seven and a half innings due to Boston's 6:15 p.m. Sunday curfew.

Date: July 4, 1942 (second game)
Teams: Boston Red Sox vs. New York Yankees (American League)
Perpetrator: Boston shortstop Johnny Pesky

Victim: Tommy Henrich, New York

Henrich was nabbed by Pesky in the eighth inning of the second game. Per *Sporting News*, "Henrich's hit to right scored [Frank] Crosetti and, when [Red Sox right fielder Lou] Finney's throw home got away from [catcher Johnny] Peacock, [Buddy] Hassett also tried to score. [Pitcher Tex] Hughson took the ball from Peacock and went back to the hill. Standing behind the mound, he conferred with Pesky and slipped the ball to him while so doing. Pesky ran back to short with Hughson still standing behind the mound. Henrich stepped off second, Pesky leaped at him for the tag, and Henrich was declared out. It was an unusual double play which had to be scored—Hughson to Peacock to Pesky."[15] The Red Sox won, 6–4.

Pesky later recalled the incident for biographer Bill Nowlin: "The best one of all was when Ed Rommel was the umpire. . . . The ball went down the right field line, and I was in the middle between second base and third, and I cut [the throw] off. Tommy Henrich was on second base, talking to Eddie Rommel. The pitcher was off the mound somewhere. Rommel knew I had the ball. You had to alert the umpire. [Indians shortstop Lou] Boudreau had pulled the hidden-ball trick the week before, and Henrich had read about it. I was behind them, and he gets off the base about four or five feet and says to Rommel, 'Eddie, that Boudreau's been pulling that hidden-ball trick. This is how far off I'm going to get, so they won't get me.' Just as he got it out of his mouth, I tagged him. Rommel was laughing, and Henrich wanted to kill me!"

An article in a 1946 edition of *Baseball Digest* has it a bit differently: "Henrich, on second base, had just commented to umpire Ed Rommel, 'I'm not going to get more than two yards off this base, like [Cleveland second baseman] Ray Mack, so they can't pick me off.' Just as he finished speaking and took one step off the base, Pesky jammed the ball into the small of his back. Henrich nearly had a fit, and later, when Pesky sent a line drive down the right field foul line, the outfielder nearly ran through the wall trying to reach the ball."[16]

Date: August 22, 1942
Teams: Cleveland Indians vs. Chicago White Sox (American League)
Perpetrator: Cleveland shortstop Lou Boudreau
Victim: Don Kolloway, Chicago

Hall of Famer Boudreau caught Kolloway on the "moth-eaten hid-den-ball trick," writes the *Chicago Daily Tribune*: "The hidden-ball item (wasn't) unveiled until the ninth. (Pitcher Eddie Smith's triple) was the opening incident, after which [Vern] Kennedy walked Kolloway and Wally Moses. Myril Hoag flied to center but too close in for Smith to break for the plate. The ball was thrown around after the catch, and Kennedy acted as if he might be ready to pitch, so Kolloway strolled off second. The ball was in Manager Lou Boudreau's hands, and Kolloway was a dead duck."[17] The White Sox managed to win anyway, 3–1. Bou-dreau had also pulled a trick the previous year.

Date: June 2, 1943 (second game)
Teams: Boston Red Sox vs. St. Louis Browns (American League)
Perpetrator: Boston second baseman Bobby Doerr
Victim: Denny Galehouse, St. Louis

According to Harold Kaese's *A Rooter's Guide to the Red Sox*, Hall of Famer "Doerr worked a hidden ball on Denny Galehouse at first base. Because the Red Sox first baseman didn't know Doerr had the ball, the second baseman had to keep edging over until he could pounce on the unsuspecting St. Louis pitcher."[18] Per *Sporting News*, it happened on this date: "Bobby Doerr, Red Sox second sacker, pulled the old hidden-ball trick on Brownie pitcher Denny Galehouse in the eighth frame of the nightcap at Fenway Park, June 2."[19] Boston won, 3–2, in ten innings.

Date: April 17, 1945
Teams: Chicago White Sox vs. Cleveland Indians (American League)
Perpetrator: Chicago third baseman Tony Cuccinello
Victim: Lou Boudreau, Cleveland

On Opening Day, Cuccinello nabbed the Indian player-manager in the sixth inning. Oscar Melillo, an Indian scout, recollected the incident three years later in *Sporting News*, saying, "With him on third and none out, we felt we were home free. The stands were packed, and they were all cheering Lou as he brushed himself off. And then Cuccinello eased over and put the ball on him! It's a long walk back to the bench in that Cleveland park, and I could see Lou hunching up his shoulders and trying to make himself smaller and smaller as he went back to the bench. If it was one more step, I doubt if he could have made it, because the wolves were on him something fierce. And poor old Barney [Burt Shotton, the coach] at third! Boudreau was the first batter, and Shotton had to stay there and take the abuse of the fans for the rest of the inning."[20]

Cuccinello remembered it a bit differently. The night before the game, at a gala dinner, Boudreau was asked about the HBT. He said, "Oh, that's obsolete. They don't do that anymore." The next day, Boudreau slid into third on a teammate's hit and represented the tying run with one out. Tony argued with the umpire and then returned to his position, pounding his glove as if it were empty. Boudreau took a few steps off the base, and Cuccinello dove at him. Umpire Cal Hubbard yelled, "He's out, if you got the ball."[21] A *Baseball Digest* article names Red Jones as the umpire, with a similar quote.[22] Arthur Daley recalls the play at least twice in his *New York Times* column (September 17, 1945; February 1, 1962), first naming Hubbard and then Jones as the ump.

The play is also detailed by Cuccinello in the book *Baseball Chronicles*, although the date is mistakenly listed as April 18, 1944: "I was playing third base for the Chicago White Sox, and we were opening the season in Cleveland. The night before the opener, the Cleveland Club held a father-and-son dinner, and Lou Boudreau, the Indians' player/ manager, was the guest speaker. Lou made a short speech and afterward asked the kids if they had any questions about baseball. One kid asked Lou about the hidden-ball trick, and Boudreau said, 'We don't pull that off anymore; it's obsolete.' The next day, we were leading Cleveland by one run in the eighth inning, and Lou was up at bat. He singled to right field, and that makes him the tying run. The next hitter also got a base hit, sending Lou to third; we made a play on him, and he slid in just ahead of my tag. Now he is the tying run at third base, and the winning run is standing at first. It looks like we are in trouble. Thornton Lee, our pitcher, walks by me to get the ball and I whispered, 'Stay off the rubber,' and I kept the ball. I put the ball in my bare hand and put my glove on over the ball so you couldn't see it. I walked over to third base so Lou could see my hands (the ball being hidden) and went to my position behind the bag. I kept my eye on Lou, and sure enough, he started to take his lead. When I thought I had him, I made a dive for third base. Lou sensed there was something wrong, and he slid head-first right into me. I could hear umpire Cal Hubbard running to call the play, and as he got close, he said to me, 'He's out if you got the ball.' I took the ball out of my glove and showed it to him, and Hubbard hollered, 'Yer out.' I saw the pained expression on Lou's face as he got up. It was a long walk back to the dugout, and I couldn't help thinking that I never would have pulled the play on him if he hadn't said it was obsolete."[23]

According to *Sporting News*, neither Hubbard nor Jones was the umpire: "It seems that when Chicago's Tony Cuccinello worked the hidden ball on Cleveland's Lou Boudreau recently, even the umpires were fooled. Charley Berry, who had to call the play, saw Cuccinello pounce on Boudreau two feet from the bag. . . . 'You're out,' Charley shouted, adding, 'if he's got the ball.'"[24] To add injury to insult, Lou was hurt on the play. Per another *Sporting News* account, "Boudreau himself sprained his wrist in the opening game, and while the injury kept him out of action only one day, it has handicapped him at the plate since. The accident occurred when the manager attempted to scramble back to third base after he discovered that Tony Cuccinello was about to tag him. Chicago's veteran third baseman got away with the ancient hidden-ball trick at the expense of one of the most alert base runners in the business, and right under the embarrassed nose of Coach Burt Shotton."[25]

Date: May 13, 1945 (first game)
Teams: Chicago White Sox vs. Washington Senators (American League)
Perpetrator: Chicago second baseman Roy Schalk
Victim: Harlond Clift, Washington

Schalk caught the veteran Clift in the first game of a doubleheader. Writes *Sporting News*, "Harlond Clift of the Senators was caught by the White Sox with the hidden-ball trick May 13, the second time the Hose secreted the ball this season. [Gil] Torres and Clift had singled and advanced on a sacrifice in the sixth inning of the curtain-raiser, when Roy Schalk, who made the putout at first base, sauntered back to his second base position without tossing the ball to the pitcher. Thornton Lee began to act as if ready to resume pitching, Clift stepped off second, and Schalk jabbed the ball into the Washington third baseman's side."[26] Per the *Washington Post*, "Besides the double defeat, the Nats were further humiliated by the Chisox working the ancient 'hidden-ball' trick. . . . (It) stopped a promising Washington rally in the sixth. Torres and Clift singled, and both moved along on [George] Binks's sacrifice; however, second baseman Schalk had the ball in his glove, and when Clift sauntered off the bag, he tagged him for the surprise out."[27] Chicago won, 5–1.

Lyall Smith of the *Detroit Free Press* editorializes, "Just about once a year some team in the majors will pull the hidden-ball trick on an embarrassed opponent. That's the maneuver, you know, when a base runner thinks the ball is some place other than where it actually is, and when he takes a lead off his base, somebody steps up and gleefully tags him out. The play is as moth-eaten as football's Statue of Liberty gesture. It is such an oldie that when it is pulled successfully, it's definite news. And it also is one of several reasons the White Sox, ranked early as a second division club, are leading the American League and feeling very cocky about the whole thing. The Sox have used the hidden-ball trick twice, and the faces of Cleveland's Lou Boudreau and Washington's Harlond Clift still are rosy red."[28]

Date: May 23, 1945
Teams: Chicago Cubs vs. Philadelphia Phillies (National League)
Perpetrator: Chicago shortstop Bill Schuster
Victim: Jimmie Foxx, Philadelphia

According to the book *Even the Browns*, "The Phillies bought Foxx, 37, for the 1945 season. In May, he led off second base and was tagged out, victim of the hidden-ball trick."[29] As documented by *Sporting News*, the incident occurred on this date: "The Cubs pulled the hidden-ball trick on Jimmie Foxx, veteran of 21 campaigns, in the sixth inning with the Phillies, May 23. Jimmie had opened the inning with a single and stopped at second on Vince DiMaggio's blow to left, Peanuts Lowrey throwing the ball to Bill Schuster. As soon as John Antonelli stepped up to the plate, Foxx led off second and was promptly tagged by Schuster. . . . Turning the hidden-ball trick is old stuff to Bill Schuster, shortstop of the Cubs, who caught Jimmie Foxx, veteran of the Phillies, on the play. . . . The Bruin short fielder once did it twice in one game for Los Angeles of the Pacific Coast League. One of his victims was Hall of Famer Earl Averill, who had scolded his teammate for the earlier victimization."[30]

Schuster was out of the majors after 1945, but that didn't stop him from turning tricks. Says a 1947 *Baseball Digest* article, "Manager Jimmie Dykes of the Hollywood [Pacific Coast League] club was so mad when that little cutie Bill Schuster worked the hidden-ball trick this spring that he fined the two base coaches, who were Harry Danning, and, that's right, Jimmie Dykes!"[31] Schuster's obituary says, "Schuster was an excellent base runner and defensive infielder, adept at . . . pulling the hidden-ball trick (he usually stuffed the baseball in his armpit during a visit with the pitcher at the mound)."[32]

Date: September 2, 1946 (first game)
Teams: New York Giants vs. Boston Braves (National League)
Perpetrator: New York third baseman Bill Rigney
Victim: Billy Herman, Boston
Call it Billyball! According to *Sporting News*, "Billy Herman, veteran second baseman of the Braves, was caught off third on the ancient hidden-ball trick, September 2—right under the nose of Manager Billy Southworth. And a rookie pulled the trick. The guy who made the two Billys' faces red was freshman third sacker Bill Rigney of the Giants."[33] The play apparently occurred in the first inning of the first game of the day's doubleheader. Herman was in the waning days of his Hall of Fame career, and Southworth would also make the Hall.

Date: July 6, 1947 (first game)
Teams: Boston Red Sox vs. Washington Senators (American League)
Perpetrator: Boston shortstop Johnny Pesky
Victim: Buddy Lewis, Washington
Per *Sporting News*, "The Red Sox executed a unique double play against the Senators, July 6, with the aid of the ancient hidden-ball play worked by shortstop Johnny Pesky in the opening round of the lid-lifter. With the bases loaded, Stan Spence skied to Dom DiMaggio, whose rifle throw to catcher Roy Partee kept Eddie Yost glued to third. Instead of returning the ball to pitcher Mickey Harris, Partee tossed to Pesky, who returned to his position and tagged Buddy Lewis when he stepped off the bag."[34] The Sox won.
Lewis wrote me more than a half century later, typing, "I remember Pesky and the RED SOX very well, and it would not surprise me that I was victim of such a sly and capable man as J. PESKY. Most of this type

thing went its merry way when it was deemed by UMPs to be a balk when the pitcher touched the rubber without the ball."[35] Pesky recalled the incident for biographer Bill Nowlin, stating, "Mickey Harris was pitching, and he had the bases full. No outs. I got the ball from the outfield, and I think I'd already made an error in that inning—screwed up a ground ball or something. . . . Lewis was on second base (and) didn't even look to see where I was. . . . (The umpire) knew that I had the ball, but he didn't say anything. I was bluffing (Lewis) a little, getting him to go back to second; then I tagged him with the ball, and that took us out of the inning."

Date: May 12, 1948
Teams: Brooklyn Dodgers vs. Cincinnati Reds (National League)
Perpetrator: Brooklyn shortstop Pee Wee Reese
Victim: Johnny Vander Meer, Cincinnati

According to *Sporting News*, "Johnny Vander Meer, losing pitcher in the game with the Dodgers, May 12, was the victim of the hidden-ball trick in the fifth inning. After he had doubled, Claude Corbitt bounced a single over Billy Cox's head, but Vandy held second. Pee Wee Reese retrieved the ball, without the Cincinnati southpaw noticing, and tagged Vander Meer out when he stepped off the base."[36]

Date: July 25, 1948 (second game)
Teams: Boston Braves vs. St. Louis Cardinals (National League)
Perpetrator: Boston second baseman Connie Ryan
Victim: Del Rice, St. Louis

In a 1951 *Sport* article, Ryan claims to have pulled the trick three times in the majors;[37] however, only two had been documented. A *Sporting News* article about Ryan's May 6, 1951, trick narrowed down the possibilities considerably. It quotes umpire Al Barlick as saying, "I had seen Ryan pull the trick on Del Rice of the Cardinals two years ago and I've been watching him closely ever since."[38] The *St. Louis Post-Dispatch* pinned it down, stating, "Ryan worked the hidden-ball trick on Del Rice in the second inning of the second game, picking the Redbirds' catcher off second after having acquired the ball while covering first on a sacrifice. One umpire was fooled, too."[39]

Date: July 27, 1948

Teams: Chicago Cubs vs. Philadelphia Phillies (National League)
Perpetrator: Chicago second baseman Gene Mauch
Victim: Dick Sisler, Philadelphia

Per a 1961 *Baseball Digest* article, Mauch—who had pulled the trick in the American Association on August 18, 1946—performed two on successive days in the majors: "We're playing in Philadelphia, and I pulled the play on Harry Walker. The Phillies are wild at me, and the next day Dick Sisler hits a double. I took the throw in from the outfield and ran over to Roy Smalley, the shortstop, as if I had something important to tell him. On my way back I see Dick step off the bag about a foot, and I reached over and tagged him."[40] *Sporting News* indicates that the Walker incident did not result in an out and suggests that the Sisler one came in July: "The Cubs second baseman tried the hidden-ball trick twice on the Phillies this season. Once he caught both Harry Walker and umpire Butch Henline by surprise, and the ruse didn't work because the arbiter failed to see the trick. Recently, he trapped Dick Sisler neatly off second."[41] The *Chicago Daily Tribune* nailed it down, writing, "The Chicago Cubs . . . started the ceremonies by working the musty hidden-ball trick in the second inning."[42] The Cubs won, 3–2.

II

1950–1959: "STEP OFF THE BASE A MINUTE, WILL YA?"

A surprising number of tricks, especially in the 1950s, were made possible by an infielder suckering a base runner on the old "step off the base so I can clean it off" trick. There were 16 hidden-ball tricks during the decade, ten by American League players, and Billy Hitchcock was the leader, with four. After completing just two tricks in 23 years, first basemen started getting back into the act in the 1950s.

Date: July 1, 1950
Teams: Philadelphia Athletics vs. Washington Senators (American League)
Perpetrator: Philadelphia second baseman Billy Hitchcock
Victim: Eddie Yost, Washington

According to Hitchcock in a letter to me written more than a half century after the fact, "In 1950—Griffith Stadium—A's vs. Senators, I pulled it. . . . I was playing second base and covered first base on a bunt. Kept the ball in my glove. He strolled off the base, and I tagged him."[1] *Sporting News* concurs: In the seventh inning, "Billy Hitchcock . . . worked the hidden-ball trick on Eddie Yost at Washington, July 1, though the Senators beat the A's . . . 3–2. Covering first base on Merrill Combs's sacrifice to Bobby Shantz, Hitchcock faked a handoff to the pitcher, and the latter played his part like a consummate actor, preparing to step onto the rubber as though ready to pitch. When Yost took a lead off second, Hitchcock tagged him."[2]

The *Philadelphia Inquirer* adds more details: "Shantz, [first baseman Ferris] Fain, and Hitchcock all crisscrossed on the way back to their positions, and Yost somehow received the impression that the pitcher had the ball. Bobby heightened the impression by preparing to ascend the hill and, gazing at [catcher Joe] Astroth, beginning his crouch. Yost took a lead off second—and with that, Hitchcock jumped up behind him with the ball and tagged him out. As they realized what had happened, the onlookers guffawed, but Yost, going to the dugout, considered it nothing less than a dirty trick."[3] According to Shirley Povich, recalling the play three years later, Hitchcock had some words for Yost as he applied the tag: "Meet Mr. A. J. Reach."[4] The official American League baseball was stamped with the insignia of A. J. Reach & Company in those days.

Date: July 18, 1950
Teams: Cincinnati Reds vs. New York Giants (National League)
Perpetrator: Cincinnati second baseman Connie Ryan
Victim: Monte Kennedy, New York

According to *Sporting News*, pitcher "Kennedy was tagged off second base in the July 18 game, a victim of the old hidden-ball trick. . . . New Yorkers also threatened in the seventh, placing runners on second and third with one out, but Ryan pulled the hidden-ball trick on Kennedy for a second out."[5] The Reds won, 1–0. Says Shirley Povich, "Ryan mosied over to Kennedy, who was taking a conventional lead off second, and started to make small-talk conversation. Kennedy looked at him inquiringly, whereupon Ryan said, 'And look what I have here in my hand.' Kennedy looked, saw a baseball, froze in his tracks, and was promptly tagged out."[6]

Date: September 8, 1950
Teams: Philadelphia Athletics vs. Washington Senators (American League)
Perpetrator: Philadelphia second baseman Billy Hitchcock
Victim: Mickey Grasso, Washington

Date: May 6, 1951 (first game)
Teams: Cincinnati Reds vs. New York Giants (National League)
Perpetrator: Cincinnati second baseman Connie Ryan

Victim: Whitey Lockman, New York

Lockman singled to open the tenth inning and was sacrificed to second. Ryan covered first on the play and then returned to his normal position. Suddenly, he whipped out the ball and tagged Lockman. According to *Street & Smith's Official 1953 Baseball Yearbook,* "The Giants' Whitey Lockman obliged Connie Ryan, then with Cincinnati, by stepping off the bag so that he, Ryan, could straighten it. Ryan then tagged him out with the hidden ball."[7] The *New York World-Telegram-Star* writes, "According to one version . . . Ryan lured Lockman into the trap by saying to him, 'Step off the bag a minute, will you, Whitey? I want to kick it and straighten it out.' Lockman denied this. 'He said nothing to me. And even if he had, do you think I would have stepped off just because he asked me to? Don't be silly. He said nothing, and I didn't step off. . . . Connie Ryan is bush, that's all I got to say.'"[8] Giant manager Leo Durocher was ejected during the ensuing argument, and the Reds won, 4–3. "Why do they try to blame a thing like this on the umpires?" asked Al Barlick, who called the out from third base. "Where were the coaches on the play?" Durocher was fined $50 and Lockman $25 in the aftermath, according to the *New York Times.*

Ryan, who developed the play in the minors, who also tricked the Giants a year earlier, and who just missed getting the Phillies' Del Ennis a few days prior, said he tried it only when he made the putout on a bunt. "It don't cost anything. If it works, it can mean a ball game. And if it misses, the worst you can get is a laugh from the stands."[9]

Sport magazine also ran an article describing Ryan's version of the play and the trick in general: "The best time to attempt the play is after a sacrifice bunt, when the second baseman has had to cover first base. Often the first base coach's eye is diverted for a second or two when he yells at the hitter coming up to get a hit. And that's the time to try and hide the ball. There's really no technique to the trick. It's usually accomplished on the spur of the moment—most of the time in a close game. There's no sense in trying to catch a base runner in a high-scoring contest when you're either way ahead or way behind. . . . When I get possession of the ball at first base, I either hide it in the fold of my glove or in the palm of my gloved hand—then just hope for luck. I try to amble toward second base as nonchalantly as possible and look as though I'm not doing anything much. The pitcher is really the key to the play. He has to put on an act on the mound and stall as long as possible. Of course, it's always better for the rest of the infield to know what you're up to. Someone is liable to call time just when you're set to pull the trick and you're stuck. But you really don't have to tip them off. Most fielders are usually alert to what's going on. In (the May 6, 1951, game), our third baseman, Grady Hatton, saw me palm the ball and told umpire Al Barlick to watch me. Actually, you're not obligated to warn the umpire. He's supposed to keep his eyes on the ball at all times. I just take it for granted that they're on their toes and watching. The play can be pulled any time it strikes you as an opportune moment—and you think you can get away with it. There are times when I've had the intention of trying it and would walk toward second with the ball hidden from view only to have the first base coach holler a warning to the runner. In that setup, not many of the fans are aware of what's going on. There are also times when the play fouls up just as it appears successful. Those are the most frustrating experiences. I tried it in Philadelphia this spring just before I worked it in New York, but it misfired. Del Ennis jumped back to the bag just in time. The coaches hadn't hollered a warning or anything, either. Del took two steps off the bag, but I had strayed too far away myself trying to coax him off, and I just couldn't get back in time. I hear a lot of pros and cons on the merits of the play. After it was pulled this year against the Giants, they immediately branded it as a 'bush-league stunt.' The detractors claim it's unsportsmanlike. But when you're trying to win a ball game, you don't care what tricks you use as long as you win. It's nice to be a sportsman, but it's nicer to be a winner. Anyway, this isn't foul play. It's a perfectly legitimate maneuver. Remember, the runner and his coach have the obligation to be on their toes to prevent it from happening. I'll keep on using the hidden ball whenever I get a chance and whenever I think it will help the team. It could mean a ball game—and we need all the victories we can get." [10]

Date: August 7, 1951 (first game)
Teams: Boston Braves vs. Philadelphia Phillies (National League)
Perpetrator: Boston first baseman Earl Torgeson
Victim: Willie Jones, Philadelphia

Torgeson nailed Willie "Puddin' Head" Jones in the eighth inning. Jones then went off on the umpire and was ejected, according to the *Boston Herald. Sporting News* lists the "Most Embarrassed Players" for

1951, declaring a "tie between Whitey Lockman of the Giants and Willie Jones of the Phils, both of whom were victims of baseball's oldest gimmick, the hidden-ball trick. Perpetrators were . . . Earl Torgeson of Braves (against Jones)."[11] *Sporting News* remarked two years later that, "Earl Torgeson works the hidden-ball trick to perfection."[12]

Date: June 15, 1952 (second game)
Teams: Philadelphia Athletics vs. St. Louis Browns (American League)
Perpetrator: Philadelphia third baseman Billy Hitchcock
Victim: Darrell Johnson, St. Louis
    According to the *Philadelphia Inquirer*, "The A's even pulled the hidden-ball trick. With runners on first and third, thanks to two hits and an error with one out in the sixth inning of the afterpiece, Billy Hitchcock held onto the ball while catcher Joe Astroth conferred briefly with [pitcher Harry] Byrd. When Astroth returned to his station and Byrd squinted plateward as though to catch his signal, the Brownies' advanced runner, Johnson, took a lead off third base. He had no chance to get back; Hitchcock, who worked the hoary stunt twice in 1950, ungloved the ball and tagged him. The stratagem prevented the St. Louisans from scoring in the frame despite three singles and the miscue."[13] *Sporting News* adds, "When Billy Hitchcock worked the hidden-ball trick on St. Louis' Darrell Johnson, June 15, that rookie catcher should not have felt too embarrassed. Hitchcock pulled the stunt against a couple of far more experienced performers in the course of the 1950 season, his first year with the Mackmen."[14] St. Louis did wind up winning, 7–6, in 11 innings.

Date: July 14, 1952
Teams: Philadelphia Athletics vs. Chicago White Sox (American League)
Perpetrator: Philadelphia first baseman Ferris Fain
Victim: Ray Coleman, Chicago
    Per a 1980 *Baseball Digest* article, "Ferris Fain, one-time American League batting champion with the old Philadelphia A's, used a dandy when a 19-year-old phenom came in to pinch run in a crucial situation. Fain was playing first base and, during a bit of a lull, mentioned to the youngster that the strap on the bag was broken. Fain got on his knees and worked with the base strap furiously. 'Excuse me, son,' he said,

finally, gently easing the kid a few steps away. 'Sure, Mr. Fain,' said the youth. 'Can I help?' 'No,' replied Fain, 'but you can go sit down now because this here is the baseball and you're out.'"[15]

This more or less matches a trick described in *Sporting News*, although the victim was ten years older than 19: "To compound his misery, Coleman fell for one of the oldest tricks in baseball when he was victimized by the 'hidden-ball' gag. Ferris Fain of the A's pulled it after Coleman had forced [Sam] Mele at second base in the eighth inning of the July (14) game, lost eventually by the Comiskeys, 2–1. Everyone of the White Sox bench was yelling 'Fain has the ball.' But in the hubbub neither Coleman nor first base coach Jimmy Adair heard the warning. 'Would you move over a minute while I straighten the bag?' Fain politely inquired of Coleman. And Coleman just as politely stepped off to be tagged very unpolitely by the grinning Fain."[16]

Date: July 20, 1952 (second game)
Teams: Philadelphia Athletics vs. Detroit Tigers (American League)
Perpetrator: Philadelphia third baseman Billy Hitchcock
Victim: Fred Hatfield, Detroit

In correspondence from 2001, Billy Hitchcock comments on the HBT, writing, "I pulled the hidden-ball trick on Fred Hatfield, Tiger infielder. I was playing third base, and he had just tripled to right-center field, sliding into third base in a cloud of dust. I asked him to step off the base so I could kick the dirt off. He did, and I tagged him!"[17] *Sporting News* concurs: "Third baseman Billy Hitchcock of the Athletics successfully pulled the hidden-ball trick on Fred Hatfield of the Tigers in the third inning of the July 20 nightcap. Hatfield had just tripled to drive in a run and stepped off the bag to be tagged by Hitchcock, who had hidden the ball in his glove after the relay."[18] The play was a crucial one, as the game wound up tied, 3–3, before being stopped due to the local curfew rule.

Date: August 31, 1952
Teams: Detroit Tigers vs. St. Louis Browns (American League)
Perpetrator: Detroit shortstop Neil Berry
Victim: Vic Wertz, St. Louis

Wertz walked in the seventh inning and was advanced to second on Clint Courtney's single, but he was promptly tagged out by Berry. St. Louis won anyway, 7–4.

Date: April 30, 1953
Teams: Milwaukee Braves vs. New York Giants (National League)
Perpetrators: Milwaukee catcher Del Crandall and first baseman Joe Adcock
Victim: Sal Yvars, New York

According to the *New York Times*, the Braves duped the Giants in the fourth inning, with Whitey Lockman and manager Leo Durocher again in the thick of it: "With Whitey Lockman on second, the result of a pass and an infield out, Sal Yvars slammed a sharp single to center. Once again, as on Wednesday's final out, Leo elected to send the runner home on what threatened to be another close and extremely doubtful play. And once again Bill Bruton's arm won, as Lockman was tagged out. Nor did matters stop there. Before Leo had a chance to figure what was coming off next, catcher Del Crandall had flipped the ball to first sacker Joe Adcock, who then nonchalantly walked back to first base and, a moment later, sprang the 'hidden-ball' trick on unsuspecting Yvars for the third out."[19] The Giants won, however, 1–0.

Date: June 21, 1953
Teams: St. Louis Browns vs. Boston Red Sox (American League)
Perpetrator: St. Louis shortstop Billy Hunter
Victim: Jimmy Piersall, Boston

This is one of the most written-about HBTs in history, appearing in many articles and at least two books, but neither has the details right. According to *The Baseball Hall of Shame 2*, Piersall represented the tying run at second base in the seventh inning of a game against the Browns on August 4, 1953: "After center fielder Johnny Groth caught a fly ball for the second out, he threw to shortstop Billy Hunter, who then walked to the mound to talk with pitcher Duane Pillette. Hunter pretended to give the hurler the ball, but in actuality, the crafty infielder concealed it in his glove. As Hunter walked back to his position, he quietly alerted umpire Bill Summers to be ready for a trick play. Hunter then ambled up to his easy mark and struck up a friendly chat with the unsuspecting Piersall. 'Hey Jim, there's dirt all over that bag,' said

Hunter. 'Why don't you kick it and get the dirt off.' Like a trusting soul, Piersall obligingly stepped off the base to give it a boot. Before Jimmy had a chance to move another muscle, Hunter quickly tagged him, and Summers called him out. Red-faced, Piersall didn't say a word. He just glared at the smirking Hunter. But Piersall got the last laugh moments later. In the top of the eighth, Hunter led off with a single and was sacrificed to second. Given the steal sign, he took a big lead—and was promptly picked off." [20]

Says Piersall in *It Ain't Cheatin' If You Don't Get Caught*, "I hit a double off the wall. After sliding in, I got up and dusted myself off, and then Billy Hunter, their rookie shortstop, asked me to step off the base and kick the bag into line. I looked over at the umpire, Charlie Berry, and I got the feeling it was all right. So I stepped off the base, and Hunter, who had the ball hidden in his glove, tagged me out. That was the most embarrassing play of my life." [21]

Among discrepancies are that the play happened on June 21, not August 4; the event did not occur following a Piersall double, as there was a runner on first; and Johnny Groth was not involved in the play. According to a contemporary account in *Sporting News*, "Piersall was on second base, with Dick Gernert on first and one out, when George Kell fouled out to Dick Kryhoski. The first baseman threw the ball to third baseman Jim Dyck, who, in turn, tossed it to Hunter. 'Give the bag a kick for me, I want to straighten it out,' said Hunter, who moved in behind Piersall at second base. 'Straighten it out yourself,' retorted Piersall. 'I can't,' Hunter answered, 'you're standing on it.' When Piersall obliged, Hunter promptly put the tag on him. The result was a double play, and the side was out." [22] Shirley Povich's column gives essentially the same account. [23]

The *Elyria Chronicle Telegram* editorializes, "Not too long ago this season, shortstop Billy Hunter of the St. Louis Browns pulled the 'hidden-ball' trick on outfielder Jim Piersall of the Boston Red Sox. Hunter asked Piersall to step off second base while he straightened the bag. Piersall obligingly complied and was promptly tagged out by Hunter. As far as this corner is concerned, Hunter is lucky Piersall didn't punch him in the nose. If it had been anyone except Piersall, that's probably what would have happened. But Piersall, the Red Sox 'problem child' of 1952, happens to be on his good behavior, and Manager Lou Boudreau might have sent him back to the bushes had he hit the Browns' rookie.

[Piersall's 1952 battle with mental illness was well documented and became the subject of a major motion picture, *Fear Strikes Out*.] Sure, the 'hidden-ball' trick is baseball, and Hunter was perfectly within his rights. But the kind of baseball I call it is 'bush.'"[24]

A month later, on July 21, 1953, National League president Warren Giles wrote the following letter:

TO ALL NATIONAL LEAGUE UMPIRES:

On one or two occasions last year and one occasion this year, the so-called "hidden-ball" trick has been used. In some cases fielders have induced base runners to step off the bag by saying, "Get off the bag a minute, I want to straighten it," or something to that effect, and then tagging them. In one instance the base runner was not called out and, I understand, the umpire involved in the play applied Rule 4.06I and explained that a player could not, by calling time, or the use of any other phrase, create a situation where he could tag a man out.

Rule 4.06I applies specifically to causing a pitcher to "balk" and does not apply to any other play. Accordingly, in the National League, if a player is off the base while the ball is in play, he may be tagged out, even though the defensive player "tricked" him into stepping off the base by asking him to get off. If base runners are not alert enough to avoid this thing, they should be put out. An umpire should keep his eye on the ball at all times. Time should not be called until no further action on the play is possible—see Rule 5.10(b).

It is not up to an umpire to listen to conversation between the base runner and the defensive player. Consequently, he could not possibly decide whether the man stepped off the bag because he was asked to do so or because of stupid baserunning. At any rate, there is no rule against the hidden-ball trick; it is a good play, and with four umpires working, should not be missed. If a defensive player can, by conversation or any other legal method, induce a base runner to step off the base so he can be tagged, the runner shall be called out.[25]

Date: June 24, 1955
Teams: Chicago White Sox vs. Boston Red Sox (American League)
Perpetrator: Chicago shortstop Chico Carrasquel
Victim: Sammy White, Boston

According to *Sporting News*, "One of the oldest plays in the book, the hidden-ball trick, was a major factor in snapping the Red Sox five-game winning streak, June 24, at Fenway Park. In the ninth inning, with the White Sox leading, 3–2, one out and Boston runners Sammy White and Faye Throneberry on second and first base, respectively, Chico Carrasquel, Pale Hose shortstop, called time and strolled to the mound for a conference with Sandy Consuegra [Note: If indeed Carrasquel had called time, the trick couldn't have been pulled, according to the rules]. As 28,628 spectators watched, Consuegra slipped the ball to Carrasquel, who trotted back to his position. When White edged off the keystone, Chico tagged the Red Sox catcher out."[26] Similar accounts can be found in the *Bridgeport Post*[27] and the 1974 *A Rooter's Guide to the Red Sox*.[28] Carrasquel later claimed that he asked White to step off the base so he could dust it off.

Date: May 13, 1956
Teams: Detroit Tigers vs. Chicago White Sox (American League)
Perpetrator: Detroit first baseman Earl Torgeson
Victim: Minnie Minoso, Chicago
     According to the *Chicago Daily Tribune*, "Minoso fell victim to a hidden-ball trick by Torgeson in the first inning."[29]

Date: June 5, 1958
Teams: San Francisco Giants vs. Milwaukee Braves (National League)
Perpetrator: San Francisco rookie first baseman Orlando Cepeda
Victim: Wes Covington, Milwaukee

Date: July 29, 1959
Teams: Washington Senators vs. Kansas City Athletics (American League)
Perpetrator: Washington third baseman Harmon Killebrew
Victim: Harry Chiti, Kansas City
     Killebrew got Chiti in the sixth inning, after Chiti had gone from first to third on Joe DeMaestri's single to left.

Date: August 11, 1959
Teams: Milwaukee Braves vs. Cincinnati Reds (National League)
Perpetrator: Milwaukee first baseman Joe Adcock

Victim: Vada Pinson, Cincinnati

Per *Sporting News*, "Vada Pinson suffered a humiliating experience on his 21st birthday, August 11, when he became the victim of the hidden-ball trick. In the opening inning of the twin-bill nightcap against the Braves, the Cincinnati outfielder was on first base when Gus Bell [sacrifice] flied to center. Milwaukee first baseman Joe Adcock kept the ball when it was returned to the infield, and when Pinson stepped off first, Adcock tagged him out."[30] The scoring was 8–6–4–3.

12

1960–1969: STICK WAS SLICK

The 1960s saw 20 hidden-ball tricks, 12 by American League players. Gene "Stick" Michael notched his first two in 1968 and 1969, tying Joe Adcock for the decade leadership.

Date: August 31, 1960 (second game)
Teams: Milwaukee Braves vs. Chicago Cubs (National League)
Perpetrator: Milwaukee first baseman Joe Adcock
Victim: George Altman, Chicago
   In the ninth inning of the second game, Adcock nailed Altman to end the doubleheader.

Date: June 23, 1961
Teams: Milwaukee Braves vs. Chicago Cubs (National League)
Perpetrator: Milwaukee first baseman Joe Adcock
Victim: Billy Williams, Chicago
   For the third consecutive year—the second straight against the Cubs—Adcock executed the HBT. According to *Sporting News*, "In eighth . . . [rookie Billy] Williams was caught off first base on the hidden-ball play by Adcock."[1] The Cubs won anyway, 5–3.

Date: June 30, 1961
Teams: Philadelphia Phillies vs. Los Angeles Dodgers (National League)

Perpetrators: Philadelphia second baseman Tony Taylor and first baseman Pancho Herrera
Victim: Willie Davis, Los Angeles

Per *Sporting News*, in the seventh inning Dodger rookie "Willie Davis . . . suffered the embarrassing experience of being picked off first base by the hidden-ball ruse. Tony Taylor, Phil second baseman, took a throw from right field and hid the ball in his glove. When Davis took a lead off first, Taylor whipped the ball to Herrera at first, and the startled Willie was out in a quick rundown." This was Herrera's last season in the majors, but he was still at it more than a decade later in the minors. With Key West in the Florida State League in 1972, writes *Sporting News*, Herrera was "leading the league in one category—the hidden-ball trick. He . . . caught no fewer than 16 base runners with the antiquated trick. . . . In fact, he surprised Orlando runners twice in one game this year."[2]

Date: July 16, 1961
Teams: Los Angeles Angels vs. Washington Senators (American League)
Perpetrator: Los Angeles second baseman Billy Moran
Victim: Gene Green, Washington

Date: August 14, 1961
Teams: Washington Senators vs. Los Angeles Angels (American League)
Perpetrator: Washington third baseman Danny O'Connell
Victim: Leon Wagner, Los Angeles

Avenging the team's humiliation from the prior month, O'Connell got Wagner in the fifth inning.

Date: August 16, 1961
Teams: Minnesota Twins vs. Kansas City Athletics (American League)
Perpetrator: Minnesota second baseman Billy Martin
Victim: Gene Stephens, Kansas City

Stephens was tagged out at second by Martin in the ninth inning, after Martin said he wanted to clean the bag. Martin, who was in the final weeks of his 11-year playing career, afterward professed remorse at tricking his good friend.

Date: July 1, 1962 (first game)
Teams: Chicago White Sox vs. Cleveland Indians (American League)
Perpetrator: Chicago second baseman Nellie Fox
Victim: Al Luplow, Cleveland

According to *Sporting News*, "Nellie Fox pulled the hidden-ball trick in the first game of the July 1 doubleheader when he tagged out Cleveland rookie Al Luplow after Luplow had gone to second on Tito Francona's sacrifice fly."[3] The White Sox won, 5–4.

Date: July 27, 1963
Teams: New York Mets vs. Houston Colt .45s (National League)
Perpetrator: New York first baseman Frank Thomas
Victim: Jimmy Wynn, Houston

Wynn, 21, had made his big league debut earlier in the month. Per *Sporting News*, "Jim Wynn, who had just been called up from the minors, was victimized by the Mets' Frank Thomas in 1963. Thomas was playing first base and asked Wynn to step off the base so he could clean the bag. Jim did."[4] The contemporary *Sporting News* account reads, "Jim Wynn, 21-year-old Colt rookie outfielder, was the victim of one of the game's oldest tricks on July 27. Wynn reached first base on a fielder's choice in the second inning and was standing on the bag when Frank Thomas, playing the sack for the Mets, said, 'Step off the bag a minute, Jim. I want to kick the dust out of it.' Wynn politely moved back a few steps, and Thomas, who had the ball hidden in his glove, put the tag on the youngster. Jocko Conlan, the first base umpire, didn't call the play immediately. He conferred with plate umpire Ken Burkhart to make sure that 'time' had not been called, then flashed the 'out' sign, and the embarrassed Wynn walked back to the dugout, vowing he'd never fall for the trick again."[5] The Colt .45s later became the Astros.

Date: September 20, 1963 (first game)
Teams: New York Yankees vs. Kansas City Athletics (American League)
Perpetrator: New York second baseman Pedro Gonzalez
Victim: Ken Harrelson, Kansas City

According to *Sporting News*, "Outfielder Ken Harrelson of the Athletics was the embarrassed victim of the hidden-ball trick at Yankee

Stadium, September 20. He singled in the eleventh inning of a twin-bill opener and advanced to second on a sacrifice. Believing the ball had been returned to the mound, Ken stepped off the bag and was tagged by Pedro Gonzalez, the Yankee second baseman, who had hidden the ball in his glove. The Yankees won, 5–4 in 13 innings."[6] Gonzalez—like Harrelson, a rookie—played only seven games in the field all season.

Date: July 17, 1966 (second game)
Teams: Detroit Tigers vs. Cleveland Indians (American League)
Perpetrator: Detroit first baseman Norm Cash
Victim: Chico Salmon, Cleveland

Date: September 4, 1966
Teams: San Francisco Giants vs. St. Louis Cardinals (National League)
Perpetrators: San Francisco third baseman Jim Ray Hart and short-stop Hal Lanier
Victim: Orlando Cepeda, St. Louis
   Hart and Lanier conspired to nab former teammate Cepeda in the eighth inning. Cepeda had previously pulled the trick himself on June 5, 1958, and been caught with it during a winter league game on January 6, 1962.[7]

Date: September 12, 1966
Teams: New York Mets vs. Los Angeles Dodgers (National League)
Perpetrators: New York shortstop Bud Harrelson and second base-man Ron Hunt
Victim: Lou Johnson, Los Angeles

Date: June 16, 1967
Teams: Cincinnati Reds vs. Los Angeles Dodgers (National League)
Perpetrator: Cincinnati second baseman Chico Ruiz
Victim: John Roseboro, Los Angeles
   Per *Sporting News*, "Veteran Los Angeles catcher John Roseboro was the victim of the age-old hidden-ball trick, June 16, when Chico Ruiz, Cincinnati second baseman, caught Roseboro and the Dodger coaches napping. Roseboro opened the second inning with a single and moved up on pitcher Bill Singer's sacrifice. Ruiz took pitcher Mel Queen's throw at first, kept the ball as he returned to his position at

second, then tagged Roseboro as the Dodger strayed off the bag."[8] It was a big play, as the Reds won, 3–2.

Date: May 8, 1968
Teams: California Angels vs. Chicago White Sox (American League)
Perpetrator: California first baseman Don Mincher
Victim: Sandy Alomar Sr., Chicago
   Mincher caught Alomar Sr. in the ninth inning, after Alomar had singled as a pinch hitter.

Date: June 5, 1968
Teams: Houston Astros vs. St. Louis Cardinals (National League)
Perpetrator: Houston second baseman Julio Gotay
Victim: Julian Javier, St. Louis
   Julio hoodwinked Julian. Writes *Sporting News*, "Julio Gotay is an artist with the ancient 'hidden-ball' ruse. The trick, a popular one in playground baseball but a rarity in the major leagues, was worked successfully by Gotay on the Cardinals' Julian Javier June 5. Gotay had covered first on a sacrifice in which Javier was moved to second base. Julio walked toward pitcher Larry Dierker and pretended to give him the ball but kept it concealed in his glove as he trotted back to his position. First baseman Rusty Staub came over and engaged Dierker in conversation. Javier lifted one foot off the bag, and Gotay was quickly behind him with the tag. Gotay said he thought he had worked it twice before in the majors and maybe ten times in all in professional baseball. 'He did it all the time in winter ball,' the Cardinals' Orlando Cepeda confirmed."[9] This trick came in the seventh inning. One person recalled hearing that Gotay let out a blood-curdling yell, scaring Javier off the bag, while another stated that someone had arranged tongue depressors like a cross on the bag, causing the religious player to shy away from it.

Date: September 17, 1968
Teams: New York Yankees vs. Detroit Tigers (American League)
Perpetrator: New York shortstop Gene Michael
Victim: Tom Matchick, Detroit
   Says *Sporting News* in 1970, "Michael had previously pulled (the hidden-ball trick) on Zoilo Versalles and Tom Matchik [*sic*]."[10] The

incident was found on this date, as Michaels nabbed the Tigers' rookie in the seventh frame.

Date: September 18, 1968
Teams: Boston Red Sox vs. Baltimore Orioles (American League)
Perpetrator: Boston third baseman Joe Foy
Victim: Merv Rettenmund, Baltimore

According to *A Rooter's Guide to the Red Sox*, "Merv Rettenmund was being complimented on his fine baserunning by coach Billy Hunter [a perpetrator of the trick in 1953], when third baseman Joe Foy interrupted, 'Hey, get me the bag, will you.' Rettenmund stepped off, and Foy tagged him. It helped the Red Sox to a 4–0 defeat of Baltimore in 1968."[11] The play occurred in the fifth inning. Says *Sporting News*, "Coy Joe Foy, they're calling him in Boston these days, and Baltimore rookie Marv [*sic*] Rettenmund will have to agree. In a key spot of a game which the Red Sox won from the Orioles, Rettenmund went from first base to third on a single. He decoyed Boston outfielder Ken Harrelson on the play, and drew a well-deserved accolade from Baltimore coach Billy Hunter. Foy had the baseball in his hand, but Rettenmund did not know it. 'Say, kid, will you step off the bag for a minute so I can straighten it out?' Foy asked the rookie. Obligingly, Rettenmund stepped off. Foy tagged him, and umpire John Rice called him out."[12]

Date: June 21, 1969 (first game)
Teams: Boston Red Sox vs. New York Yankees (American League)
Perpetrator: Boston first baseman George Thomas
Victim: Jerry Kenney, New York

In the 11th inning of the first game, Thomas—playing first base for one of only 20 times in his 13-year career—nabbed the Yankee rookie. It was one of two HBTs on the day.

Date: June 21, 1969
Teams: Washington Senators vs. Detroit Tigers (American League)
Perpetrator: Washington second baseman Tim Cullen
Victim: Willie Horton, Detroit

Date: June 28, 1969
Teams: New York Yankees vs. Cleveland Indians (American League)

Figure 12.1.   Shortstop Gene Michael revived the hidden-ball trick in the late 1960s. "I had five of them, but I could have had 15," he said. "If you did it too much, they'd think you were trying to be smarter than they were, so I stopped doing it." Topps baseball card, used courtesy of Topps Company, Inc.

Perpetrator: New York shortstop Gene Michael
Victim: Zoilo Versalles, Cleveland

According to a 1970 *Sporting News* article, "Michael had previously pulled (the hidden-ball trick) on Zoilo Versalles."[13] It was found in this game, Michael getting Versalles in the sixth frame.

13

1970–1979: ELEMENTARY, MY DEAR WATSON

Gene Michael again led the way, notching three of the 13 hidden-ball tricks in the 1970s. Bob Watson also had a pair. The American League again dominated, with ten of the 13.

Date: April 26, 1970
Teams: Montreal Expos vs. San Francisco Giants (National League)
Perpetrator: Montreal shortstop Bobby Wine
Victim: Willie Mays, San Francisco

Date: June 13, 1970
Teams: New York Yankees vs. Kansas City Royals (American League)
Perpetrator: New York shortstop Gene Michael
Victim: Joe Keough, Kansas City
According to noted journalist Bob Addie, "Kansas City's talented sophomore Lou Piniella started the sixth inning with a double and scored the tying run on a single by Joe Keough. While Keough was congratulating himself for getting Kansas City back in the game, Michael palmed the relay from the outfield. Keough, concentrating on (pitcher Gary Waslewski), took his lead, and Michael then stepped in and tagged the embarrassed Keough"[1] Per *Sporting News*, "Gene's mates call him Stick because of his build, but many opponents refer to him as Slick for the bag of tricks he unfolds. Joe Keough of Kansas City was the latest victim of Gene's hidden-ball stunt recently. . . . He does it

with a sheepish grin. 'I'd never do it just to embarrass a guy,' Michael said. 'If it might help win a game, then I'll try it. I guess all's fair in love or war.'"[2] According to a 1980 article in *Baseball Digest*, "Gene Michael once used the hidden-ball trick [against the Royals] . . . twice in the same game."[3] It seems highly unlikely that the contemporary publications would have failed to mention the second trick.

Date: July 27, 1970
Teams: New York Yankees vs. California Angels (American League)
Perpetrator: New York shortstop Gene Michael
Victim: Jarvis Tatum, California

Says *Sporting News*, "Gene Michael pulled the hidden-ball trick for the second time this year, and it helped beat the Angels. He got pinch runner Jarvis Tatum to blunt an Angel rally. . . . Shortstop Gene Michael of the Yankees was up to an old trick against the Angels July 27. Michael pulled the ancient hidden-ball trick on pinch runner Jarvis Tatum, who had strayed off second base, to help Mel Stottlemyre out of a ninth-inning jam. 'That was the fourth time I've pulled it in the major leagues,' said Michael. Earlier this season he nailed the Royals' Joe Keough."[4]

According to Bob Addie, "Jarvis Tatum was put in to run in the ninth inning of a tie game when Yankee pitcher Mel Stottlemyre was in a jam. Jarvis represented the winning run. Michael palmed the ball and bluffed Jarvis back to second. Michael then strolled back to second, and Jarvis, intent on Stottlemyre, didn't bother going back to second base. Michael put the tag on, and the inning was over. The Yanks won with three runs in the tenth. . . . 'I make sure the second base umpire knows I'm going to pull the hidden-ball trick,' Michael said. 'If you don't warn the umpire, it could get a little confusing. I must say the umpires have been great actors. It's tough to keep a straight face when it's going on.'"[5] Three decades later, Michael recalled, "One time I knew there was a runner I could get, but I looked and the umpire, Emmett Ashford, was in right-center. I yelled to him, and he came trotting to second. I showed him the ball, and his eyes got real big. The runner didn't see it. He took a couple more steps, and I trotted over and tagged him."[6]

Date: June 9, 1972
Teams: Texas Rangers vs. Baltimore Orioles (American League)

Perpetrator: Texas shortstop Toby Harrah
Victim: Paul Blair, Baltimore

After Ranger third baseman Dave Nelson threw to catcher Dick Billings in the sixth inning, Billings fired the ball to Harrah. Moments later, Harrah tagged Blair with the HBT.

Date: June 6, 1973
Teams: New York Yankees vs. Texas Rangers (American League)
Perpetrator: New York shortstop Gene Michael
Victim: Vic Harris, Texas

Michael scored his fifth successful trick, more than anyone else since 1940, and a record that has remained unapproached since. The Yankee shortstop took the relay from left fielder Roy White following a sacrifice fly by the Rangers' Toby Harrah (the trick's most recent perpetrator), kept the ball, and nabbed Harris at second base. According to *Sporting News*, "The Yankees pulled the old hidden-ball trick on the Rangers in a 5–2 victory June 6. With Texas runners at first and second base, two out, and Rico Carty prepared to bat in the fifth inning, New York right-hander Steve Kline circled the mound pretending to rub the baseball. When Vic Harris led off second base, shortstop Gene Michael moved in for the tag, and the inning was over. 'Michael had the ball, but I had to make it look good,' said Kline."[7]

A decade later, Michael seemed embarrassed to discuss his prowess: "Heck, I only pulled it five times in my career, no big deal. But the truth is I could have done it a lot more times if I'd wanted to. It's always easier to pull it at second base because the runner usually has to do something 'extra' to get there (hit a double, steal, etc.), and it seems to cause a temporary loss of his concentration. But if you keep doing it, you run the risk of antagonizing the player you fool. He thinks you are showing him up. The first time I worked the hidden ball was against Zoilo Versalles of the Twins. He told the press I was bush. And I said 'Why? He was the guy who made the mistake.' Why didn't I pull the hidden-ball trick more often? Why didn't I want to run the risk of antagonizing people? I don't know. Human nature, I guess."[8] Three decades later, Michael reflected, "I had five of them, but I could have had 15. If you did it too much, they'd think you were trying to be smarter than they were, so I stopped doing it."[9]

Date: June 14, 1974
Teams: Texas Rangers vs. Milwaukee Brewers (American League)
Perpetrator: Texas second baseman Dave Nelson
Victim: Bob Coluccio, Milwaukee

Per *Sporting News*, "Coluccio's face had to be red when Dave Nelson of the Rangers pulled the hidden-ball trick on him at second base recently in the Ranger pasture. 'Could you step off the bag?' Nelson asked Bobby. 'I want to dust it off.' Coluccio obliged, and, presto, he was tagged out. Coluch was so embarrassed, he got into a debate with Nelson later and told him he'd get him next time he got down. Nelson suggested now would be the time. They rapped for a while, and that's how it ended."[10] Retrosheet indicates that it happened in the third inning, after Coluccio had walked and stolen second with two out, although it describes it as "picked off second, unassisted." Texas won, 7–2.

Date: August 1, 1975
Teams: Minnesota Twins vs. Chicago White Sox (American League)
Perpetrator: Minnesota first baseman Jerry Terrell
Victim: Nyls Nyman, Chicago

In the sixth inning, Terrell faked a throw back to the pitcher after a third pickoff attempt, and rookie Nyman moved off the bag too quickly. First base coach Alex Monchak was ejected in the ensuing argument.

Date: June 22, 1976
Teams: Chicago White Sox vs. Kansas City Royals (American League)
Perpetrator: Chicago second baseman Jack Brohamer
Victim: Hal McRae, Kansas City

Date: August 29, 1976
Teams: Houston Astros vs. St. Louis Cardinals (National League)
Perpetrator: Houston first baseman Bob Watson
Victim: Jerry Mumphrey, St. Louis

According to *Sporting News*, in the third inning, Mumphrey beat out an infield hit, and coach Johnny Lewis went down the line to retrieve his batting helmet and congratulate him. Watson then tagged Mumphrey out when he took a lead. "I've been trying to do that for three years," said Watson. "That play can only work when the coach isn't watching."[11] The Astros won, 6–0. Watson executed the play again less than a year later.

Date: April 17, 1977
Teams: Houston Astros vs. Atlanta Braves (National League)
Perpetrator: Houston first baseman Bob Watson
Victim: Pat Rockett, Atlanta

Date: July 9, 1977
Teams: Chicago White Sox vs. Detroit Tigers (American League)
Perpetrator: Chicago first baseman Jim Spencer
Victim: Ron LeFlore, Detroit
A *This Week in Baseball* episode depicts this play, in which Spencer nabbed LeFlore after faking a throw back to pitcher Ken Kravec in the third inning. Retrosheet has it as a pickoff.

Date: May 6, 1978
Teams: New York Yankees vs. Texas Rangers (American League)
Perpetrator: New York second baseman Willie Randolph
Victim: Bump Wills, Texas
Randolph nabbed Wills in the first inning. One scoresheet has "hit by batted ball." Randolph was later victimized by the play in 1980.

Date: August 27, 1978
Teams: Toronto Blue Jays vs. Minnesota Twins (American League)
Perpetrator: Toronto first baseman John Mayberry
Victim: Hosken Powell, Minnesota
Mayberry caught rookie Powell in the first inning. Writes Dan Gutman in *It Ain't Cheatin' If You Don't Get Caught*, "John Mayberry, who played first base, wasn't so subtle. He'd simply ask the runner to move his foot so Mayberry could use the base to tie his shoe. The runner stupidly would, and Mayberry would tag him out."[12]

14

1980–1989: HAPPY BIRTHDAY, KID!

The hidden-ball trick had a resurgence in the 1980s, with 22 incidents, the most since the 1920s. Marty Barrett's three led the way, helping the American League to a 17–5 advantage. One of the most memorable tricks happened on Gary "The Kid" Carter's birthday.

Date: June 29, 1980
Teams: San Francisco Giants vs. Los Angeles Dodgers (National League)
Perpetrators: San Francisco first baseman Rich Murray and shortstop Johnny LeMaster
Victim: Dusty Baker, Los Angeles
　　In the eighth inning, Murray and LeMaster caught Baker. Rich, brother of Eddie Murray, was in his first month in the majors.

Date: July 3, 1980
Teams: St. Louis Cardinals vs. Philadelphia Phillies (National League)
Perpetrators: St. Louis shortstop Garry Templeton and second baseman Ken Oberkfell
Victim: Bake McBride, Philadelphia
　　McBride led off the seventh inning with a single and stole second base, but Templeton kept the ball and, when McBride led off the bag, fired it to Oberkfell for the out. The Phillies won anyway, 8–1.

Date: October 4, 1980 (first game)

Teams: Detroit Tigers vs. New York Yankees (American League)
Perpetrator: Detroit second baseman Lou Whitaker
Victim: Willie Randolph, New York

Date: April 10, 1981
Teams: Oakland A's vs. Minnesota Twins (American League)
Perpetrator: Oakland second baseman Brian Doyle
Victim: Glenn Adams, Minnesota

According to *Sporting News*, "Minnesota threatened in sixth with runners on first and second and no outs. But second baseman Doyle employed the hidden-ball trick and tagged out Adams at second base. A double play then ended the inning."[1] They expand on the story in the following issue: "A's second baseman Brian Doyle caught the Minnesota Twins by surprise April 10, when he worked a rare hidden-ball trick against Glenn Adams. The play killed a Minnesota rally. . . . Adams, the Twins' designated hitter, drew a walk from Rick Langford to lead off the seventh inning. The A's were leading, 5–3. The next batter, Gary Ward, hit a grounder in the hole between short and third. Third baseman Wayne Gross knocked down the ball and was unable to make a play and was charged with an error. What happened next was missed by almost everyone in Metropolitan Stadium, especially Adams. Gross threw the ball to Doyle at second. Doyle looked at Langford, who was standing behind the mound. When Langford saw that Doyle had no immediate intention of returning the ball, he turned his back on the outfield and pretended he had the ball. Meanwhile, Adams took a lead off the bag but returned when Doyle circled behind him. Adams took another lead, and Doyle applied the tag. Mickey Hatcher then grounded into a double play to end the inning."[2]

Baseball Digest editor John Kuenster recalled the play later that year, writing, "During training camp last spring, (Oakland manager Billy Martin) devoted time one day to teaching his players—you won't believe this—the hidden-ball trick! Ye, gads! Your author has to go back in memory 20 years to recall the last time he saw the hidden-ball trick pulled off in a game. Yet, in the second game this season, the A's embarrassed the Minnesota Twins with the play and perhaps averted a loss. With the Twins trailing, 5–3, in the sixth inning, Minnesota had runners on first and second with nobody out. It was the kind of crisis on which Martin thrives. He flashed a signal to third baseman Wayne

Gross, whose error had put a Twin on first. Gross flipped the ball to second baseman Brian Doyle. Evidently, the unalert Twin coaches and base runners did not see the throw or simply ignored the fact that Doyle had the ball. A few seconds later, Doyle walked over and tagged Glenn Adams, who had taken a slight lead off second. The next Minnesota batter hit into an inning-ending double play, and the A's, who appeared to be headed for serious trouble, escaped undamaged and with the ball game as well. Martin shrewdly downplayed the hidden-ball trick after the game, but deep inside he had to be pleased with the obvious payoff."[3] Martin had used the trick as a player two decades earlier.

Date: April 14, 1981
Teams: California Angels vs. Oakland A's (American League)
Perpetrator: California first baseman Rod Carew
Victim: Mike Heath, Oakland

Four days later, Martin's team was the victim of the trick, at the hands of one of his former players. Heath, who had been caught stealing earlier in the game, was now caught dozing by Carew after a one-out single in the eighth inning. The A's still won, 5–2.

Date: June 12, 1982
Teams: Houston Astros vs. San Diego Padres (National League)
Perpetrator: Houston second baseman Phil Garner
Victim: Ruppert Jones, San Diego

Date: June 21, 1982
Teams: Cleveland Indians vs. Baltimore Orioles (American League)
Perpetrators: Cleveland first baseman Mike Hargrove and second baseman Alan Bannister
Victim: Al Bumbry, Baltimore

With one out and Lenn Sakata on first base in the second inning, Bumbry hit a grounder to short. Sakata was retired at second, but the speedy Bumbry beat the throw to first. Hargrove kept the ball, however, and when Bumbry left the base he had him, although he had to throw to Bannister for the out. Rich Dauer, the batter at the time, apparently wasn't paying close attention, as he would be victimized on the trick 17 days later. The Orioles won this game, 7–0.

Date: July 8, 1982
Teams: Seattle Mariners vs. Baltimore Orioles (American League)
Perpetrator: Seattle first baseman Bruce Bochte
Victim: Rich Dauer, Baltimore

Date: September 27, 1982
Teams: Chicago White Sox vs. Seattle Mariners (American League)
Perpetrators: Chicago first baseman Mike Squires and shortstop Vance Law
Victim: Todd Cruz, Seattle

Date: August 17, 1984
Teams: Boston Red Sox vs. Minnesota Twins (American League)
Perpetrator: Boston shortstop Jackie Gutierrez
Victim: Tim Teufel, Minnesota
According to the *Red Sox Media Guide*, Gutierrez nabbed Teufel. The *Boston Globe* confirms it: "Leading off second as Minnesota was trying to build on its 6–1 lead in the seventh, Teufel was victimized by the ol' hidden-ball trick. Shortstop Jackie Gutierrez pulled the surprise. 'Wade Boggs told me I ought to do it,' Gutierrez said. 'So I hid the ball and told [pitcher Steve] Crawford, "Let's go." I heard somebody yelling for him to get back, then I tagged him. I was really excited. It's the first time I've done that.' Teufel wasn't smiling. 'I'll talk with Jackie about it,' he said. 'It turned out to be a big play. But at the time, it seemed meaningless because the score was 6–1 [the Twins wound up winning, 6–5]. I was thinking they should have saved it for a closer game.'"[4]

Date: July 7, 1985
Teams: Boston Red Sox vs. California Angels (American League)
Perpetrator: Boston second baseman Marty Barrett
Victim: Bobby Grich, California
Sporting News, talking about Barrett's July 21 trick, mentions, "Two weeks earlier, Barrett had caught Bobby Grich snoozing."[5] Writes the *Boston Herald*, "Marty Barrett pulled the hidden-ball trick on Bobby Grich in the second, tagging him when he stepped off second base, while [first baseman] Bill Buckner was near the mound talking with [pitcher] Jim Dorsey. Barrett had covered first when Brian Downing

beat out a bunt trying to sacrifice and held the ball in his glove. It was poetic justice since Grich has made a career out of pulling it on people."[6] That same day's *Boston Globe* also refers to Grich as "long a master of the same play." No trick by Grich has been turned up during my research. "I knew Barrett had it all the time," claimed Grich. "I just had to go to the bathroom. I haven't seen the play for so long, and my mind wasn't ready for it. It's kinda funny, now."[7] The Angels won, 8–3. Barrett had pulled the trick as early as 1980 in the Eastern League.[8]

Date: July 21, 1985
Teams: Boston Red Sox vs. California Angels (American League)
Perpetrators: Boston second baseman Marty Barrett and shortstop Glenn Hoffman
Victim: Doug DeCinces, California

Barrett duped the Angels for the second time in two weeks, nabbing DeCinces. Marty hung on to the ball in the sixth inning after Dick Schofield flied to left fielder Jim Rice, and Rice relayed it in. Shortstop Glenn Hoffman is quoted in the *Boston Herald* as saying, "In order to make the play work, you've got to have a real sneaky type like Marty involved. I saw Marty show the ball to the umpire and knew something was up. I waited for him to make a move, but he kept walking further and further away from second base. Finally it dawned on me he wanted to throw the ball to me. So I ducked behind DeCinces and we picked him off, and then I got out of there just as fast because I figured Doug wouldn't be very happy."[9] Boston won, 8–4. "That may be Barrett's best play; that's all I've got to say about it," Angel manager Gene Mauch fumed (probably repeating what someone said when Mauch pulled the trick in 1948). Pitcher Al Nipper said, "I didn't get the ball back and knew something was up. I didn't want to give it away. I just stepped on the mound—didn't straddle the rubber—and just kind of stood there to bide my time and wait until things happened."[10]

As the *Boston Globe* points out, "Neither coach was looking. Nor was Mauch. 'I saw Nipper on the mound,' said DeCinces, 'and figured everything was normal. I'm at fault; I didn't know the rule. I know now the pitcher has to be right near the rubber. Barrett had left, there was no one around. . . . He just barely got me as it was.'"[11] In the same paper, Barrett gives his version: "Jimmy threw to me trying to get DeCinces out. I looked around to see if any of the base coaches were

looking. They weren't. So I went back to my position. I yelled at Hoffman and showed it to the umpire, [Nick Bremigan], real quick. With
[lefty Rod] Carew up, there was no need for me to be close to second,
so Hoffy started shifting over, and when he got off a little further, Hoffy
broke. I just flipped it to him, and (DeCinces) didn't have time to
react. . . . I used to do it about 15 times a year in the minors."[12]
According to *Sporting News*, "After becoming the second Angels player
this season to fall for Red Sox second baseman Marty Barrett's hidden-
ball trick, Doug DeCinces vowed revenge. 'I don't get mad, I get even,'
he said."[13] DeCinces tried in the 1986 American League Championship
Series (see the later discussion of foiled tricks) but failed.

Nearly a decade later, in *Sports Collectors Digest*, Barrett says he
learned the trick "from a guy named Buddy Hunter in the Red Sox
organization," adding, "I did it a lot in the minor leagues, because they
have a little different rule there. I think I pulled it three times in the
major leagues. I did it once to Bobby Grich, and he took it real well. He
said he had to go to the bathroom anyway; he was glad to get off base.
But the funny thing is, Doug DeCinces (Grich's teammate with the
Angels) really rode him the whole trip from Anaheim to Boston, because they played us (again) a week later. He told him, 'You better
watch out, they'll get you twice.' I ended up getting DeCinces; he was
really embarrassed. He was telling the umpire, 'How come you let him
get away with that Little League stuff?' Well, he was saying that because after giving Grich so much grief that he was going to get a lot. I
played golf with Bobby Grich about two months ago, and he said that
was the best thing that could've happened to him because he was the
type of guy who always popped off. From then on, any time he tried to
get on someone the rest of his career, they'd say 'hidden-ball trick,' and
he couldn't say a whole lot. Actually, (how I executed the trick is) a kind
of thing I told Buddy Hunter I'd keep to myself. You end up keeping
the ball, but the situation and stuff that happens, I'm keeping to myself
because I'm going to teach it (in the minor leagues). The bottom line is
the base coaches are responsible for picking it up, but they never do."[14]

Date: September 26, 1985
Teams: Minnesota Twins vs. Texas Rangers (American League)
Perpetrator: Minnesota first baseman Kent Hrbek
Victim: Bill Stein, Texas

Hrbek caught Stein in the seventh inning. Stein was in the final days of a 14-year career and would reach base just one more time.

Date: June 17, 1986
Teams: Detroit Tigers vs. Baltimore Orioles (American League)
Perpetrator: Detroit first baseman Dave Bergman
Victim: Alan Wiggins, Baltimore
Bergman got Wiggins in the third inning, as described earlier in this book. Supposedly, the next time Wiggins encountered Bergman, Alan said, "If you pull that shit again, I'll kill you."

Date: June 30, 1986
Teams: Minnesota Twins vs. Texas Rangers (American League)
Perpetrator: Minnesota second baseman Steve Lombardozzi
Victim: Mike Stanley, Texas
According to *Sporting News*, "Texas rookie Mike Stanley was Chris Lombardozzi's roommate when the two played at the University of Florida. Lombardozzi's brother, Steve, is the Twins' second baseman. When the Twins defeated Texas, 5–2, on June 30 in Arlington, Lombardozzi ended a Rangers rally [in the eighth inning] when he pulled the hidden-ball trick on his brother's old roommate. After he returned to the Twins' hotel, Lombardozzi called Stanley. 'The first thing I said is, "This is Lombo. Don't hang up,"' Lombardozzi said. 'I told him I didn't try to pull it on him because he was a rookie or anything, that it just came to me instinctively.' Lombardozzi kept the ball after taking a throw at first on a sacrifice bunt. No one on the Texas bench or in the coaching boxes noticed, and when Stanley strayed off second, Lombardozzi raced over from a normal second base position and tagged him out."[15] Stanley had made his major league debut just six days earlier, and Lombardozzi was also a rookie.

Date: April 8, 1988
Teams: Philadelphia Phillies vs. New York Mets (National League)
Perpetrator: Philadelphia shortstop Steve Jeltz
Victim: Gary Carter, New York
Jeltz ended the game by tagging out Carter in the ninth inning. To add insult to injury, it was Carter's 34th birthday. The play was featured

in the 1989 *Sports Illustrated*/Major League Baseball Productions video *Super Duper Baseball Bloopers*.

Date: May 8, 1988
Teams: Kansas City Royals vs. Milwaukee Brewers (American League)
Perpetrator: Kansas City second baseman Brad Wellman
Victim: Dale Sveum, Milwaukee

Wellman kept the ball after a sacrifice hit and nabbed Sveum in the eighth inning.

Date: September 5, 1988
Teams: Boston Red Sox vs. Baltimore Orioles (American League)
Perpetrators: Boston second baseman Marty Barrett and shortstop Jody Reed
Victim: Jim Traber, Baltimore

According to *Sporting News*, "The Orioles were the victim of the old hidden-ball trick in a Labor Day game with Boston. After Larry Sheets and Jim Traber opened the second inning with singles, Rene Gonzales bunted, forcing Sheets at third. [Boston third baseman] Wade Boggs threw to second baseman Marty Barrett, who was covering first in an attempt to complete a double play. Gonzales was safe at first, but Barrett held on to the ball and walked back to his position at second. He waited a few seconds then tagged out Traber, who had led off the base, not realizing Barrett still had the ball [Retrosheet says Barrett tossed to rookie shortstop Jody Reed for the out]. 'I don't know if (the play) was bonehead,' said [manager Frank] Robinson. 'You have to stay on the base and always know where the ball is. The coaches should never lose sight of the ball.' The Orioles got the last laugh on Barrett two days later. They . . . beat the Red Sox, 4–3, scoring the winning run on a wild throw by the Sox' second baseman."[16]

Date: October 2, 1988
Teams: Kansas City Royals vs. Chicago White Sox (American League)
Perpetrator: Kansas City first baseman George Brett
Victim: Mike Diaz, Chicago

Brett caught Diaz—playing his final major league game—in the sixth frame. Diaz batted one more time and flied out.

Date: June 23, 1989 (second game)
Teams: Milwaukee Brewers vs. Chicago White Sox (American League)
Perpetrator: Brewers' first baseman Greg Brock
Victim: Ozzie Guillen, White Sox

A *This Week in Baseball* episode depicts this play, in which Brock nabbed Guillen after a fake throw back to the pitcher. It was in the ninth inning of the doubleheader's second game.

Date: August 5, 1989
Teams: Detroit Tigers vs. Chicago White Sox (American League)
Perpetrator: Detroit first baseman Dave Bergman
Victim: Ozzie Guillen, Chicago

A *This Week in Baseball* episode also depicts this one, in which Guillen was caught on the same play for the second time in 43 days. This time, Bergman was the perpetrator, smacking the ball hard on Guillen's helmet in the seventh inning. Retrosheet calls it a pickoff.

Date: August 11, 1989
Teams: Atlanta Braves vs. San Diego Padres (National League)
Perpetrator: Atlanta second baseman Jeff Treadway
Victim: Marvell Wynne, San Diego

Wynne led off the ninth inning with a pinch single, and Bip Roberts sacrificed him to second, Treadway covering first for the putout. Wynne represented the tying run with one out and future Hall of Famers Roberto Alomar and Tony Gwynn due up. But Treadway had kept the ball and tagged Wynne out. Suddenly there were two out and nobody on. Alomar fanned, and the Padres lost, 6–5.

15

1990–1999: MASTER MATT

Before Matt Williams executed the play in 1994, no third baseman had pulled off the hidden-ball trick in more than a quarter-century. Williams had two of the 11 tricks in the 1990s, tying Delino DeShields for the decade lead. They helped the National League finally top the American League in this category, 7–4.

Date: May 18, 1990
Teams: Montreal Expos vs. San Francisco Giants (National League)
Perpetrator: Montreal second baseman Delino DeShields
Victim: Terry Kennedy, San Francisco
   Montreal rookie DeShields caught Kennedy after a sacrifice hit in the second inning.[1]

Date: April 27, 1991
Teams: Atlanta Braves vs. Houston Astros (National League)
Perpetrator: Atlanta second baseman Jeff Treadway
Victim: Eric Yelding, Houston
   Yelding was out on a HBT by Treadway well after a fly out in the sixth inning; no double play was scored.

Date: May 13, 1991
Teams: Boston Red Sox vs. Chicago White Sox (American League)
Perpetrator: Boston second baseman Steve Lyons
Victim: Ozzie Guillen, Chicago

Steve "Psycho" Lyons duped Guillen in the fourth inning. It was the third time Guillen had been caught in a two-year span.

Date: July 8, 1992 (second game)
Teams: Montreal Expos vs. Los Angeles Dodgers (National League)
Perpetrator: Montreal second baseman Delino DeShields
Victim: Jose Offerman, Los Angeles

In the third inning, DeShields completed a delayed double play, nabbing Offerman at second base after a sacrifice bunt.

Date: June 28, 1994
Teams: San Francisco Giants vs. Los Angeles Dodgers (National League)
Perpetrator: San Francisco third baseman Matt Williams
Victim: Rafael Bournigal, Los Angeles

Apparently 1992 victim Jose Offerman didn't offer the benefit of his experience to his understudy, nor did DeShields—by this time Offerman's teammate—impart his wisdom. According to *USA Today Baseball Weekly*, "Rookie shortstop Rafael Bournigal, who replaced Offerman, was victimized by the old hidden-ball trick after tripling in a run in the sixth inning of the Dodgers' 7–4 victory against San Francisco June 28. Seconds after he reached third base, the 28-year-old infielder moved off the bag and was tagged out by Giants third baseman Matt Williams. 'I saw it happen, and I was surprised. That's a veteran move,' Dodger second baseman Delino DeShields said. 'He asked me to step off the bag so he could clean it,' said Bournigal. 'You have no friends in this business.'"[2]

Date: June 28, 1995
Teams: Colorado Rockies vs. San Francisco Giants (National League)
Perpetrator: Colorado third baseman Vinny Castilla
Victim: Darren Lewis, San Francisco

On the anniversary of the last successful HBT, Castilla got Lewis in the first inning. *Rocky Mountain News* beat writer Jack Etkin checked his scoresheet and reported, "Lewis led off with a walk and stole second with Robbie Thompson batting. Thompson grounded out to third, and after Castilla's throw, Lewis took third. Mark Hirschbeck was the third

Figure 15.1.   Second base belonged to Delino DeShields. He pulled a couple of tricks there in the 1990s. Topps baseball card, used courtesy of Topps Company, Inc.

base umpire. The hidden-ball trick took place with [Barry] Bonds batting."

Date: May 30, 1996
Teams: Los Angeles Dodgers vs. Philadelphia Phillies (National League)
Perpetrator: Los Angeles first baseman Eric Karros
Victim: Glenn Murray, Philadelphia

In the fourth inning, Karros tricked Murray. Murray, who had made his debut earlier that same month, went on to play only 38 games in his career.

Date: August 19, 1997 (first game)
Teams: Chicago White Sox vs. Toronto Blue Jays (American League)
Perpetrators: Chicago third baseman Robin Ventura and second baseman Ray Durham
Victim: Jose Cruz Jr., Toronto

In the third inning of the first game, Ventura and Durham conspired to nail rookie Cruz.

Date: September 19, 1997 (second game)
Teams: Cleveland Indians vs. Kansas City Royals (American League)
Perpetrator: Cleveland third baseman Matt Williams
Victim: Jed Hansen, Kansas City

According to *USA Today Baseball Weekly*, "After Royals rookie second baseman Jed Hansen stole third base (in the first inning of the second game) Friday, he turned to talk to third base coach Rich Dauer [a 1982 victim]. Enter Indians third baseman Matt Williams. 'He said, "Why don't you step off the bag, so I can clean it off?" I was gullible enough to step off,' Hansen said. 'I was not paying attention and talking to Rich Dauer. I learned something. I didn't expect that'—a polite tag by Williams. Hansen was called out. 'He caught me by surprise. I was upset about that. Hopefully, it won't happen again.'"[3] Williams supposedly told Hansen that big league basemen were expected to keep the bases as white as possible.[4]

Date: April 25, 1998
Teams: Baltimore Orioles vs. Oakland Athletics (American League)

Figure 15.2.   Matt Williams was the first third baseman since the 1960s to execute the play, which he carried out using the old "step off the base a minute, I want to clean it" trick on multiple occasions. Topps baseball card, used courtesy of Topps Company, Inc.

Perpetrator: Baltimore first baseman Rafael Palmeiro
Victim: Rickey Henderson, Oakland

Oakland's Rafael Bournigal lofted a fly ball to Oriole center fielder Jeffrey Hammonds, advancing Ryan Christenson to third base. That left Henderson on first base, with second open and two out in a scoreless game. The crowd of 46,206 buzzed with anticipation, as the owner of 1,236 major league stolen bases conferred with his coach about the situation. Palmeiro ambled back to his position from second base, where he had backed up the throw from Hammonds to shortstop Mike Bordick. And suddenly, the inning was over. Palmeiro had tagged Henderson out with the ball he had concealed in his mitt. The greatest base-stealer of all time had fallen victim to the old HBT.

"'When the ball came back to the infield, I had no intentions of doing anything,' Palmeiro said. 'I was going to call time and give the ball to the pitcher. But when I turned around, I saw that he (Henderson) was off the bag talking to the coach. So I didn't call time. I just started walking toward first base. I didn't run. If he would have stepped on the bag, I would have stopped. But the closer I got, I thought I could touch him and get out of the inning.' . . . 'I didn't see the exchange' [from Bordick to Palmeiro, first base coach Gary] Jones admitted. . . . 'I've seen it at second (base), but never at first,' he [Henderson] said. 'Especially after the play's been made and everybody's going back. It's one of those plays. They came out lucky today.'"[5] Baltimore beat Oakland, 8–1, with the trick play occurring in the third inning of Cal Ripken's 2,500th consecutive game.

Labeling this a hidden-ball trick is a borderline call, but the story was too good to pass up. More than 15 years later, Henderson remained the last American League player to be caught with the trick.

Date: June 26, 1999
Teams: San Francisco Giants vs. Los Angeles Dodgers (National League)
Perpetrator: San Francisco first baseman J. T. Snow
Victim: Carlos Perez, Los Angeles

In the fourth inning, Snow embarrassed the Dodger pitcher, who had just beaten out a bunt single, been congratulated by his coach, and taken a healthy lead off first. According to USA *Today Baseball Weekly*, "The hidden-ball trick rarely works, but the Giants pulled it off against the Dodgers when first baseman J. T. Snow stunned Carlos Perez. Snow hid the ball in his glove and waited for Perez, who had singled, to step off the bag. Once he did, Snow applied the tag. First base umpire Charlie Reliford immediately called Perez out to end the inning. 'I was nervous,' Snow said. 'I felt like I was stealing something and running out of a store.' After Perez singled, he chatted with first base coach John Shelby as Snow and pitcher Chris Brock signaled to each other that the play was on. Brock walked behind the mound for the resin bag (if he's on the mound without the ball a balk would be called), and Perez was trapped."[6]

16

2000–PRESENT: A DYING ART?

Since the turn of the millennium, only five hidden-ball tricks have been executed, indicating that the play is dying out. With two in 2013, however, there is hope that it isn't entirely dead. Mike Lowell had two of the five tricks, leading the National League to a 3–2 advantage. Both of the American League tricks occurred in interleague games, so all of the victims in this century have been National League players.

Date: September 15, 2004 (first game)
Teams: Florida Marlins vs. Montreal Expos (National League)
Perpetrator: Florida third baseman Mike Lowell
Victim: Brian Schneider, Montreal
　　Per MLB.com, the "Marlins successfully pulled off a hidden-ball trick against the Expos on Wednesday in game 1 of a doubleheader at Pro Player Stadium. All-Star third baseman Mike Lowell caught the Expos napping, enabling the Marlins to pull off a sandlot play. To set the stage, the Expos went ahead, 2–1, on Brian Schneider's double. With two outs in the fourth inning, Maicer Izturis was intentionally walked, bringing up pitcher John Patterson. Patterson lined a single to left field. Expos third base coach Manny Acta held Schneider at third, and left fielder Miguel Cabrera ran the ball in. Cabrera flipped the ball to shortstop Alex Gonzalez, who quickly tossed it to Lowell at third. . . . To keep the Expos off guard, Lowell trotted to pitcher Carl Pavano, and the play was on. In the confusion, the Expos never detected Pavano didn't have the ball. Lowell returned to third, and Pavano milled about

the grass around the mound. When Schneider took a one-step lead, Lowell snapped a quick tag, and third base umpire Paul Emmel pumped out Schneider. The play even fooled the television crew, who were showing a replay when it happened."

According to the *Palm Beach Post*, "The play ended an inning in which the Expos would have had the bases loaded with the top of the order due up. When Lowell saw Schneider talking with his third base coach and not paying attention to the ball, he walked over to the bag and made eye contact with the umpire. 'He just took his foot off and put his other foot on the base, and I just touched him,' Lowell said. 'It's not anything I practice.'"[1] Marlin manager Jack McKeon, quoted in the *Chicago Sun-Times*, said, "Give Mike credit. . . . It was a good, smart play on Mike's part, and nobody called time. That was the key."[2]

Date: August 10, 2005
Teams: Florida Marlins vs. Arizona Diamondbacks (National League)
Perpetrator: Florida third baseman Mike Lowell
Victim: Luis Terrero, Arizona

Lowell, to this point the only major leaguer to successfully pull off the HBT in the new millennium, did it for the second time, nabbing Terrero in the eighth inning of a 10–5 Florida victory. The Fish were clinging to a 6–5 lead at the time, and the D'backs had runners on the corners, with one out. According to the Associated Press story, "Terrero hit a leadoff single against Marlins closer Todd Jones. Terrero advanced on Quinton McCracken's sacrifice and went to third on Tony Clark's pinch-hit single to left. Lowell . . . quickly sized up another opportunity to pull the rare trick after catching [Miguel] Cabrera's throw to the infield. 'I looked to first to see if Tony Clark was going to advance, then I looked at third base,' Lowell said. 'Both guys had their heads down so I just held onto the ball to see what would happen.' Despite the absence of any signal from Lowell, Jones—who said he hadn't seen the play since 1986—when he was in high school—understood what his teammate was up to. 'When I didn't get the ball, I figured it out by the process of elimination,' Jones said. 'I just walked around and tried to stall. I was running out of things to do. I was going to touch my toes.' Just as Jones was getting ready to give up the charade, Terrero took his lead off third base. Lowell sauntered over and tagged the stunned base-

Figure 16.1.   Between 1999 and 2007, the hidden-ball trick was executed successfully only twice—both times by third baseman Mike Lowell. Courtesy of the National Baseball Hall of Fame Library, Cooperstown, New York.

runner, who was immediately called out by third base umpire Ed Rapuano."

In his *Sporting News* column "The Closer," Jones expanded on the play, saying, "As I was on my way back to the mound after backing up home plate on Clark's hit, I noticed that no one was looking to throw the ball back to me. I knew either our shortstop, Alex Gonzalez, or third baseman Mike Lowell had it. When I checked Gonzalez and saw that he didn't have it, I knew Mike had kept it. My job then was to sell the play. There would be only a few seconds before everyone would wonder where the ball was. I started walking around the mound. About all I could think to do was to not go on the dirt of the mound. The play wouldn't have been legal if I had been on the mound when Mike tagged the runner. So now I was behind the mound. I picked up the rosin bag, figuring that looked innocent enough. Then I got the bright idea to make hand gestures to the catcher, like we were going over where I was going to throw the ball if it was hit back to me. Then I turned to the shortstop as if to tell him, 'Hey if it's hit to me, I'm throwing it to you to start the double play.' Now I've done all that, and the runner still was on the base. Well, just at that time, Terrero stepped off and—boom!— Mike tagged him. Perfect. . . . The lesson is when you're in trouble, use whatever you can to get out of it—even if you have to go back to your Little League days."[3]

Terrero, quoted in the *Miami Herald*, said, "I was in shock. It was a really smart play by (Lowell), and he got me. It had never happened to me before." Lowell added, "If I'm the cutoff, I always look to see if (the base runner) is paying attention. . . . It might have been 15 seconds, but it felt like 15 minutes. . . . I've got nothing to lose. What's the worst that can happen? I throw it back to the mound. . . . I give credit to Ed Rapuano. He was on the play the whole way."[4] Lowell, quoted in the *Arizona Republic*, said, "I looked over to third, and both guys [Terrero and third base coach Carlos Tosca] had their heads down. I didn't want to give it away, but Jonesy was awesome. He really sold it."[5]

The Society for American Baseball Research's Bill Nowlin interviewed Lowell about the play a year later. "I got the cutoff, and I was going to throw it right to Todd Jones, but he's way back there, so I decided to wait," recalled Lowell. "Jonesy sold it perfect. . . . He started, like, stretching and walking around the mound . . . just trying to buy time. After the fact he said, 'I didn't know what else to do. Maybe start to do jumping jacks or something. It was too much time.'"

Date: June 8, 2007
Teams: Boston Red Sox (American League) vs. Arizona Diamondbacks (National League)
Perpetrator: Boston shortstop Julio Lugo
Victim: Alberto Callaspo, Arizona
   Lugo turned the trick on rookie Callaspo in an interleague game. Callaspo singled to open the third inning, and Chris Snyder followed with a ground single to right field. Callaspo took a wide turn at second but had to scramble back to the bag when right fielder J. D. Drew threw to Lugo behind him. According to the *Boston Globe*, "The hidden-ball trick is baseball burlesque, a sight gag that seldom appears on the big stage anymore but never fails to draw a guffaw when it does. . . . Callaspo was unaware that Lugo had not returned the ball to the mound. As long as [pitcher Josh] Beckett wasn't standing on the dirt of the mound, the ball was still in play, as a red-faced Callaspo belatedly discovered when Lugo, still lurking behind him, slapped the tag on him. 'I wasn't expecting it,' Beckett said. . . . 'I was actually back there, trying to get him to throw me the ball. I'm glad he didn't.'"[6]

Date: August 10, 2013
Teams: Tampa Bay Rays (American League) vs. Los Angeles Dodgers (National League)
Perpetrators: Tampa Bay first baseman James Loney, shortstop Yunel Escobar, and third baseman Evan Longoria
Victim: Juan Uribe, Los Angeles
   The Rays pulled off an impressive display of sleight of hand in an interleague game in Los Angeles, with three infielders conspiring to record the major leagues' first successful HBT in more than six years. It started when the Dodgers' A. J. Ellis hit a bases-loaded sacrifice fly. As Tampa Bay center fielder Wil Myers threw plateward, the other runners moved up, with Uribe reaching third. Loney wound up with the ball near the mound. For no apparent reason, he deftly tossed the ball to Escobar, and Escobar followed by flicking it to Longoria. Longoria stood by the bag as Uribe chatted with Coach Tim Wallach, with umpire Angel Hernandez watching closely. Uribe shifted his weight, lifting

his foot just off the bag, and Longoria quickly tagged him for the out. It was about the Rays' only highlight in a 5–0 loss.

"It's a play that I always have in my mind through the course of a game," said Escobar through a translator. "Guys were going everywhere, so it happened to be a good situation where I thought we might be able to tag Uribe out. The umpire was standing there and knew what was going on right away, and the only one who didn't know what was going on was Uribe. I've tried it four or five other times this year and never got anybody out in the big leagues. But in the minor leagues, I got four or five guys out."

"I know that Yuni is always looking to do it," Longoria said. "Usually when a play like that happens, the pitcher is right around the mound, and you don't have a whole lot of time before the umpires call time. I had just walked around behind Uribe, and [pitcher Roberto] Hernandez was still walking back from behind the plate to the mound. I was just kind of waving my hand to see if Loney would see me, and he did. But he threw the ball to Yuni, which was the best part of the play, because it was indirect. Once I got the ball, I just kind of waited there. He barely took his foot off the base, and I tagged him."

"It's a good play," said Uribe, taking some ribbing in the clubhouse after the game. "They did a good job. I made a mistake. Every day you see something different. I've never seen it before. I got surprised."[7]

Date: September 19, 2013
Teams: Colorado Rockies vs. St. Louis Cardinals (National League)
Perpetrator: Colorado first baseman Todd Helton
Victim: Matt Carpenter, St. Louis

Helton, in the waning days of his 17-year career, finally achieved a longtime dream. After a pickoff attempt by pitcher Roy Oswalt in the first inning, Helton pretended to throw the ball back to the pitcher and then tagged Carpenter out after he took a step off the bag. "It had never worked, that was the first time," said Helton afterward. "Five or six times I've given it a halfhearted effort. I can't believe it worked."[8] The Rockies ended up winning in 15 innings.

17

TRICKS GONE AWRY

Of course, the play doesn't always work as planned. The section includes some foiled tricks.

In an 1889 National League game, Cleveland tried to take advantage of deaf Washington player Dummy Hoy, but Hoy got the last laugh, according to *Sporting Life*: "The mute had reached second base on a passed ball. The ball was thrown down to second, and [Cleveland shortstop Ed] McKean, [center fielder Jimmy] McAleer, and [second baseman Cub] Stricker handled the ball alternately, until Stricker got hold of it and crept up behind Hoy, hoping that the latter would step off his base. The mute was onto the little game, and when Stricker stood beside him, he smacked the hand that held the ball and the dogskin rolled several feet away. Before Stricker realized what had happened, Hoy was safe on third base. Captain [Jay] Faatz made a vigorous kick, but umpire [Lon] Knight held that there was no rule to cover such a play. It was simply a case of dog eat dog. [Third baseman Patsy] Tebeau captured the ball during the dispute and concealed it under his arm with the intention of getting even with the mute. The latter was wide awake as usual and deliberately squatted down on the base and would not move until he saw the ball returned to [Henry] Gruber, who was pitching. This exhibition of dirty work occupied nearly ten minutes."[1]

On July 11, 1892, Phillie second baseman Bill Hallman tried unsuccessfully to catch Cleveland's Cupid Childs at first base.

Per *Sporting Life*, on June 14, 1893, St. Louis shortstop Jack "Glasscock worked a trick in the ninth inning that did not count, because he fooled the umpire as well as [Boston base runner Billy] Nash, whom he clearly put out. [Umpire Jack] McQuaid did not see the play and consequently refused to give the out. It was the old trick of concealing the ball while the pitcher pretended to have it. Had it not been for this decision, St. Louis would have won the game."[2] The Cards lost, 11–10.

Author Ira L. Smith says that Red first baseman Jake Beckley tried it against Louisville rookie Honus Wagner in 1897, but Wagner wouldn't fall for it.[3] Bill James writes, "Beckley attempted to work the hidden-ball trick on every rookie in the National League at least once, and often succeeded; he had several variations of the ruse. When he tried it on Honus Wagner, Wagner sniffed it out, so Beckley tried a second version. He snuck an extra baseball on the field and hid it under his armpit, allowing it to stick out far enough that Wagner could spot it. When the umpire turned his back, Wagner grabbed the extra ball and tossed it into the stands, then lit out for second base—only to discover that the pitcher had the legal ball."[4]

On July 30, 1898, Cleveland's Cupid Childs caught Baltimore's Gene DeMontreville, apparently evening the score for a trick DeMontreville had pulled on Childs in 1896, but the call was changed from "out" to "safe," as Childs was ejected while holding the ball.

Bill Coughlin, who pulled the trick at least three times in 1902, almost had another one that year. Neither of the two umpires saw it, and one report says fans accused him of "reading history books" in trying the ruse.

In April, 1905, Detroit third baseman Bill "Coughlin almost worked the 'hidden-ball' trick on [White Sox player-manager Fielder] Jones in the eighth inning, with [Nixey] Callahan coaching not ten feet from third base. Jones gave Callahan a deserved call down for neglecting the coacher's first duty—to 'watch the ball.'"[5]

On August 2, 1905, the Tigers' Bill Coughlin tried the trick twice in one game, failing to nab Washington's Jake Stahl or John Anderson at third base.

On August 16, 1907, the Reds' Miller Huggins drew a walk, but Giant catcher Roger Bresnahan held on to the ball. When Huggins led off first, Bresnahan fired the ball there, but first baseman Frank Bowerman was at least as surprised as Huggins, and the Mighty Mite advanced to second.

On August 26, 1909, according to the *Chicago Tribune*, Cub second baseman "John Evers worked the moss grown hidden-ball trick on [Phillie rookie Pep] Deininger at second base in the fifth inning so plainly that everyone in the ball yard saw him do it except [umpire Bill] Klem. . . . [T]hat ocular failure cost the Cubs a victory and possibly a pennant."[6] Deininger scored, and the Cubs lost in ten innings, 8–7. They lost the pennant to Pittsburgh by six and a half games, however.

On May 18, 1910, per the *Washington Post*, Cleveland's George "Perring tried to work the hide-the-ball trick on (Washington's Red Killefer) in the third, but 'Red' refused to move from the base. The lesson did not get Street's attention."[7] Gabby Street was caught on the trick later in the same game.

On July 22, 1910, writes the *New York Times*, Cardinal rookie shortstop Arnold "Hauser worked the hidden-ball trick on [the Giants' Fred] Snodgrass. [Umpire Bob] Emslie waved the runner out, [while ump Cy] Rigler declared him safe. This gave rise to a long argument. [Cardinals player–manager Roger] Bresnahan produced a book and asked Rigler to read the rules. Rigler refused."[8]

On August 28, 1910, the Giants' Josh Devore was apparently caught by Cub first baseman Jimmy Archer, but pitcher Ed Reulbach was called for a balk and Devore was awarded second base by umpire Cy Rigler.[9]

On September 3, 1910, the Cubs' Harry Steinfeldt caught the Cardinals' Miller Huggins, one of the play's top practitioners. According to the *Chicago Daily Tribune*, Cub pitcher Ed Reulbach "was yanked out of one deep hole in the first inning by that hoary-headed hidden-ball trick chaperoned by Harry Steinfeldt. Huggins started the game with a walk and, after [Rube] Ellis flew out, went all the way to third on [Mike] Mowrey's single. Right there Steiny took the ball as it was returned from the field and stuck it under his arm until Huggins innocently strolled off third, whereupon he was a dead Cardinal, for ump [Mal] Eason happened to be looking."[10] Nevertheless, the feat was nullified when the game was rained out after three innings.

The play was attempted in the 1910 World Series, writes the *Washington Post*.[11]

On June 8, 1918, per the *New York Times*, "In the opening game, Heinie [Zimmerman of the Giants] was the victim of the old hidden-ball trick, for he was touched out by [the Cardinals' Rogers] Hornsby when Zim thought that (pitcher Bill Sherdel) had the ball. Umpire [Bill] Byron saved Zim a heap of embarrassment when he discredited the trick, as the ball was not in play at the time the ancient joker was brought into use. Following the dispute between Manager [John] McGraw and umpire Byron, someone in the upper tier of the grand stand . . . heaved a glass down on to the field at the umpire while his back was turned."[12]

Babe Pinelli claimed to have caught Babe Ruth with the trick in 1920 but says, "I didn't get away with it," adding, "I had my foot between his foot and the bag, and he was kicking his way back and I was yelling for the umpire, but he didn't see it and Babe got back."[13] *Baseball Magazine* adds that Pinelli "had a neat trick of walking over to his pitcher, pretending to toss him the ball. But all the time he would keep it to himself, then walk back to third and, by conversation, take the runner's mind off the game. One step off the base and the runner was a dead duck. Pinelli still talks about the day he caught Babe Ruth off third. 'The umpire didn't see it and, therefore, couldn't call it,' Pinelli explains. 'But I got a lot of satisfaction out of knowing I had actually caught the big guy off. He didn't make many mistakes, nor was he often caught napping in his career.'"[14] Umpire Billy Evans corroborated the incident: "He all but pulled the stunt one day in New York before a 30,000 crowd on Babe Ruth with Manager [Miller] Huggins coaching third. So excited did Huggins get when he realized Pinelli had the ball he executed a hook slide in the coacher's box in the general direction of third that equaled anything he ever pulled in a regulation game. It was a close decision."[15]

On May 23, 1922, the Cubs' John Kelleher reportedly nabbed the Dodgers' Hank DeBerry, but the umpires missed it.

Between 1922 and 1924, Pinelli of the Reds tried it on Ivy Olson of the Dodgers, who had executed the trick himself on three occasions in the 1910s. "Ivy stood there on the base and looked at me with great scorn," Babe recalled. "Then he sneered: 'Say, you busher, don't you know I *invented* that play?'"

In early June, 1923, there was a foiled trick, according to the *Washington Post*.[16]

On June 24, 1923, following a protested call, Pittsburgh's Rabbit Maranville apparently worked the trick on the Cardinals' Rogers Hornsby, but it was not allowed.

On July 7, 1923 (second game), Red Sox shortstop Howie Shanks tried to work the trick on Cleveland's Homer Summa and then threw the ball into the grandstand in trying to return it to pitcher George Murray.

On July 17, 1923, asserts the *Pittsburgh Gazette Times*, Brooklyn's Tommy Griffith drew a walk off Pittsburgh's George Smith, pushing Gene Bailey up a base. "As Bailey went to second base, [catcher Johnny] Gooch threw to Rabbit [Maranville, the shortstop,] who touched Bailey after the latter had stepped off second base in the direction of third base, according to the claim of the Pirates. The umpires refused to allow the claim."[17]

On September 24, 1923, Washington shortstop Roger Peckinpaugh tried to work the trick against Chicago but threw the ball into the Washington dugout.

On October 8, 1924, in Game 5 of that year's World Series, Senator first baseman Joe Judge tried to work the trick on the Giants' Travis Jackson in the sixth inning, but Judge dropped the ball, tipping off the play.

On August 5, 1926, the Reds' Babe Pinelli tried to add to his résumé at the expense of Giant future Hall of Famer Fred Lindstrom. According to the *New York Times*, "Pinelli tried to take advantage of Lindstrom at the Polo Grounds yesterday by reviving the hidden-ball trick, but Lindy wasn't caught. If ballplayers resurrect old plays like this it won't be surprising to see them wear mustaches again." [18]

On April 30, 1932, per the *New York Times*, Dodger third baseman "Joe Stripp, aided by the excellent acting of Joe Shaute, who started the game, worked the hidden-ball trick successfully on (Phillie rookie Kiddo) Davis in the fourth inning, but umpire Charley Pfirman called Davis safe. The Brooklyn third baseman threw the ball violently to the ground in protest against the decision. This gave the Phils a run instead of their being retired, and Stripp was banished from the game." [19]

Jimmy Dykes recalled that the Senators' Buddy Myer once tried it on him between 1925 and 1939: "He was giving me a lot of palaver around second base, but I kept edging back to the bag. 'I know you've got that ball in your hand,' I finally said, and Buddy had to grin as he fished it out." [20]

On June 30, 1936, the Yankees' Frankie Crosetti tried the hidden-ball trick on Boston's Bing Miller in the fifth inning, but coach Al Schacht spoiled it. According to the *New York World-Telegram*, "Schacht got wise and shouted to Bing, who thumbed his nose at Frankie." [21]

In September 1937, Crosetti failed once more. According to *Sporting News*, "Frankie Crosetti has worked the old corner-lot hidden-ball trick three times this year and nearly got away with it again the other day, with Wally Moses as the intended victim." [22]

The Yankees' Frank Crosetti tried to trick the Giants twice in the 1937 World Series, says the *New York Times*. In Game 2 on October 7, the Yanks, "supposedly most modern, reached back to the era of Abner

Doubleday by attempting to pull the hidden-ball trick on Jo-Jo Moore in the eighth. Had Frankie Crosetti worked it this would have been the final ignominious touch to the rout of the Giants."[23] *Sporting News* writes, "After Jo Jo Moore doubled in the eighth Crosetti unsuccessfully tried to pull the hidden-ball trick on the Texan."[24] Two days later, in the second inning of Game 4, "Crosetti tried the hidden-ball trick [on Hank Leiber], and the fans laughed when it did not work." There might even have been a third attempt. According to *Baseball Magazine*, "Crosetti actually tried to pull the trick in one of the Yankee–Giant World Series conflicts last fall. And who do you think Frankie picked out as a prospective victim? None other than Dick Bartell, his rival shortstop. 'Dare Devil Dick' took a short lead off second base. He happened to catch a glimpse of Crosetti making a thrust at him. Dick hotfooted it back to second base, arriving just in the nick of time."[25]

On May 29, 1938, according to the *New York Times*, Cro tried again, this time on the Athletics' Sam Chapman: "Crosetti then tried the hidden-ball trick, but his deception was discovered before [pitcher Eddie] Smith singled to score Chapman."[26]

On August 25, 1940, Cardinal shortstop Jimmy Brown palmed the ball after an infield single by the Bees' Bama Rowell, plotting to nab Rowell after he took a lead, but St. Louis pitcher Clyde Shoun took his position on the mound and was called for a balk by umpire Larry Goetz.

On May 18, 1941, per the *New York Times*, "Practically everything happened, including an attempt at the hidden-ball trick by [the Dodgers' Cookie] Lavagetto with [Cub rookie Lou] Stringer on third in the sixth."[27]

On June 3, 1941, writes the *New York Times*, Yankee freshman first baseman Johnny "Sturm tried the hidden-ball trick when [Tiger rookie Pat] Mullin beat out a bunt in the seventh, but Paddy didn't fall for it."[28]

In Game 3 of the 1941 World Series on October 4, according to the *New York Times*, following a force out, "[i]n the fourth inning [Dodger first baseman] Dolph Camilli tried to work the 'hidden-ball' trick on [the Yankees' Tommy] Henrich. He didn't come close. Smart fellows, these Yankees."[29] The article neglects to mention that the brainy Henrich was promptly picked off first by catcher Mickey Owen. Henrich would also be caught on a successful trick nine months later.

On May 2, 1942, per *Sporting News*, the Red Sox' Johnny "Pesky pulled the hidden-ball trick on [the Browns' Glenn] McQuillen in the hectic ninth, but it availed him nothing. After Tony Criscola had been forced at third, Johnny hid the ball in his glove and moved back to short. But just as Johnny sprinted towards McQuillen and tagged him, [Sox second baseman Bobby] Doerr called for time out, not being aware of Pesky's plan."[30]

On May 15, 1942, Pittsburgh attempted the ruse against the Dodgers, according to the *New York Times*. Brooklyn's Billy "Herman was at the plate ten minutes before he whacked a double in the sixth. [Bucs' pitcher Rip] Sewell tried repeatedly to pick Pee Wee Reese off second base, [shortstop] Pete Coscarart even attempting the hidden-ball trick. Then Reese made a clean steal of third."[31]

On June 23, 1942, says the *New York Times*, the Giants' Johnny "Mize tried the hidden-ball trick on [the Reds'] Eddie Joost, only to have Joost reach around, pluck the ball out of John's glove, and toss it back to [pitcher Jack] Lohrman. Mize blushed and then grinned."[32]

On May 5, 1948 (second game, eighth inning), pitcher Mel Parnell was called for a balk while the Red Sox were attempting the ploy on the Tigers. Detroit had Johnny Lipon on first with one out. According to *Sporting News*, "Eddie Mayo came to bat, took his position in the box, called for time, and stepped out. John Stevens, the plate umpire, waved Lipon to second on a balk. . . . A wild argument followed. . . . Stevens said that Parnell had taken his position on the rubber without having possession of the ball. The Red Sox claimed that Mayo had called for time before Parnell took his position. . . . Boston was trying to work the hidden-ball trick. Mayo suspected it (and) called for time. Parnell was on the pitching rubber when Mayo made his request. This was proved to the satisfaction of the umpires [who reversed the decision and then reversed it back to the balk call]."[33] Parnell promptly balked again on the next pitch, sending Lipon to third, from where he scored on a sacrifice fly.

Sporting News tells of a foiled trick by Gene Mauch in 1948: "The Cub second baseman tried the hidden-ball trick twice on the Phillies this season. Once he caught both Harry Walker and umpire Butch Henline by surprise, and the ruse didn't work because the arbiter failed to see the trick."[34]

On August 26, 1948, per the *New York Times*, an attempt by the St. Louis Browns versus the Washington Senators led to a balk call and a rhubarb. Pitcher Al "Widmar's balk precipitated a Brownie flare-up which saw second baseman Gerry Priddy waved out of the game. He then shoved plate umpire Bill McKinley. Priddy and the Browns contended time had been called, but the umpires ruled that Widmar stepped on the mound without the ball. The Browns were trying to pull the hidden-ball trick."[35] *Sporting News* adds that "Priddy, attempting the hidden-ball trick, held onto the ball while Al Widmar went back to the mound. The pitcher picked up the resin bag and accidentally stepped on the rubber. Then umpire Bill Summers waved [Al] Kozar to third on a balk. . . . The Browns claimed that time had been called, as [manager] Zack Taylor came out of the dugout to talk with his pitcher, but Summers said there had been no interruption and declared that there was nothing he could do but call a balk on Widmar."[36]

On May 11, 1949, the Gus Zernial of the White Sox reached third base on a one-out bloop triple in the sixth inning. Red Sox third baseman Johnny Pesky held the ball, waiting for a chance to nab Zernial with the trick, but BoSox pitcher Jack Robinson stepped on the rubber, and plate umpire Bill McGowan called a balk, sending Zernial home with a crucial run. The ChiSox won, 12–8.

According to Shirley Povich's July 20, 1950, column, "Al Rosen of the Cleveland Indians almost pulled it on Eddie Stewart of the Nats at third base in Cleveland last month. 'The only reason he didn't get away with it,' said [Washington manager Bucky] Harris, 'was because I had a hunch and called time just before Stewart stepped off the bag. Rosen used to try to pull it when he was playing for me at San Diego last year, and it just happened I got curious about where the ball was at the right time.'"[37]

In early 1951, Connie Ryan tried it on Del Ennis.

According to Gordon McClendon's play-by-play, there was a foiled trick during the October 3, 1951, National League playoff game between the Giants and Dodgers.

On April 24, 1952, Brave pitcher Vern Bickford was ejected by umpire Art Gore after a attempt against the Giants. According to *Sporting News*, "Bickford was banished from the bench in the second inning when he claimed that first baseman Earl Torgeson had tagged Max Lanier on a hidden-ball play. Gore explained that he had stopped play, before the tag, because the batboy was running to the bag with a jacket for the Giants' pitcher."[38]

In 1952 or 1953, a trick was pulled off but improperly nullified by the umpire, citing Rule #4.06(c), according to National League president Warren Giles in a July 21, 1953, letter (reprinted in chapter 11 of this book).

In Game 4 of the 1953 World Series on October 3, asserts Roger Kahn of the *New York Herald Tribune*, "A strange thing happened after [the Dodgers' Junior] Gilliam got his hit [, a two out, second-inning Texas League double. Billy] Martin, the Yankee second baseman, had the ball hidden and was hoping to catch Gilliam off base with the hidden-ball trick. But Bill Stewart, a National League umpire at second base, not knowing who had the ball, kept calling to [pitcher Tom] Gorman to show it to him for examination. . . . The game was stopped, and Martin was forced to produce the ball. Annoyed, Martin complained [to no avail] to Ed Hurley, an American League umpire at third base."[39] The *New York Times* describes the play differently: "Billy tried to pull the hidden-ball trick. 'I had the ball hidden in back of my glove,' he said, 'but I guess Chuck Dressen spotted it and spoiled everything by calling for time. I'm sure Gilliam would have stepped off the bag, and I'd have had him. My discussion with the umpire was that Dressen had no right to ask for time while the ball was in play.'"[40] *Sporting News* writes, "The

Yankees also complained about a National League custom of discouraging the hidden-ball trick. When Billy Martin tried it in the Saturday game, umpire Bill Stewart asked for the ball. In the American League, the umpires are not permitted to interfere."[41]

According to *A Rooter's Guide to the Red Sox*, by Harold Kaese, White Sox pitcher Dick Donovan balked when first baseman Jim Rivera plotted a hidden-ball trick on Boston's Sammy White on June 5, 1957.[42]

On July 19, 1957, Kansas City tried the move in the ninth inning against Baltimore's Joe Durham, but it backfired, with a runner advancing and no out made.

Noted practitioner Joe Adcock feared the Yankees were trying to pull the trick on him in either the second or fourth inning of Game 2 of the 1957 World Series on October 3, according to the *New York Times*: "The country boys from Milwaukee are mighty suspicious of the city slickers from New York. When Joe Adcock of the Braves wandered a few steps off second base the other day, he leaped frantically back as soon as [shortstop] Gil McDougald sauntered toward him. 'You wouldn't pull the hidden ball on me, would you?' asked Adcock. 'Not me,' said McDougald, 'I'm not that tricky.' But Adcock still was worried when he next went to bat and he mentioned his fears to [catcher] Yogi Berra, a free-for-all conversationalist at all times. 'We never do nuthin'' like that,' said Yogi. 'At least we'd never do it in anything as important as the World Series.'"[43]

Per *Sporting News*, "The Giants tried to pull the hidden-ball trick on John Edwards of the Reds, August 12 [1961]. Everybody on the field and in the stands seemed to know [rookie shortstop] Jose Pagan had the ball but pitcher Jack Sanford. He was busy leveling off the mound with his feet. As a result, a balk was called because he was 'on or astride' the rubber without the ball."[44]

Writes *Sporting News*, in the top of the tenth inning of the second game of a doubleheader on August 1, 1962, the "Indians attempted to pull the hidden-ball trick, but a disputed balk was called on [Ruben] Gomez, allowing [the Angels' Bob] Rodgers to score tie-breaking run. The Angels then went on to add three more runs,"[45] padding an 8–4 win.

According to *Sporting News*, Oriole first baseman Boog Powell feigned an exchange of the ball to pitcher Eddie Watt with the Yanks' Joe Pepitone on first base in the eighth inning, August 4, 1968. "'I walked around behind the mound, smoothing grass, killing time,' Watt said. 'Suddenly, umpire Emmett Ashford threw up his hands at second base, yelling "Time!" I said, "Emmett, why are you calling time?" He replied, "Because Boog's got the ball, that's why!" It spoiled our plot for a surefire hidden-ball trick.'"[46]

The Stick tried for his third trick in eight weeks on August 7, 1970, according to a picture caption in that day's *New York Times*: "THE OLD HIDDEN BALL PLOY—FAILS: Gene Michael, Yankees' shortstop, who was successful twice recently in fooling base runners, was unable to entice the Tigers' Elliott Maddox off second base in the second inning at the Stadium."[47]

According to umpire Ron Luciano in *The Umpire Strikes Back*, "First baseman Jim Spencer was with the Rangers in 1974, when he successfully pulled off the hidden-ball trick. The runner wandered off base while Spencer was holding the ball, and Jim tagged him. . . . Unfortunately, I was in the middle of an important conversation with the first base coach at the time and missed it completely. . . . 'Jeez,' I told him later, 'next time you're going to do that you've got to warn me.'"[48] A fan recalls a different play described in Luciano's book, saying he remembers it as Reggie Jackson being victimized while talking to Luciano.

In June 1984, writes the *Boston Globe*, Boston's Marty "Barrett pulled Buddy Hunter's old hidden-ball trick in Toronto and caught Dave Collins. Problem is, he also caught the umpires off guard, and they blew the call."[49]

On April 10, 1986, according to the *Boston Globe*, "Marty Barrett tried a hidden-ball trick on [Detroit's] Darnell Coles in the seventh. It didn't work."[50]

In an American League Championship Series game on October 8, 1986, says the *Boston Globe*, "Angels third baseman Doug DeCinces tried a hidden-ball trick when Spike Owen was on third in the eighth, but third base coach Rene Lachemann shrewdly alerted Owen."[51] DeCinces, in the final days of his career, had been victimized by the Sox in 1985 and vowed revenge.

States the *Boston Globe*, Boston's Marty Barrett wanted to pull off the trick on Oakland's Carney Lansford in the eighth inning of the May 21, 1989, 5–4 Sox loss, but second base umpire Dan Morrison foiled the plan: "Lansford was on second after Dwight Evans dropped Tony Phillips's fly ball with one out. Barrett went to tell Morrison he was going to pull a hidden-ball play, but Morrison called time."[52]

On May 11, 1992, the Cubs attempted the play during an intentional walk against Houston, but no out was made.

On April 2, 1998, Arizona third baseman Matt Williams nabbed Colorado's Neifi Perez, but pitcher Felix Rodriguez was called for a balk.

On July 4, 2002, Phillie second baseman Tomas Perez apparently caught the Expos' Brian Schneider, but after a discussion, it was ruled that "time" had been called by Philadelphia catcher Mike Lieberthal.

On August 18, 2005, the Mariners attempted the trick. Rookie Yuniesky Betancourt held the ball at second base while pitcher Ryan Franklin, who had been backing up the catcher, walked from behind home plate toward the mound. But Franklin cut across the right side of the mound without the ball and was called for a balk.

On July 12, 2013, in the top of the fifth inning, Pablo Sandoval hit an RBI double off Padre pitcher Sean O'Sullivan to bring the Giants to within one, 2–1. Padre shortstop Everth Cabrera then apparently tagged the runner out with the trick, but umpire Laz Diaz ruled that he had given time out to Sandoval.

18

UNSUBSTANTIATED POSSIBILITIES

Oftentimes I'll find a great story, sometimes multiple versions, about a hidden-ball trick of the past. Naturally, these stories don't include a date, and I'm left to try to deduce when it could have happened based on the details provided. Sometimes the process produces a handful of possible dates to check, and other times hundreds of possible dates surface in as long as a 15-year period. Many of the stories have started out with such a search; many others could not possibly have happened as reported. And then there are those that I believe may have happened but I just can't pin down the specifics—I call them "unsubstantiated possibilities." I keep these listed separately in hopes that I'll someday get another lead to fine-tune or conclude my search.

The following are notes on possible HBTs that I have not been able to verify. I would be grateful for any information that can help me confirm, refute, or investigate these instances; if you can assist, please contact me at Bill Deane, 408 Christian Hill Rd., Cooperstown, NY 13326; (607) 547-4426; billdeane14@gmail.com.

August 1879 According to the September 6, 1879, edition of the *New York Clipper*, Troy's Al "Hall was caught napping at first base by [Boston's Ed] Cogswell's concealing the ball in a recent game at Boston, and some critics condemned Cogswell for playing a legitimate and sharp point."[1] The most likely dates are August 19, 20, 28, 29, or 30.

August 1881 This trick supposedly occurred in a Buffalo at Cleveland game, the only possibilities being August 20 (the victim's first game for Cleveland), 23, or 25. Cleveland played at Buffalo on August 27, 29, 30, and 31. The event is well described (in an item reprinted from the *Cleveland Voice*) in the *Buffalo Courier* and the *Chicago Tribune*: "Buffalo's Big (Dan) Brouthers played an old but successful trick on [Billy] Taylor, Cleveland's 'fresh' left fielder. Taylor overran first base and, while returning, saw Brouthers apparently throw the ball to [Pud] Galvin, the pitcher. Galvin faced the batsman, as if to pitch the ball, and Taylor innocently touched first base and stepped off a pace again. Brouthers, who had the ball under his armpit, quietly reached out and touched Taylor. The umpire said 'out,' Taylor hung his head and walked home, nine Buffalos 'snickered,' and 700 Cleveland people said something which doesn't look well in print."[2] In checking the three possible dates, I found nothing in the *Cleveland Plain Dealer, Cleveland Press*, or *Cleveland Leader*. The *Leader*'s account of the August 20 game (in which Taylor went 1-for-5) mentions that "Taylor played a pretty game," and with regard to the August 23 game, it says, "Taylor will do." Nothing was found in the *Buffalo Morning Express, Buffalo Courier*, or *Buffalo Evening News*, but the August 25 game appears to be the best bet since it was the least thoroughly covered of the three games, and the attendance is mentioned by the *Morning Express* as being "about seven hundred," although Taylor was 0-for-4. It also mentions that Taylor reached and died at third base in the August 23 game, decreasing the likelihood of that being the game, since he was 1-for-3.

July 8, 1887 In the bottom of the seventh inning of an American Association game, Cleveland shortstop Jim Toy tagged Philadelphia pitcher Ed Seward off second base. Seward evidently thought "time" was called during an argument at third base, where Chippy McGarr had just bowled over Ed McKean. It doesn't sound as if there was any trickery involved or that Seward thought the Cleveland pitcher had the ball.

April 1891 Bill Dahlen biographer Lyle Spatz believes that Dahlen may have been victimized on April 24 or 25 of this year. Dahlen's Cubs were playing in Pittsburgh on those dates. Nothing was found in *Sporting News, Sporting Life*, or the *Boston Herald*. The *Chicago Tribune* points to the April 25 date, although it sounds more like a pickoff than a HBT: "Dahlen hit safe. Anson . . . struck out, and a moment later Dahlen was caught asleep on first base."[3] It's not likely there would be a HBT executed after a strikeout. The *Chicago Times* expands, saying, "Dahlen made a dash for second just as Anson struck out, but [catcher Connie] Mack took quick for him, cutting him off to [first baseman Jake] Beckley before he could recover."[4] Spatz doesn't think this is the play, because here Dahlen was being aggressive, not "napping."

April 25, 1891 According to the *Washington Post*, in an American Association game, Washington's Gil "Hatfield went to sleep at second base and was touched by [Philadelphia left fielder George] Wood to [second baseman Bill] Hallman."[5] It's unlikely that an outfielder would be involved in a HBT.

April 14, 1904 The Giants' Billy Gilbert was "caught napping" by Brooklyn in this Opening Day game, but it remains unclear whether this was a HBT or something else. Nothing was found in the *Brooklyn Daily Eagle*. Retrosheet lists it as a pickoff.

1905–1909 Per the *Washington Post*, "Del Howard also has used (the hidden-ball trick) to advantage on several occasions."[6] Howard played in the National League during these years, a total of 187 games at first base, 48 at second, and 14 at shortstop, with Pittsburgh (1905), Boston (1906–1907), and Chicago (1907–1909).

August 19, 1907 Sam Lanford pitched in his first of two major league games on this date. Sixty-one years later, he recalled the occasion for the *Spartanburg Herald-Journal*: "I had been with Washington for three or four days. We were in Chicago, and I got a chance to [play] because we were behind by eight runs or so. Doc White was pitching. I got a two-base hit off him. But do you know what they did to me? They pulled the hidden-ball trick on me. They showed the rookie up. I'll never forget that."[7] Lanford's recollection of details six decades after the fact is remarkable: The game *was* in Chicago, Doc White *was* pitching, and the score was 14–2 when Lanford came in. Lanford actually singled in the seventh inning in his only at bat of the game. The game was ended by darkness after eight innings with the Sox ahead, 16–2, by which time most of the press corps had apparently long since called it a day. Consequently, there seems to be no source that can confirm or refute the HBT taking place on that date. Chicago's *Daily News, American, Tribune, Inter-Ocean, Evening Post, Daily Journal,* and *Record-Herald* have been consulted, as have Washington's *Post, Star, Herald,* and *Times.* Interestingly, two other Senators made their major league debuts in this game, including Clyde Milan, who would amass 2,100 hits and 495 stolen bases during his career.

1911–1913 The Phillies' Mickey Doolan reportedly executed the trick. According to legendary pitcher Grover Cleveland Alexander, quoted in the *Waukesha Daily Freeman* in 1923, "The funniest hidden-ball trick I ever saw pulled was by our shortstop, Mike Doolan, when I was with the Phillies. A youngster being tried out by the team we were playing reached second base and failed to notice Mike had taken the ball and hidden it. The recruit led off the base several feet. Mike casually walked up to the lad, took off his cap, and banged him on the head with the ball, saying, 'You must learn to watch where the ball is if you want to stay up here, my young man.'"[8] As Alex's teammate, Doolan played 145 games at shortstop for the Phillies in 1911, 146 in 1912, and 148 (plus three at second base) in 1913.

1916 Casey Stengel, quoted by Leonard Koppett in the *New York Post,* reprinted in a 1955 *Baseball Digest* article, said, "Now I say there is no excuse for one of your players to get picked off second base by a hidden-ball trick. . . . It never happened to me when I was playing except one time when I stepped off second and oops! There I felt the tag on the back, and it caused me to make a study on how to prevent it."[9] An earlier *Baseball Digest* article, reprinted from a story by Arch Ward in the *Chicago Tribune,* pins down the year and teams involved, quoting Stengel: "I made a mistake as a player I thought I'd never live down. It almost cost Brooklyn the National League pennant in 1916. We were playing the St. Louis Cardinals. I doubled in the ninth inning and would have scored the winning run if I had kept my wits about me. I sneaked off second to get a lead when I thought the pitcher was ready to go into his windup. Then something hit me in the back that felt like a gun. I turned around, and there was the shortstop grinning and holding the ball in his glove. 'This,' he said, 'is a baseball.' My Brooklyn teammates were so furious at me I was almost afraid to go into the clubhouse. [Manager] Wilbert Robinson wouldn't even speak to me. We were neck and neck with the Phillies in the pennant fight. That boner of mine looked like it had ruined us. But we finally beat out the Phillies for the title by three games anyway, so the boys started talking to me again."[10]

Stengel's details don't wash, however. He hit doubles against St. Louis that year on May 16, June 14 (two), July 13 (second game), July 27, and September 21. Stengel definitely scored following his two-baggers of May 16 and September 21. All six doubles were in Dodger victories, except the earliest, hardly a "pennant fight" time of year, and nothing could be found in *Sporting News* or *Sporting Life* for any of the five dates. Also checked were the *New York Herald Tribune*, *New York Times*, and *New York World*. Other games Stengel played against the Cardinals (with losses denoted by an asterisk) were on May 13* and 15; June 10* and 13; July 11, 13 (1)*, 14*, 26 (1)*, 26 (2), and 28; August 28*, 29, and 30; and September 20 and 22. The July 14 and August 28 losses were by four runs each.

1916 Giant second baseman Larry Doyle reportedly caught the Boston Braves' Rabbit Maranville. According to *The Baseball Hall of Shame's Warped Record Book*, "Rabbit Maranville felt like crawling into a rabbit hole when New York Giants second baseman Larry Doyle tagged him out in a 1916 game by using the oldest sucker play in the book—the hidden-ball trick. Teammates razzed Rabbit unmercifully the rest of the game. But then they quit, and the relieved Boston Brave thought he'd heard the last of it. That evening, as Rabbit and some teammates were dining at their hotel, another player raved about the chef's 'special' dessert that wasn't on the menu. Rabbit promptly ordered it, and the waiter brought him a huge mound of ice cream topped with fresh cherries and whipped cream. Rabbit dug in with gusto—and dug out a baseball hidden inside. His teammates had given him his just desserts!"[11] This again sounds suspiciously like the July 15, 1931, Maranville story. The possible 1916 dates are April 25 or 27; May 4, 6, 8, 26, or 27 (both games); or June 20 (both games) or 21. Nothing was found in *Sporting News*, *Sporting Life*, the *New York Times*, the *New York World*, or the *Boston Globe*.

1920 Said Babe Pinelli, quoted in a 1948 issue of *Baseball Digest*, Ossie Vitt "was very popular in Boston, and the first day I went in there with the Tigers he hit a triple the first time up. The crowd is cheering as he pulls into third base standing up, and he has his back to me as I take the throw from the outfield. He stands there, tipping his cap and bowing to the crowd back of third base, and I say to myself, 'Here's one I can't miss.' I don't, either. When he is through bowing, he takes a short lead, and I give it to him. Oscar and I always have been friends, and I didn't like to do it to him, but I never saw anybody who asked for it like he did. He says, 'You know what you are, don't you?' And I says, 'Yes. But the next time keep your mind on the ball game.'"[12] Unfortunately, Vitt never tripled in the majors with Pinelli on the field. On the chance that Vitt's "triple" was actually a two-bagger with third on a throw or error, his 1920 doubles were checked. The only one Vitt got for the Red Sox with Pinelli on the field was in the second game on August 17, but nothing was found in *Sporting News*, and the *Boston Post* indicates that Vitt was left on base after the double. It's possible that Pinelli was recalling his trick on Stuffy McInnis on June 19, 1920; Vitt was reportedly coaching third at the time.

1921–1924 Writes *Sporting News*, Gene Mauch's 1948 HBT "attempts recalled to Manager Charlie Grimm the time Rabbit Maranville worked the hidden-ball trick on Hy Myers. Maranville stepped between Myers and the bag and asked, 'Why, Hy, what are you doing standing clear out here?' Myers inquired where the Rabbit wanted him to stand. 'What?' said Maranville, 'and with me holding the ball?' There was a wild scramble as the Rabbit tagged out Hy."[13] This must have happened between 1921 and 1924 (Grimm wasn't Maranville's teammate prior to 1921; Maranville didn't play against Myers in 1925). Maranville was with Pittsburgh during those years; Myers was with Brooklyn (1921–1922) and St. Louis (1923–1924). There are approximately 62 possible dates.

1922–1936 According to Ed Pollock in the *Philadelphia Bulletin*, reprinted in a 1951 *Baseball Digest* article, "There's a hidden-ball story about Travis Jackson, the old New York Giant shortstop, in which the batter had smacked a double and went sliding into second base a moment before Jackson took the throw. . . . It was a late inning of a long doubleheader afternoon." While Jackson held the ball, he and the runner discussed favorite foods, and the runner mentioned he liked little pearly onions. "Jackson turned his glove, exposing the ball. 'How do you like this onion?' he inquired."[14] Jackson played short for the Giants in 1,326 games during these years.

1923–1926 White Sox third baseman Willie Kamm, quoted in the book *Rowdy Richard*, said, "One time I pulled it and George Moriarty was the umpire. He said to me, 'If I was the manager of a team and that happened to one of my baserunners, I'd fine the coach $500.'"[15] There are approximately 60 possible dates, including 14 in 1926: April 16, 19, 22, 25, 28; May 1; June 10; July 22; August 4, 7 (1), 9, 12; September 20 (2), 25 (1). There is no mention of the trick in the *Boston Globe*.

1926–1929 A 1945 *Sporting News* article by Francis J. Powers of the *Chicago Daily News* quotes Jimmy Dykes as saying, "I remember pulling the hidden-ball once when I was playing second for the A's. I forget who the guy was, but he was getting a lead when I walked between him and the sack. He said, 'Get the hell out of there, fellow,' but I just said, 'Brother, you get the hell out of here,' as I tagged him."[16] Another *Sporting News* article from four weeks later narrows down the possible dates: "During his entire 22-year playing career he pulled the play successfully only once—on Bill Regan of the Red Sox."[17] The 49 possible dates follow:

> 1926 (12) June 2 (2), 21; July 1, 2, 3 (both), 7 (both), 26; August 14 (both)
>
> 1927 (14) April 26; July 4 (both), 5, 6 (both); August 10, 11 (both), 12, 13; September 29; October 1 (both)
>
> 1928 (10) May 3, 29; July 2 (both), 3; August 31; September 1, 7 (both), 8 (both)
>
> 1929 (13) April 28, 30; May 1, 2, 20, 22; June 24, 25 (both); August 29; September 26, 28, 29.

Actually, Dykes played second base in only three of those games: July 26 and August 14 (second game), 1926, and April 26, 1927 (in which Regan was 0-for-1 as a pinch hitter). Nothing was found in *Sporting News* or the *Boston Globe* for any of these 49 dates.

1931–1940 Tony Cuccinello claimed to have pulled a trick on Ernie Lombardi: "There was a close play at second, and I missed him sliding in. The pitcher was standing nearby. While Ernie's getting up I told the pitcher to stay off the rubber. I hid the ball in my glove. The pitcher went toward the mound, picked up the resin bag, and looked in at the catcher like he's looking for the sign, and Ernie walked off the bag. When I had enough room I ran over to him and showed him the ball. Oh, he was mad. He said to me, 'You tag me and I'll punch you right in the nose.' I never tagged him. He just walked back to the dugout."[18] Lombardi played for Brooklyn (1931) and Cincinnati (1932–1940), while Cuccinello played for Cincinnati (1931), Brooklyn (1932–1935), Boston (1936–1940), and New York (1940), producing approximately 140 possible dates. I eliminated 1943 as a possibility.

1933–1937 Yet another version of the 1931 Rabbit Maranville story appears in the "Millennium Edition" of Dan Schlossberg's *The Baseball Catalog*: "Years earlier [prior to pranks pulled by Moe Drabowsky], Leo Durocher was a victim twice—the first time as a Cardinal base runner put out by the hidden-ball trick. That night, he dined with the manager of the St. Louis hotel where he was living. Knowing Leo liked chocolate ice cream, his host had two huge portions brought to the table. The delighted Durocher dug in with enthusiasm—until his spoon struck a solid object: a hidden baseball."[19]

September 11, 1936 According to a 1951 article by John Carmichael in *Baseball Digest*, condensed from the *Chicago Daily News*, "The late Pat Malone of the Chicago Cubs was closing out his career as a relief hurler for the New York Yankees . . . and one day he found himself breathing noisily on second base as the result of an unexpected two-base hit. 'Hey, that was a pretty good clout,' called Billy Rogell, the Detroit shortstop." Rogell then engaged Malone in conversation about how long the latter had been in pro ball. "Billy nodded reflectively, then suddenly whipped a hand from behind one leg. It was holding a base-ball, which he clapped against Malone's nearest arm. 'That's too long,' said Rogell happily, 'for you to be fooled like this.'"[20] Malone's only double (a bases-clearing two-bagger) as a Yankee came in the second inning on this date at Detroit, but nothing about a HBT was found in *Sporting News*, the *New York Times*, the *New York Herald Tribune*, the

New York Sun, the *Detroit Free Press*, the *Detroit Times*, or the *Detroit News*.

1942 Johnny Pesky, recalling the trick he pulled on July 4, 1942, said that Tommy Henrich—just before he was nabbed—was discussing the fact that Indian shortstop Lou "Boudreau had pulled the hidden-ball trick the week before." An article in a 1946 edition of *Baseball Digest* has it a bit differently: "Henrich, on second base, had just commented to umpire Ed Rommel, 'I'm not going to get more than two yards off this base, like [Cleveland second baseman] Ray Mack, so they can't pick me off.' Just as he finished speaking and took one step off the base, Pesky jammed the ball into the small of his back."[21] Indian games played between June 19 and July 3 were checked, with no luck.

1951 The Athletics' Billy Hitchcock is said to have pulled the trick once in 1951. He played 77 games that year.

May 30, 1951 Phil Rizzuto supposedly nabbed Walt Dropo after Dropo had hit a double off the Green Monster. Eliminated were April 23–24, 1949; May 30 (1st), June 30 (1st), July 2, and September 7, 1950; and September 22, 1951. This leaves the New York at Boston (American League) game of May 30 (1st), 1951, but nothing has been found in the *Boston Globe*, *New York Times*, or *New York Herald Tribune*, among other sources.

1955–1969 On a *Costas Now* TV interview, Willie Mays told Bob Costas that he had once been victimized by the HBT perpetrated by Ken Boyer. Boyer and Mays competed against one another in the National League from 1955 to 1969.

1956–1963 According to *The New Dickson Baseball Dictionary*, "One of the oddest versions of the hidden-ball trick came in 1958, when [White Sox second baseman] Nellie Fox asked Billy Gardner to step off the bag for a moment while he cleaned it off. Gardner obliged and got tagged out by Fox."[22] Writes author Paul Dickson, this came from *Baseball Lite* (1986), a 90-page booklet by pro baseball announcer Jerry Howarth. Checked, to no avail, were 20 possible dates in 1958: April 30; May 22, 23, 24; June 13, 15 (2), 20, 21, 22; July 15, 16 (both), 17, 22, 23,

24; August 24, 25; September 16, 18. Nothing was found for the possible 1956 dates in the *Chicago Tribune*. Dave Anderson recalls a play by Fox between 1957 and 1963; Fox did have a HBT against Cleveland in 1962. John Kuenster tells this tale as if he witnessed it at Comiskey Park in the May 2009 installment of *Baseball Digest*. Based on the Retrosheet holdings, David Smith is certain this is apocryphal.

1960–1966 A fan recalled Ken Hamlin being tricked by the Yankees: "I think it was in 1961, when he was a member of the Angels. It was after he hit a double." When that didn't pan out he wrote, "It's possible it could have happened when Hamlin was a member of the Senators, as it was 1962 when I began to follow baseball closely. . . . I also think it did not happen during July or August. What I'm sure about it: It happened against the Yankees. (I was watching on television.) It was after he hit a run-scoring double. It was the third out of the inning." Dave Smith checked every game Hamlin in played against the Yankees in 1961–1962, finding nothing remotely related. I suspect the fan is misremembering a trick pulled by the Yankees on Ken *Harrelson* in 1963. For the record, Hamlin played for Kansas City (1960), Los Angeles (1961), and Washington (1962, 1965–1966), with respective doubles totals of 10, 3, 12, 21, and 7.

1961 According to the *Washington Post*, Senator Danny O'Connell "was the only one who successfully pulled off the hidden-ball trick [for the Senators in 1961], accomplishing this against Detroit's Norm Cash."[23] Following are the 13 possible dates: May 2, 3, 4, 9 (both), 10, 11; June 11 (both), 20, 22; August 2 (1), 27 (1). O'Connell was at second base for the first seven games plus June 11 (2), and at third base in the rest. Nothing was found in *Sporting News*. O'Connell did trick the Angels' Leon Wagner on August 14, 1961; that this isn't mentioned, and no evidence is found on catching Cash, leads one to believe that author Bob Addie confused Wagner for Cash, although it is admittedly difficult to imagine mixing up those two players.

1968–1982 One person recalls a trick featured on *This Week in Baseball*. It was performed by first baseman Jim Spencer, after faking a throw to the pitcher. Spencer played 1,221 games at first in the American League between 1968 and 1982.

1968–1982 According to *Baseball: The Biographical Encyclopedia*, John Mayberry may have victimized Bobby Grich. It quotes Grich as saying, "Big John is so nice and easygoing you don't suspect anything when he asks you to take your foot off the bag to kick the dust away—until he tags you." [24] Mayberry played in the American League with Kansas City (1972–1977), Toronto (1978–1982), and New York (1982), while Grich was with Baltimore (1972–1976) and California (1977–1982). A fan recalls seeing a feature about Mayberry in a Blue Jays' program/scorecard, claiming that he successfully pulled the trick four times. Only one has been verified.

1973–1975 When Mike Lowell pulled his second trick for the Marlins in 2005, Florida manager Jack McKeon said, "I've seen Cookie Rojas pull it a couple of times, and Mike a couple of times; those are the only ones I know of in the big leagues." Rojas played from 1962 to 1977, but the only years McKeon would have been around to see him would have been between 1973 and 1975, when Jack managed the Royals. Rojas played second base in 137, 141, and 116 games, respectively, during those years; McKeon was fired on July 24, 1975.

1977–1981 A fan recalls a trick during a Cleveland at Texas game, possibly by Mike Hargrove, Texas first baseman, on Andre Thornton, Cleveland, which would make it 1977–1978. The possible dates in 1977 (April 11, 13; July 15 [both], 16, 17), 1978 (April 26, 27; August 4, 5, 6), 1979 (April 10, 11, 12; August 10, 11, 12), 1980 (April 14, 15, 16; August 12, 13, 14), 1981 (April 14, 15), and 1982 (April 20, 21, 22; August 13, 14, 15) have been checked in *Sporting News*, with no success.

1977–1988 One person recalls a trick by Eddie Murray with Baltimore, leaving a mere 1,608 possibilities.

June 29, 1978 In the sixth inning, Atlanta shortstop Pat Rockett put out the Dodgers' Johnny Oates at second, with no indication of how the putout came about. Nothing was found in *Sporting News*, the *Atlanta Constitution*, or the *Los Angeles Times*.

1981–1983 San Diego's Alan Wiggins may have been the victim of San Francisco's Dave Bergman, a precursor to the same combination when the two were in the American League on June 17, 1986. One fan "seem(s) to remember the announcer saying that this was the second time this has happened to Alan, the other time when he was with San Diego." Another person, a rabid Oriole fan, recalls that following the 1986 trick, "Bergman was asked whether he had ever done the trick before and refused to talk about it to avoid embarrassing Wiggins—and the researchers at the time determined that Bergman had, in fact. caught Wiggins before, when both were in the National League." If so, it could have happened in one of only eight Padres–Giants games in 1981 (September 26, October 4), 1982 (July 4, September 19), or 1983 (April 14, June 26–July 2, September 20–21); however, nothing was found in *Sporting News*, the *San Francisco Chronicle*, or Retrosheet's holdings.

1985–2000 In *The New Bill James Historical Baseball Abstract*, James writes, "Ozzie [Guillen] once made the hidden-ball trick work twice in two days, against the same team."[25] I questioned this tale, advising the author that I had documented three tricks pulled *on* Guillen but none *by* him. I asked, "What is the source of this fact? Is it possible you have confused his victimization for perpetration?" James replied, "I'm sure I was just repeating something I read, but I don't know where I read it. I suspect you are probably right."

1987–1997 An account of Matt Williams's 1997 HBT says that it was his third; only two have been found.

1988–1992 When Florida's Mike Lowell tricked the Diamondbacks in 2005, Arizona color commentator Mark Grace claimed that he had once caught Mike Scioscia on the trick. It would have to have been between 1988 and 1992, when Grace was the Cubs' first baseman and Scioscia was playing for the Dodgers.

1991–1998 A correspondent recalled seeing a play involving "Boston vs. ? at home in the mid-1990s," adding, "I think it was a day game, too. Mo Vaughn at [first base] hid the ball [and] chatted it up with the base runner while the ump stood close by, obviously aware of the deception.

Once the runner brushed himself off and came off the bag to talk, Mo put the tag on him." Vaughn played 928 games at first base for the Red Sox between 1991 and 1998.

1994 A fan recalls that Houston's Orlando Miller was caught twice in the same game shortly after he came up on July 8. Nothing was found in *USA Today Baseball Weekly* or the 1994–1995 Astros' scoresheets.

19

ODDS AND ENDS

This chapter includes descriptions of some hidden-ball tricks that took place in games outside of the major leagues, plays that were described as HBTs but turned out to be something else, or just fun little stories.

May 19, 1873 According to the *Brooklyn Daily Eagle*, Philadelphia's Bob "Addy was caught off second base in the Atlantic and Philadelphia [National Association] match. . . . Addy had reached second base safely on the ball being thrown by [third baseman Bob] Ferguson to [second baseman Jack] Burdock, but seeing Burdock standing apparently without the ball in hand, he stepped off the base, when Burdock touched him with the ball, which he had quietly held."[1] Earlier in the same issue it says, "In the Mutual and Baltimore match of last week [May 13 or 16], Joe Start played it upon Lip Pike in a way that the latter 'despised.' In the second portion of the sixth inning, Pike overran first base, and in passing it was touched by Start with the ball, but the umpire, Mr. N. Young, decided the player entitled to his base. Start, however, held on to the ball and performed as clever a piece of baseball generalship as could be wished for. He argued with Pike that he had been put out, whereupon Pike left his base for the purpose of explaining how he had overrun the base, and no sooner had Pike stepped from the sand bag than the wily Start touched him with the ball, thus putting him out, and it was so declared by the umpire. It is not often Lip gets caught napping in this style."[2]

July 4, 1874 The Mutuals' Jack Burdock tagged the Atlantics' Charlie Hodes off third base—the third trick by New York in ten days. Per the *New York Clipper*, it followed an argument with umpire A. Allison: "While this was going on, Burdock had quietly held on to the ball, and Hodes, forgetting the important fact and seeing (pitcher Bobby Mathews) walk back to his position apparently ready to deliver the ball, walked off his base and then Burdock touched him with the ball, and the umpire decided him out. On the principle that all tricks are fair in war, this was a 'point to play,' but it did not raise Burdock in the estimation of the reputable portion of the spectators. When appeals are made on decisions in regard to a reversal or when a player is hurt, the umpire should promptly call time so as to make the ball dead until the talk is over or the injured player can resume his position. Twice this last week have the Mutuals benefited by the failure of the umpire to attend to this part of his duties."[3] The Atlantics won, 3–2. Burdock was considered a pioneer of the play, not necessarily a compliment. An 1878 article remarks, "We regretted to see [Herm Doscher, who is not a major leaguer,] resort to one of Burdock's old tricks of hiding the ball under his arm."[4]

September 10, 1874 According to the *Hartford Post*, in a National Association game, Hartford's Tom Barlow hid the ball under his arm instead of handing it to the pitcher and returned to his position. When Chicago's Paul Hines led off third base, Barlow snuck over and tagged him several times, screaming for the umpire's attention. The ump called Hines out. Barlow had reportedly become notorious for this trick.[5] Nothing was found in the *Hartford Courant* or *Chicago Tribune*, and there is a question as to whether Barlow was at shortstop or third (Steve Brady may have been at third). *Sporting News* wrote in 1888, "It was the late little Tommy Barlow who introduced the trick of hiding the ball under his arm after it was returned from the outfield when the hit had been made and then catching the base runner napping on a neat throw to the baseman, who would be on the lookout."[6] Disregarding his games as a catcher, Barlow played only 41 contests in the field during his National Association career: four at shortstop and one at third base for the 1872 Athletics; one each at short and second for the 1873 A's; 32 at short for the 1874 Hartford team; one at short for New Haven in 1875, and one at second for the A's that same year.

July 21, 1875 Boston's George Wright, by some accounts the inventor of the play, became a victim at the hands of Bill Hague of St. Louis in a National Association game. Writes the *St. Louis Republican*, Wright led off the game with a triple, "but a shout of 'how's that' from Hague let us know for the first time that the 'old woman' had tucked the ball under his arm when it was thrown in from the outfield and touched George with it the moment he stepped off the base. . . . George was terribly crestfallen. He said 'he had been tried a hundred times before but that was the first time he had ever been caught.'"[7]

September 20, 1875 Philadelphia first baseman Tim Murnane—the same one who 33 years later declared the play "unsportsmanlike" in print—caught Cincinnati's Emmanuel Snyder in the final inning of an exhibition game. According to the *Cincinnati Enquirer*, "Murnan [*sic*], on first base, got the ball and hid it under his arm. Snyder was told that the ball was in the pitcher's hand and stepped off his base. . . . Murnan, quick as a flash, touched his man, and the Reds were beaten."[8]

October 18, 1875 In a game between amateur teams, New York hosted Brooklyn. According to the *New York Clipper*, future National League shortstop Pete "Treacey marred his fine play by a trick in putting out Brasher, unworthy of a fair and manly player, by pretending to have thrown the ball to the pitcher while holding it under his arm. This is not legitimate ball-play."[9]

April 1877 Cincinnati pulled a trick play in a nonleague game. Red catcher Nat "Hicks turned about carelessly and, without calling time, purposely walked toward the grandstand. [Base runner Mike] Golden fell into the trap and started for home. [Pitcher Bobby] Mitchell, having the ball in his hand, easily ran in and caught him before he reached . . . home plate."[10] Obviously, this is not a HBT, since the pitcher had the ball.

September 26, 1879 Henry Chadwick writes, "A queer decision was made by the umpire in the Albany–Worcester (National Association) game on September 26. [Lou] Say had secreted the ball about his person and, when the runner stepped off the base, touched him. The umpire would not allow the out, although we are at a loss to understand why."[11] Historian Lee Allen called this the earliest reference to the hidden-ball trick, although we now know that isn't true.

Other minor league tricks include the following, reported in *Sporting News*: August 1926 (Pacific Coast League [PCL]); May 1941 (Southern Association [SA]); August 27, 1944 (International League triple play); May 1945 (Eastern League [EL]); June 6, 1946 (IL); June 21, 1947 (PCL); July 28, 1949 (Central League); August 15, 1952 (PCL); April 13, 1954 (SA); May 9, 1954 (by Connie Ryan in the American Association); September 20, 1956 (SA); September 11, 1958 (IL); May 17, 1974 (IL); August 23, 1976 (IL); July 24, 1979 (EL); April 20, 1980 (IL).

May 12, 1883 According to *Sporting Life*, "In the Brooklyn–Metropolitan game on the 12th, Lynch tried the little trick invented by Battin and Nolan and played by them so successfully on the Baltimores. It didn't work this time, however, as the umpire, Billy McLean, not seeing him enter the 'box,' decided the ball not in play and put the runners back. To avoid being caught napping in this way, all base runners have to do is not to leave their bases until the ball has been delivered to the bat."[12] Unfortunately, Brooklyn wasn't in the American Association in 1883, and the Metropolitans played the Athletics on May 12 (and Jack Lynch did not play for the Mets that day). Joe Battin and Edward "The Only" Nolan played together only on Pittsburgh, in 1883, and their team's only games against Baltimore to that date were on May 10, 11, and 12. In the first, "No especially brilliant plays were noted," according to the *Commercial Gazette*, and in the second, Nolan did not play.

September 10, 1884 A play at third base by Washington ended the Union Association game. With Pittsburgh's Charlie Householder "sleeping" on third, George Strief hit a foul pop "that was relayed to [pitcher Bill] Wise and on to [third baseman Jerry] McCormick." With the pitcher involved, it can't be a HBT.

April 27, 1885 Per *Sporting Life*, in the first inning of a New York–Washington National League game, "[T]he ball was passed around to [Jim] O'Rourke . . . who, it is alleged, put it in his bosom and threw out a dead ball." A "half an hour's wrangling" ensued before a new ball was put into play. [13]

October 17, 1885 According to *Sporting Life*, Washington (Eastern League) first baseman Phil Baker "worked an old 'chestnut trick'" on the same Jim O'Rourke during an exhibition series against the Giants. Baker put out O'Rourke on a HBT, "and the great manipulator of balls was out, amid the jeers of the vast audience." [14]

May 30, 1887 Cub Hall of Famer Cap Anson was the victim of a trick play. Writes *Sporting News*, "Baby Anson is a very large man, but he could have been drawn through a keyhole when in the afternoon on Decoration Day at the Polo Grounds, [the Giants' George] Gore leisurely walked in from center field and caught Anson napping off second base and put him out." [15] Nothing was found in *Sporting Life* or the *Chicago Tribune*, but the *Chicago Times* confirms it was merely a pick-off: "The greatest play ever made on a ball field was made by Gore in the sixth inning. Anson was laying off second base in the hope of a chance to get down to third when Gore worked himself in from the outfield and got the ball, which [catcher Willard] Brown threw to him and put Anson out. It was some time before the 15,000 spectators stopped yelling their delight in the clever strategy." [16]

July 8, 1887 New York's George "Gore was caught napping at second" to end a National League game against Detroit, reports *Sporting Life*. With two out and two on in the ninth inning, "Gore let himself be caught off the second bag," says the *Boston Herald*. Nothing was found in *Sporting News*. Nonetheless, the *Boston Daily Advertiser* shows it was a pickoff rather than a HBT: "Gore was caught napping at second on a throw by [pitcher Charles 'Lady'] Baldwin, and this ended the game."

April 1900 Per *Sporting News*, Phillie rookie Fred Jacklitsch "was caught by that moth-eaten trick of a player (Dolan) hiding the ball under his arm." [17] This turns out to have been an exhibition game involving the Philadelphia A's of the Atlantic League.

1902 The *Washington Post* notes, "In no previous season within the past five years has the 'hidden-ball trick' been worked so frequently as this." [18]

June 16, 1908 According to the *Chicago Tribune*, "It was no wooden horse that fooled J. Evers." There follows a description of a play in which the Cubs' second baseman was unwittingly duped by his own teammate during a game against the Phillies. Pitcher Orval Overall, coaching first, tossed a ball, which had been returned by a spectator, toward the umpire. Evers, at first base, thought it was the ball in play and made a bluff toward second, at which point he was tagged out by first sacker Kitty Bransfield. [19] Since Bransfield was making no attempt at duplicity and Evers didn't think the pitcher had the ball, I have ruled that this was not a HBT.

March 21, 1910 The University of Georgia tricked the Yankees in an exhibition game. Pitcher Rube Manning, the courtesy runner for Hal Chase, was the victim of first baseman Walker, reports the *New York Times*. [20]

April 4, 1912 Cardinal third baseman Wally Smith snookered Brown pitcher Earl Hamilton in a St. Louis City Series (exhibition) game. According to the *Washington Post*, "The hidden-ball trick was pulled on Hamilton in the third, with Monte Cross coaching. The bases were full, with Hamilton on the far corner, when Smith concealed the ball under his arm. When Hamilton wandered off he was tagged." [21]

June 19, 1913 In this date's *Detroit News* is an article entitled "Naps Have Way to Prevent Working a Hidden-Ball Trick." Datelined in Washington, the article about the Cleveland team later known as the Indians says, "There'll be no hidden-ball trick victims among the Naps this season unless someone gets careless and forgets [manager Joe] Birmingham's instructions. The Naps are directed to hug bases until the opposing pitcher takes his position at the slab, unless they positively know where the ball is. If the pitcher should take his position on the rubber and then the hidden-ball trick be tried by an opposing player, the base runners would move up a base. The taking of the pitching position without being able to deliver the ball would constitute a balk as soon as the pitcher took down his hands."[22] No HBTs against Cleveland before 1929 have been found.

March 14, 1914 The Giants' Mike Donlin was caught with the trick during a spring training game versus Dallas.

August 7, 1915 With two out in the seventh inning of a 4–4 game, the Cardinals' Miller Huggins duped Dodger rookie pitcher Ed Appleton, but the Cards were on offense and the ball was anything but hidden. Huggins, coaching third, asked Appleton to toss him the ball for inspection and then stepped aside, allowing the ball to roll away and Card runner Dots Miller to score the go-ahead run. St. Louis won, 6–4. According to the *St. Louis Globe-Democrat*, the same play was pulled against St. Louis by Baltimore in a Federal League game on July 17, 1915.[23]

July 13, 1918 A 1971 article in *Street & Smith's Official 1971 Baseball Yearbook* about the HBT says, "Even [Ty] Cobb was suckered. The Georgia Peach had a habit of making a wide turn at first base, always alert to the possibility of advancing. But it was noticed that he relaxed after rounding the base and took his eye off the ball. The Tigers were playing Washington, and Cobb singled to left. Burt Shotton, playing left field, whipped the ball to shortstop Doc Lavan, who relayed to first baseman Joe Judge. When Cobb made his leisurely turn, he was tagged out by Judge before stepping on first base. Judge skillfully had hidden the ball."[24] The *Washington Star* account of this game describes what is obviously the same play, but just as obviously not a HBT: "Cobb's third single, a rap to left, was produced in the ninth, but Ty was outsmarted and nipped off first when Shotton threw in to Lavan and Johnny whipped the ball without hesitation to Judge."[25]

June 12, 1919 According to the *St. Louis Times*, Brave shortstop "Rabbit Maranville put one on for the book in the fifth inning yesterday. [The Cardinals' Verne] Clemons opened with a single. [Lee] Meadows bunted and was thrown out by [third baseman Lena] Blackburne. With third base open, (Maranville) started from second to cover the sack. He saw Clemons approaching second and, naturally with second open, too, Clemons wasn't going to pull up at the middle station. Running but several yards in the direction of third, Maranville wheeled on his spikes and rushed back to second. He received (first baseman Walter Holke's) toss and tagged Clemons, who tried to protect himself. When [umpire Bob] Emslie called Clemons out, the catcher protested and was put out of the game."[26] It doesn't sound like a HBT to me.

May 25, 1922 According to *Sporting News*, first baseman George Lafayette of the Oakland Oaks (Pacific Coast League) "conjured the ball out of somewhere and caught [Portland's] Sammy Hale off the initial sack for the third out."[27]

August 27, 1922 The *Boston Globe* discusses a certain minor league team having pulled its 19th HBT of the season, Braunsen victimizing Spud Campbell.

June 3, 1923 Per the *Cleveland Plain Dealer*, Cleveland's Larry "Gardner was safe as [Detroit pitcher Herman] Pillette juggled [first baseman Lu] Blue's throw to first base. When Gardner walked off the bag, Pillette threw to [third baseman Fred] Haney, who tagged him out."[28] It is possible that Gardner thought the batter was out and left the bag. In any case, it doesn't qualify as a HBT because the throw came from the pitcher.

March 1931 Jimmy Dykes, later a prolific storyteller about seeing and executing the play, was victimized in a spring training intrasquad game by teammate Eric McNair.

April 16, 1931 The *New York Times* from this date discusses the origin of football's version of the hidden-ball trick, with C. V. P. Young of Cornell and Amos Alonzo Stagg of Springfield both credited with the innovation.[29] A 1942 article in the *Times* names Dr. James Johnson and Glenn Warner of Carlisle as the innovators.[30]

April 6, 1933 In an exhibition game between the Giants and Tigers, New York's "Blondy Ryan introduced the hidden-ball trick to tag [rookie Frank] Reiber at second for the third out in the sixth."[31]

March 2, (year uncertain), between 1933–1941 A gag game between mostly sportswriters was held in Hot Springs, Arkansas, with Giant pitcher Carl Hubbell reporting on the action: "They pulled the hidden-ball trick on Eddie Brannick, but there were extenuating circumstances. He thought the second baseman was asking him to autograph the ball . . . he had just hit for a double."

1936 Chattanooga shortstop (say *that* five times fast) Jose Olivares worked the trick seven times in this Southern Association season, according to the *Chicago Tribune*.

May 17, 1939 In the first televised baseball game, Princeton topped Columbia. The *New York Times* reports that, "When the age-old hidden-ball trick was worked by the third baseman, even the camera was not fast enough to turn on the quick turn of events."[32]

May 2, 1942 According to Harold Kaese, "Johnny Pesky worked the hidden-ball trick three times while with the Red Sox, on Tommy Henrich, on Buddy Lewis, and on George McQuillan, all in the pinch. Pesky had another hidden-ball set up when his partner, Bobby Doerr, called time because he wanted to talk to the pitcher." For the third-named victim, Kaese must be referring to Glenn "Red" McQuillen, since George McQuillan retired before Pesky was born. He must also be combining this one into the "almost" HBT mentioned, per *Sporting News*'s account of this game (see chapter 17, "Tricks Gone Awry"). Boston beat St. Louis, 11–10. Pesky also mentioned the "almost" HBT and a trick on McQuillen as two separate plays, the latter one occurring in 1946; the possible dates (May 6 [both], 7, 16, 18; June 5, August 20–September 2) were checked in *Sporting News*, without success. In 2002, when confronted with the evidence, Pesky conceded that he had only two successful tricks.

1946 Al Spaeter recalled his debut with the Salem, Oregon, Senators (Western International League) in this year: "I got a line-drive base hit in my first at bat. I knew better, but I led off first base a bit before pitcher Chuck Cronin was quite back on the mound. First baseman Dick Adams said, 'Hey, Spaeter,' showed me the ball, and tagged me out. They never let me forget that."[33]

August 26, 1946 Writes the *Boston Herald*, Ted Williams "kicked his glove all the way to left field after he was picked off second base by the Cleveland Indians' Bob Lemon and Lou Boudreau in 1946."[34] But while this play was described as a HBT, it was merely a pickoff.

March 22, 1948 In a spring training game against the Reds, asserts the *New York Times*, the Yankees' Frank "Crosetti capped his day by springing his favorite old hidden-ball trick to spike a Redleg rally in the tenth. His victim, of all persons, was another crafty veteran, Augie Galan, who fell into the trap after drawing a pass and advancing to second on a sacrifice."[35] According to Shirley Povich, Crosetti said, "Augie, I want you to meet an old friend of mine. This is A. J. Reach, you remember him? Sorry it had to be you, Augie, old boy."[36] (Reach was the manufacturer of the official American League ball.) The *Portland Press-Herald* reports that Crosetti actually apologized afterward: "That really was a nice gesture on the part of Frankie Crosetti in sending a note of apology to Augie Galan for picking him off second base with the hidden-ball trick. . . . Crosetti will be glad to know that it was appreciated and that Augie can laugh about the incident now. 'That would never happen to me in the regular season,' the personable Cincinnati veteran says. 'My first rule before stepping off a bag is to be sure who has the ball. I was talking to umpire Bill Stewart and wasn't paying much attention.'"[37] Galan's rule must have been enacted sometime after June 3, 1941, when he was nailed with the trick by Bobby Bragan. The text of Crosetti's letter was reprinted in *Sporting News*:

> Dear Augie:
> I presume you have been calling me all the names under the sun. I know that it was a "bush trick" to try something like that in spring training. You will admit that the game was so monotonous that something had to be done to enliven the proceedings. Too bad you had to be the one on second base—and a native Californian to boot.
> I hope you do not think too ill of me; all's fair in love and war, so the saying goes.
> You can at least console yourself by the fact that your name is added to other great stars that have fallen as my victims. Namely Cronin, Werber, Poffenberger, Goslin, Walker, and others. So you have gained some distinction in your sad experience.

You may be the last one that I will ever catch off base. When people ask me who my last victim was, naturally your name will come to me as long as I live. So there will be at least one person who will never forget you and, of course, you may never forget me, which would make us even.

Do not invite me to dinner, as I will have to refuse, as you might be tempted to put arsenic in my soup.

No hard feelings—I hope. Wishing you a very successful season, with best wishes, I am.

Sincerely,
Frankie Crosetti[38]

However, it wasn't the last time Crosetti tried the trick. On August 30, 1952, Cro apparently nabbed former teammate Tommy Henrich in an old-timers' game, but the umpire disallowed it.[39]

June 13, 1948 Third baseman Red Rolfe pulled the ruse on a Hall of Famer in the Yankees' Old-Timers' Day game. According to the *New York Times*, "Rolfe, the cad, pulled the hidden-ball play on Waite Hoyt."[40]

July 6, 1950 Per Shirley Povich's July 20, 1950, column, "The Athletics are the slickest perpetrators of the trick in the league. Second baseman Pete Suder pulled it on Gene Woodling of the Yankees last month."[41] The only 1950 dates that Suder played against Woodling prior to July 20 were May 13, May 14, May 28 (both games), and July 6 (when Suder was at first base). Checked to no avail were the *Philadelphia Inquirer*, the *New York Daily News*, the *New York Herald Tribune*, and *Sporting News*. But the July 7 *New York Times* reveals that Suder was not at second base, and it was not a HBT. In the fifth inning on the previous day, Woodling "decided it was time for a visit to the New York dugout for a drink of water. So, nonchalantly, he strolled off the bag and headed toward the bench. It would have been quite all right, except that Woodling neglected to call for time. When Gene realized his mistake, he dashed back toward the base, but by then [pitcher Bobby] Shantz had fired the ball to Pete Suder and Woodling was picked off."[42] There was obviously no deception involved, and by definition, it's not a HBT if the pitcher had the ball.

1951 According to a 1951 article in *Sporting News*, Lyle Judy had executed the trick five times in the Florida State League that year.[43]

1953 Says a 1953 article in *Street & Smith's Official 1953 Baseball Yearbook*, "Frank Verdi, Yankee third base rookie, worked the hidden-ball trick successfully seven times last season while playing with Binghamton, [New York], of the Eastern League. The hidden-ball trick is barred in the Texas League."[44]

1953 Hank Aaron, in his autobiography, recalls that he was victimized three times in one South Atlantic League game in 1953: "The first time up, I singled and stole second, and the second baseman tagged me out with the hidden-ball trick. The next time, I stole second again, and he used some other hidden-ball trick and tagged me out again. (Manager Ben Geraghty) let it go the first time, but the second time he was pretty hot. When it happened the third time, he let me have it. Of course, I deserved it. . . . I was a better base runner from that day on."[45]

1954 Red manager Birdie Tebbetts, quoted by Jack Hernon in the *Pittsburgh Post-Gazette*, reprinted in a 1955 issue of *Baseball Digest*, recalled that Bud Podbielan was pitching for him when a HBT was attempted. Podbielan was delaying pitching to the Phillies' Andy Seminick, so Tebbetts went out to the mound twice to see what was going on before learning they were trying to pull the trick. The story doesn't say whether the trick ultimately worked, but it does say that Tebbetts "spoiled the strategy."[46] Nevertheless, Podbielan never pitched for the Reds against Seminick prior to the date of this article, not to mention the rule implications of two trips to the mound by Tebbetts. In another version (an unidentified December 1954 clipping), Tebbetts said it happened in a 1954 Reds–Giants game: "Willie Mays was at bat, and the Giants had men on first and second with two out. My pitcher kept shaking off the catcher, and finally I walked out to the mound and said, 'What the hell's the matter? You've been getting this guy out all afternoon. Why don't you pitch to him?' . . . At this point, Roy McMillan ran over and said, 'Get the hell out of here, Birdie, we were trying to work the hidden-ball trick.'" In *Sporting News*, April 24, 1957 is yet another version of the Tebbetts yarn, this one involving pitcher Johnny Klippstein.

April 25, 1957 Retrosheet questioned how Whitey Herzog was put out in a Washington versus Boston game, but it turned out he was hit by a batted ball.

1964 In a New York–Pennsylvania League game, Binghamton outfielder Johnny May secreted a ball in his uniform and used it in pretending to catch a ball hit over the fence.

June 12, 1966 At Chicago, Minnesota's Cesar Tovar was out on the bases in the sixth inning. Tovar had singled and stole second with one out. Shortstop Lee Elia somehow got an unassisted putout on him. Nothing could be found in *Sporting News* or the *Chicago Tribune*. One account says that Tovar thought he was out on the steal attempt, got up and walked away, and was tagged by Elia.

August 5, 1967 In the fifth inning, the Cubs' Billy Williams was out at second base, Brave shortstop Denis Menke to second baseman Woody Woodward, with no indication in Retrosheet of how the putout came about. Nothing was found in *Sporting News*, but it was ascertained from the *Chicago American* that this was not a HBT: "Williams's short fly dropped in center, but when he attempted to stretch it into a double he was out, Menke to Woodward." [47]

1972 According to an article in *Sporting News*, first baseman Pancho Herrera of Key West in the Florida State League led the " league in one category—the hidden-ball trick. He . . . caught no fewer than 16 base runners with the antiquated trick. . . . In fact, he surprised Orlando runners twice in one game."[48] This may have been lifted from *Sports Illustrated*: "Pancho Herrera . . . has been reviving a lost art as playing manager of the Key West Conchs. Playing first base, he may have come up with a new baseball record. He has pulled off the hidden-ball trick no fewer than 16 times this season, including twice in one game against Orlando."[49]

September 14, 1980 In the eighth, Cub second baseman Mike Tyson put out the Mets' Frank Taveras, who was charged with a caught stealing. David Vincent and David Smith now say this was not a HBT.

June 1984 Marty Barrett of Boston supposedly performed the trick versus Toronto (10 possible dates: June 15, 16, 22, 23, 24; September 17, 18, 19, 24, 25), as mentioned in the *Boston Herald*, which discusses Barrett's July 7, 1985, trick: "It was the second time in two years Barrett has done it. He did it [versus] Toronto last year."[50] But Barrett himself says he "only accomplished it the three times . . . mentioned [twice in 1985, once in 1988]—never against Toronto." As described in chapter 17, "Tricks Gone Awry," this is probably referring to Barrett's unsuccessful attempt.

August 31, 1987 According to Retrosheet, the Giants' Robby Thompson was caught by Expo shortstop Tom Foley after a successful steal in the fifth; however, the play is featured on the 1989 *Sports Illustrated/Major League Baseball Productions* video *Super Duper Baseball Bloopers*, revealing it was merely a decoy pulled by Foley, followed by a tag by second baseman Casey Candaele.

September 30, 1992 According to one fan, George Brett was caught with the HBT after recording his 3,000th career hit on this date. Accounts of the game, however, make it clear that Brett was first picked off by pitcher Tim Fortugno. According to the *Riverside Press-Enterprise*, "And then Fortugno picked Brett off. . . . Said Brett, 'I was right in the middle of a sentence to [Angels' first baseman Gary] Gaetti, and then they picked me off.'"[51]

May 8, 1994 Two fans claimed that the Dodgers' Eric Karros caught the Giants' Salomon Torres after Torres singled; however, Retrosheet notes that, "Torres rounded first base too far" and was out, right field to first base.

July 14, 2003 Bo Jackson, playing first base, pulled the trick during the celebrity softball game in the All-Star FanFest.

July 19, 2003 During an American Legion–sponsored vintage baseball game between the House of David barnstorming team and a local female all-star squad (including four Illinois Softball Hall of Famers) in Geneva, Illinois, Society for American Baseball Research member Bill

Swank dressed up as Santa Claus and resurrected Eddie Deal's old "hidden-ball-in-the-beard" play. Deal was a player-manager for the storied House of David team, on which all the players wore beards. Swank played second sitting in a folding chair and lured opposing players onto his lap to offer them candy canes. Having built the girls' trust over the first five innings, Swank successfully executed the hidden-ball-in-the-beard trick in the sixth. The out was disallowed by 1860s rules for being "deceptive and unsportsmanlike."

2004 In the 2004 movie *Mr. 3000*, veteran first baseman Stan Ross (Bernie Mac) pulls off the trick to quell a rally.

April 21, 2006 The play was pulled off in a collegiate game by the University of California, Los Angeles against Arizona State.

September 19, 2007 In the bottom of the fifth inning at Toronto, Boston's Mike Lowell struck again, but I have not classified it as a HBT. Base runner Russ Adams lifted his foot off the third base bag to shift position after the play was over; Lowell, still holding the ball, tagged him out. Part of Dickson's definition is that the "base runner believes (the ball) has been returned to the pitcher." [52] It doesn't sound as if that was the case.

April 13, 2012 The Mets' Josh Thole reached on a single in the second inning and was moved to second on R. A. Dickey's sacrifice bunt. The Phillies' infielders convinced Thole that the bunt had gone foul, and he headed back toward first base, only to be tagged out.

2013 According to Yahoo! Sports, "Astros rookie Max Stassi had a strange hidden-ball encounter where the Rangers didn't even try to fool him, he just sort of fooled himself."[53] This occurred on August 20, Stassi's major league debut. With the rookie at first base, the next batter grounded to the pitcher, who threw to force the runner at second, but the throw airmailed Ranger shortstop Elvis Andrus, who leaped for the ball and came down with his empty glove on Stassi, who slid several feet short of the bag. Stassi obviously thought he was out, not looking at the umpire or for the ball—which second baseman Ian Kinsler, backing up the throw, had caught. When Kinsler saw Stassi wandering off the base, he ran up and tagged him out. There did not appear to be any deception on the part of the Rangers: Andrus appeared to be acting instinctively by completing the tag even though he had missed the ball, and Kinsler seemed shocked that Stassi had left the bag. More importantly, Stassi left the bag not because he thought the ball had been returned to the pitcher, but because he thought he was already out. Thus, this is not a HBT, but a decoy, intentional or not.

See appendix A for successful executions of the HBT and appendix B for unsubstantiated possibilities.

NOTES

INTRODUCTION

1. *Sporting News*, June 30, 1986, p. 16.

I. WHAT IS THE HIDDEN-BALL TRICK?

1. Paul Dickson, *New Dickson Baseball Dictionary* (San Diego, CA: Harcourt Brace & Company, 1999), 244–45.

2. *New York Times*, March 8, 1947.

3. *Sporting News*, November 10, 1938.

4. Clete Boyer, presentation at Utica–Cooperstown SABR Chapter meeting, August 5, 2001.

5. Edgar Munzel, "Kamm-oflage!" *Baseball Digest*, November–December 1956, p. 49.

6. Dan Gutman, *It Ain't Cheatin' If You Don't Get Caught* (New York: Penguin, 1990).

7. Clifford Bloodgood, "The Hidden-Ball Trick," *Baseball Magazine*, July 1948.

8. Jay Feldman, "The Hidden-Ball Trick, Nicaragua, and Me," *National Pastime*, Winter 1987, pp. 2–4.

2. HISTORY OF THE TRICK

1. David Pietrusza, Matthew Silverman, and Michael Gershman, eds., *Baseball: The Biographical Encyclopedia* (Kingston, NY: Total Sports Illustrated, 2000), 1,254–56.

2. *Cleveland Plain Dealer*, May 22, 1872.

3. *Sporting News*, May 15, 1919, p. 4.

4. Commissioner of Baseball, *2004 Official Rules of Major League Baseball* (Chicago: Triumph Books, 2003), 134–36.

5. *Sporting News*, May 9, 1946, p. 22.

6. *Sporting News*, February 1, 1956, p. 29.

7. *Sporting News*, November 24, 1948, p. 24.

8. *Sporting News*, May 10, 1950, p. 40.

9. *Sporting News*, January 26, 1955, p. 25.

10. *St. Louis Globe-Democrat*

11. *Washington Post*, January 30, 1910, p. M8.

12. *Washington Post*, March 20, 1910, pp. 4E, MS8.

13. *Sporting Life*, April 12, 1913.

14. *Sporting Life*, May 20, 1915.

15. *Sporting Life*, August 1915.

16. Hugh S. Fullerton, "Insubordination Hurts Baseball; Helped Yankees to Lose Series," *Atlanta Constitution*, October 20, 1922, p. 11.

17. *Sporting News*, June 28, 1945, pp. 10, 14.

18. *Sporting News*, July 12, 1945, p. 12.

3. MASTERS OF THE TRICK . . . AND THEIR VICTIMS

1. *New York World-Telegram*, March 18, 1936.

2. *Sporting News*, November 29, 1934.

3. *Sporting News*, August 20, 1942, p. 10.

4. Billy Evans, "Glad Pinelli Is Gone," *Kansas City Star*, April 9, 1921, p. 8.

5. *Sporting Life*, May 30, 1908.

6. Dick Bartell, with Norman Macht, *Rowdy Richard* (Berkeley, CA: North Atlantic Books, 1993).

7. Clifford Bloodgood, "The Hidden-Ball Trick," *Baseball Magazine*, July 1948.

4. 1876–1889: THE EARLY TRICKS

1. *Chicago Tribune.*
2. *Louisville Journal*, May 26, 1876.
3. *Chicago Tribune*, May 26, 1876.
4. *Hartford Times.*
5. *Hartford Daily Courant*, May 26, 1876.
6. *Philadelphia Press*, September 6, 1876.
7. *Boston Globe*, June 29, 1877.
8. *Chicago Times*, May 21, 1881.
9. *Chicago Tribune*, May 21, 1881.
10. *Sporting Life*, January 14, 1885.
11. *Sporting Life*, June 25, 1884.
12. *Louisville Courier-Journal*, July 5, 1884.
13. *Boston Morning Journal*, July 11, 1884, p. 4.
14. *Boston Globe*, June 26, 1886.
15. *Chicago Daily Tribune*, June 24, 1886.
16. *New York Sun*, May 22, 1887.
17. *Brooklyn Eagle*, June 18, 1888.
18. *Philadelphia Inquirer*, May 27, 1889.
19. *Sporting Life.*
20. *Sporting News*, July 20, 1889, p. 5.

5. 1890–1899: GAIETY IN THE '90S

1. *Sporting Life*, September 24, 1892, p. 2.
2. *Sporting Life*, May 27, 1893.
3. *Baltimore Sun*, May 31, 1893.
4. David Pietrusza, Matthew Silverman, and Michael Gershman, eds., *Baseball: The Biographical Encyclopedia* (Kingston, NY: Total Sports Illustrated, 2000), p. 70.
5. A. H. Tarvin, "Believe Me, These Happened," *Baseball Digest*, June 1944.
6. *Brooklyn Eagle*, June 7, 1893.
7. *Brooklyn Eagle*, June 8, 1893.
8. *New York Sun*, September 29, 1893.
9. *St. Louis Post-Dispatch*, July 4, 1894.
10. *Washington Post*, April 29, 1896, p. 4.
11. *Washington Post*, August 20, 1896.

12. *Sporting News*, May 1, 1897, pp. 5, 8.

13. *Sporting News*, June 5, 1897, p. 5.

14. *Washington Post*, May 28, 1897.

15. *Chicago Tribune*, June 3, 1897, p. 4.

6. 1900–1909: COUGHLIN CORNER TRICKS

1. *Sporting News*, January 12, 1901.

2. *Brooklyn Eagle*, July 10, 1900.

3. *Washington Post*, September 25, 1901.

4. *Sporting News*, May 3, 1902, p. 10.

5. *Detroit Free Press*, May 6, 1902.

6. *Boston Globe*, May 3, 1902.

7. *Brooklyn Eagle*, May 12, 1902.

8. *Chicago Tribune*, May 14, 1902.

9. *Washington Post*, May 16, 1902.

10. *Washington Post*.

11. *Sporting Life*.

12. *New York Evening Telegram*, June 3, 1904.

13. *Washington Post*, August 27, 1904.

14. *Chicago Tribune*, April 23, 1905.

15. *Detroit News*, April 24, 1905.

16. *Detroit News*, April 24, 1905.

17. *Sporting Life*, May 20, 1905, p. 9.

18. *Washington Post*, April 30, 1905.

19. *New York Evening World*.

20. *Detroit Free Press*, May 14, 1905.

21. *Boston Herald*, May 13, 1905.

22. *Boston Globe*.

23. *Chicago Tribune*, July 24, 1905, p. 8.

24. *Sporting Life*, May 26, 1906.

25. *Washington Post*, April 14, 1907.

26. *Detroit Journal*, August 20, 1907.

27. David Jones, ed., *Deadball Stars of the American League* (Dulles, VA: Potomac Books, 2006), 542.

28. *Chicago Daily Tribune*, September 23, 1907, p. 10.

29. David S. Neft and Richard M. Cohen, *The World Series* (New York: St. Martin's, 1990), 20.

30. *Sporting Life*.

31. Stephen D. Boren, "Blunders on the Base Paths Part of World Series Lore," *Baseball Digest*, October 1991.

32. Jones, ed., *Deadball Stars of the American League*, 552.

33. *Boston Globe*.

34. *Detroit Times*, May 16, 1908.

35. *Sporting Life*, May 10, 1913, p. 7.

36. *Sporting Life*, February 3, 1894.

37. *Cincinnati Commercial Tribune*, May 25, 1908.

38. *Cincinnati Commercial Tribune*, April 16, 1909.

39. *Sporting News*, July 29, 1909, pp. 1, 6.

40. *Sporting News*, July 29, 1909, pp. 1, 6.

41. "Play Ball," *Baseball Magazine*, June 1910, pp. 47–48.

42. John B. Foster, "Brooklyn Budget," *Sporting Life*, August 14, 1909.

43. Bob Addie, "Pickoff," *Street & Smith's Official 1971 Baseball Yearbook* (New York: Condé Nast Publications, 1971), 73.

44. *New York Times*.

7. 1910–1919: BAN TRIES TO BAN IT

1. *Washington Post*, May 19, 1910, p. 8.

2. *Washington Post*, May 19, 1910, p. 8.

3. *New York Telegram*.

4. *New York Telegram*, June 28, 1910.

5. *New York Times*, August 7, 1910.

6. *Detroit Free Press*, August 7, 1910.

7. *Chicago Tribune*, September 23, 1910.

8. *Atlantic Constitution*, June 3, 1911.

9. *Brooklyn Daily Eagle*, September 26, 1929.

10. *Washington Post*, July 10, 1911.

11. *New York Times*, June 15, 1912.

12. *Boston Herald*, June 18, 1912.

13. *Washington Post*, July 4, 1912, p. 4.

14. *New York Times*, July 15, 1912.

15. *Boston Globe*, August 30, 1912.

16. *Cincinnati Enquirer*, September 3, 1912, p. 8.

17. *Washington Post*, September 4, 1912, p. 8.

18. *Cincinnati Enquirer*, October 1, 1912.

19. *Sporting News*, April 17, 1913, p. 6.

20. *New York Times*, May 14, 1913.

21. *Frederick Post* (Maryland), May 29, 1913, p. 5.

22. *Cincinnati Enquirer*, June 1, 1913, p. 20.

23. *New York Times*, July 13, 1913.

24. *Sporting Life*, August 2, 1913, p. 9.

25. Ernest J. Lanigan, "Hidden Ball Works," *Baltimore Evening Sun*, August 12, 1919, p. 15.

26. *Sporting Life*, June 6, 1914, p. 8.

27. *Boston Globe*, May 27, 1914.

28. Ernest J. Lanigan, "Hidden-Ball Trick Has Fooled Many," *Ohio State Journal*, August 10, 1919.

29. *Boston Herald*, May 27, 1914, p. 8.

30. *St. Louis Star*, May 27, 1914.

31. *Pittsburgh Gazette Times*.

32. *Sporting News*, July 16, 1914, p. 3.

33. *Cleveland Plain Dealer*, June 24, 1914.

34. *Sporting News*, July 16, 1914, p. 3.

35. Lanigan, "Hidden Ball Trick Has Fooled Many."

36. Lanigan, "Hidden Ball Trick Has Fooled Many."

37. *Boston Post*, September 10, 1914, p. 10.

38. *St. Louis Post-Dispatch*, May 2, 1915, Sports, p. 1.

39. Lanigan, "Hidden Ball Works," p. 15.

40. *Sporting News*, August 19, 1915.

41. *St. Louis Times*, December 14, 1915.

42. *Sporting News*, December 9, 1953, p. 16.

43. *New York Times*, June 17, 1915.

44. *Washington Post*, August 30, 1915, p. 27.

45. *Sporting News*, August 17, 1916, p. 5.

46. *Detroit Free Press*, July 5, 1918.

47. *Washington Post*, July 27, 1918, p. 4.

48. *Toledo Blade*, April 20, 1925.

49. *Detroit Free Press*.

50. *Detroit News*, September 3, 1918.

51. *Boston Globe*, June 19, 1919.

52. *St. Louis Times*, June 19, 1919, p. 14.

53. *Boston Herald*, June 19, 1919, p. 16.

54. *Sporting News*, July 3, 1919, p. 4.

55. *Sporting News*, July 31, 1919, p. 5.

8. 1920–1929: A DECADE DOMINATED BY BABE WHO?

1. Mike Shatzkin, ed., *The Ballplayers: Baseball's Ultimate Biographical Reference* (New York: Arbor House, 1990).

2. *Detroit Free Press*, June 20, 1918.

3. *Toledo Blade*, April 20, 1925.

4. Billy Evans, "Glad Pinelli Is Gone," *Kansas City Star*, April 9, 1921, p. 8.

5. *Washington Post*, June 23, 1920.

6. *Detroit Free Press*.

7. *Baseball Digest*, November 1948, p. 54

8. Evans, "Glad Pinelli Is Gone," p. 8.

9. *Baseball Magazine*, December 1932, p. 312.

10. *St. Louis Post-Dispatch*, July 10, 1921.

11. *St. Louis Globe-Democrat*, July 10, 1921.

12. *Sporting News*.

13. *St. Louis Post-Dispatch*, July 10, 1921.

14. *New York Telegram*, July 12, 1921.

15. *Washington Post*, August 3, 1921, p. 10.

16. *Washington Post*, April 25, 1922, p. 14.

17. *Toledo Blade*, April 20, 1925.

18. *Washington Post*, May 27, 1923.

19. *Chicago Sunday Tribune*, May 18, 1924, sec. 2, p. 3.

20. *Chicago Tribune*, May 20, 1924.

21. *New York Times*, July 20, 1926.

22. Clifford Bloodgood, "The Hidden-Ball Trick," *Baseball Magazine*, July 1948, pp. 262, 285.

23. Dick Bartell, with Norman Macht, *Rowdy Richard* (Berkeley, CA: North Atlantic Books, 1993), 95.

24. Edgar Munzel, "Kamm-oflage!" *Baseball Digest*, November–December 1956, p. 49.

25. *Baseball Digest*.

26. *Chicago Tribune*, April 24, 1928.

27. *Baseball Digest*, July 1951, p. 72.

28. Francis J. Powers, "The Art of Nipping Base-Nappers," *Chicago Daily News*, April 26, 1945, p. 10.

29. *Chicago Tribune*, July 28, 1928, p. 15.

30. *New York Times*, September 14, 1928.

31. *New York Times*, April 21, 1929.

32. Gordon Cobbledick, "The Old Kamm-oflage," *Baseball Digest*, pp. 63–64.

33. *Elyria Chronicle Telegram*, May 1, 1929.

9. 1930–1939: THE CROW FLIES HIGH

1. *New York Times*, September 17, 1945.
2. *Boston Globe*.
3. Walter "Rabbit" Maranville, *Run, Rabbit, Run* (Cleveland, OH: Society for American Baseball Research, 1991), 73–74.
4. Sam Levy, *Milwaukee Journal*, January 1953, p. 34.
5. Shirley Povich, "This Morning," *Washington Post*, June 15, 1943.
6. *Sporting News*, July 26, 1931, p. 3.
7. *Boston Globe*, June 17, 1933.
8. *Sporting News*, June 22, 1933, pp. 1, 3, 8.
9. *Chicago Tribune*, June 16, 1933, p. 27.
10. *New York World-Telegram*.
11. *Sporting News*, August 4, 1948, p. 12.
12. *Baseball Digest*, May 1946, p. 54.
13. *Baseball Digest*, July 1951, pp. 71–72.
14. Bruce Nash and Alan Zullo, *The Baseball Hall of Shame 4* (New York: Pocket Books, 1991), p. 33.
15. *St. Louis Post-Dispatch*, May 10, 1936, p. 1B.
16. *Sporting News*, May 14, 1936, p. 8.
17. *Sporting News*, June 25, 1936.
18. *Baseball Digest*, September 1950, p. 72.
19. Povich, "This Morning," June 15, 1943.
20. *Sporting News*, November 10, 1938.
21. Clifford Bloodgood, "The Hidden-Ball Trick," *Baseball Magazine*, July 1948.
22. Telephone interview with Billy Werber, October 8, 2002.
23. *New York Times*, May 30, 1937.
24. *Sporting News*, June 3, 1937, p. 6.
25. *New York Times*, August 30, 1937.
26. *Sporting News*.
27. Bloodgood, "The Hidden-Ball Trick."
28. Edward T. Murphy, "Crosetti and His Pet Trick," *Baseball Magazine*, September 1938, p. 470.
29. Bloodgood, "The Hidden-Ball Trick."
30. Shirley Povich, "This Morning," *Washington Post*, July 5, 1938.
31. Murphy, "Crosetti and His Pet Trick," 440.
32. Murphy, "Crosetti and His Pet Trick," 440.
33. *Baseball Digest*, October–November 1960, p. 64.
34. Harold Kaese, *A Rooter's Guide to the Red Sox* (Boston: Self-published, 1974).

35. *Sporting News*, March 23, 1949, p. 28.

36. Frank Crosetti, correspondence with author, 2001.

37. Charles Segar, "Yanks Lose, 7–3, Then Win, 9–3; Henrich Hurt," *New York Mirror*, July 3, 1939, p. 23.

10. 1940–1949: PESKY HOLDING THE BALL

1. Transcript of February 24, 1990, speech by Al Brancato at the Historical Society of Pennsylvania.

2. *New York World-Telegram*, April 25, 1940.

3. *Helena Independent* (Montana), July 29, 1940, p. 8.

4. Bill Bryson, "Diamond Deceivers," *Baseball Magazine*, June 1942.

5. Shirley Povich, "This Morning," *Washington Post*, June 1, 1941.

6. Bill James, *The New Bill James Historical Baseball Abstract* (New York: Free Press, 2001), 455.

7. *Baseball Magazine*, June 1942.

8. *Sporting News*, June 12, 1941.

9. *Sporting News*, June 12, 1941.

10. *Philadelphia Inquirer*, August 14, 1941.

11. *Sporting News*.

12. Telephone interview with Bobby Bragan, January 28, 2008.

13. *Baseball Digest*, July 1946, p. 39.

14. *Washington Post*, June 1, 1942.

15. *Sporting News*, July 9, 1942, p. 2.

16. *Baseball Digest*, July 1946, p. 39.

17. *Chicago Daily Tribune*, August 23, 1942, p. B1.

18. Harold Kaese, *A Rooter's Guide to the Red Sox* (Boston: Self-published, 1974).

19. *Sporting News*, June 10, 1943, p. 8.

20. *Sporting News*, August 4, 1948, p. 12.

21. Dick Bartell, with Norman Macht, *Rowdy Richard* (Berkeley, CA: North Atlantic Books, 1993), 95–96.

22. *Baseball Digest*, July 1951.

23. Mike Blake, *Baseball Chronicles* (Cincinnati, OH: Betterway Books, 1994).

24. *Sporting News*, May 24, 1945, p. 10.

25. *Sporting News*, April 26, 1945, p. 6.

26. *Sporting News*, May 17, 1945, p. 14.

27. *Washington Post*, May 14, 1945, p. 8.

28. *Detroit Free Press*, May 18, 1945, p. 16.

29. William B. Mead, *Even the Browns* (Mineola, NY: Dover Publications, 2010).

30. *Sporting News*, May 31, 1945, pp. 6, 12.

31. *Baseball Digest*, August 1947, p. 59.

32. *Sporting News*, August 24, 1987, p. 50.

33. *Sporting News*, September 11, 1946.

34. *Sporting News*, July 16, 1947, p. 38.

35. Buddy Lewis, correspondence with author, April 2001.

36. *Sporting News*, May 19, 1948, p. 16.

37. Connie Ryan, "How I Work the Hidden-Ball Trick," *Sport*, October 1951, p. 66.

38. *Sporting News*, May 16, 1951, pp. 5, 18.

39. *St. Louis Post-Dispatch*.

40. Allen Lewis, "Fun Play: The Hidden-Ball Trick," *Baseball Digest*, June 1961, p. 63.

41. *Sporting News*, August 11, 1948, p. 7.

42. *Chicago Daily Tribune*, July 28, 1948, p. 1.

11. 1950–1959: "STEP OFF THE BASE A MINUTE, WILL YA?"

1. Billy Hitchcock, correspondence with author, February 2001.

2. *Sporting News*, July 12, 1950, p. 15.

3. *Philadelphia Inquirer*, July 2, 1950.

4. Shirley Povich, "This Morning," *Washington Post*, June 30, 1953, p. 14.

5. *Sporting News*, July 26, 1950, pp. 8, 30.

6. Shirley Povich, "This Morning," *Washington Post*, July 20, 1950, p. 19.

7. *Street & Smith's Official 1953 Baseball Yearbook* (New York: Condé Nast Publications, 1953).

8. *New York World-Telegram-Star*, May 7, 1951.

9. *Sporting News*, May 16, 1951, pp. 5, 18.

10. Connie Ryan, "How I Work the Hidden-Ball Trick," *Sport*, October 1951, p. 66.

11. *Sporting News*, January 2, 1952, Section 2, p. 3.

12. *Sporting News*, April 22, 1953, p. 12.

13. *Philadelphia Inquirer*, June 16, 1952.

14. *Sporting News*.

15. Steve Cameron, *Baseball Digest*, November 1980, p. 81.

16. *Sporting News*, July 23, 1952, p. 9.

17. Hitchcock, correspondence with author, February 2001.

18. *Sporting News*, July 30, 1952, p. 21.

19. *New York Times*, May 1, 1953, p. 26.

20. Bruce Nash and Allan Zullo, *The Baseball Hall of Shame 2* (New York: Pocket Books, 1986), 13.

21. Dan Gutman, *It Ain't Cheatin' If You Don't Get Caught* (New York: Penguin, 1990).

22. Clif Keane, *Sporting News*, July 1, 1953, p. 11.

23. Povich, "This Morning," June 30, 1953, p. 14.

24. *Elyria Chronicle Telegram* (Ohio), July 10, 1953, p. 6.

25. Warren G. Giles, July 21, 1953, letter from the National League president to National League umpires.

26. *Sporting News*, July 6, 1955, p. 19.

27. *Bridgeport Post* (Connecticut), June 25, 1955.

28. Harold Kaese, *A Rooter's Guide to the Red Sox* (Boston: Self-published, 1974).

29. *Chicago Daily Tribune*, May 14, 1956, p. E1.

30. *Sporting News*, August 19, 1959, p. 25.

12. 1960–1969: STICK WAS SLICK

1. *Sporting News*, July 5, 1961, p. 28.

2. *Sporting News*, July 12, 1961, p. 37.

3. *Sporting News*, July 14, 1962, p. 17.

4. *Sporting News*, June 22, 1968, p. 20.

5. *Sporting News*, August 10, 1963, p. 26.

6. *Sporting News*, October 5, 1963, p. 47.

7. *Sporting News*, January 17, 1962, p. 29.

8. *Sporting News*, July 1, 1967, p. 22.

9. *Sporting News*, June 22, 1968, p. 20.

10. *Sporting News*, July 4, 1970, p. 15.

11. Harold Kaese, *A Rooter's Guide to the Red Sox* (Boston: Self-published, 1974).

12. *Sporting News*, October 5, 1968, p. 56.

13. *Sporting News*, July 4, 1970, p. 15.

13. 1970–1979: ELEMENTARY, MY DEAR WATSON

1. Bob Addie, "Pickoff," *Street & Smith's Official 1971 Baseball Yearbook* (New York: Condé Nast Publications, 1971), 73.

2. *Sporting News*, July 4, 1970, p. 15.

3. *Baseball Digest*, November 1980, p. 81.

4. *Sporting News*, August 15, 1970, pp. 13, 30.

5. Addie, "Pickoff," 73.

6. *New York Times*, July 7, 2002.

7. *Sporting News*.

8. *Sporting News*, April 4, 1983, p. 19.

9. *New York Times*, July 7, 2002.

10. *Sporting News*, July 6, 1974, p. 22.

11. *Sporting News*, September 18, 1976, pp. 22, 28.

12. Dan Gutman, *It Ain't Cheatin' If You Don't Get Caught* (New York: Penguin, 1990).

14. 1980–1989: HAPPY BIRTHDAY, KID!

1. *Sporting News*, April 25, 1981, p. 32.

2. *Sporting News*, May 2, 1981, p. 56.

3. *Baseball Digest*, July 1981, p. 16.

4. *Boston Globe*, August 18, 1984, p. 29.

5. *Sporting News*, August 5, 1985, p. 24.

6. *Boston Herald*, July 8, 1985, p. 50.

7. *Boston Globe*, July 8, 1985, p. 30.

8. *Sporting News*, August 16, 1980, p. 41.

9. *Boston Herald*, July 23, 1985, p. B3.

10. *Boston Globe*, July 22, 1985, pp. 26, 32.

11. *Boston Globe*, July 22, 1985, pp. 26, 32.

12. *Boston Globe*, July 22, 1985, p. 32.

13. *Sporting News*, August 5, 1985, pp. 22, 24.

14. *Sports Collectors Digest*, September 16, 1994.

15. *Sporting News*, July 14, 1986, p. 23.

16. *Sporting News*, September 19, 1988, p. 22.

15. 1990–1999: MASTER MATT

1. *Sporting News*, May 28, 1990, p. 19.

2. *USA Today Baseball Weekly*, July 6–13, 1994, p. 23.

3. *USA Today Baseball Weekly*, September 24–30, 1997, p. 3.

4. *Baseball Digest*, January 1998, p. 63.

5. *San Francisco Examiner*, April 26, 1998, p. D-6.

6. *USA Today Baseball Weekly*, June 30, 1999–July 6, 1999, p. 17.

16. 2000–PRESENT: A DYING ART?

1. *Palm Beach Post*.

2. *Chicago Sun-Times*.

3. Todd Jones, "The Closer," *Sporting News*, August 26, 2005.

4. *Miami Herald*.

5. *Arizona Republic*.

6. *Boston Globe*, June 9, 2007.

7. ESPNLosAngeles.com, August 10, 2013.

8. Thomas Harding, "Dickerson's Walk-off Triple Ends 15-Inning Marathon," *MLB.com*, September 20, 2013. Available online at http://colorado.rockies.mlb.com/mlb/gameday/index.jsp?gid=2013_09_19_slnmlb_colmlb_1&mode=recap&c_id=col (accessed October 13, 2014).

17. TRICKS GONE AWRY

1. *Sporting Life*, September 11, 1889.

2. *Sporting Life*, June 17, 1893, p. 4.

3. Ira L. Smith, *Baseball's Famous First Basemen* (New York: A. S. Barnes and Company, 1956).

4. Bill James, *The New Bill James Historical Baseball Abstract* (New York: Free Press, 2001), 452.

5. *Chicago Tribune*, April 24, 1905.

6. *Chicago Tribune*.

7. *Washington Post*, May 19, 1910.

8. *New York Times*, July 23, 1910.

9. *New York Times*, August 29, 1910.

10. *Chicago Daily Tribune*, September 4, 1910, p. C1.

11. *Washington Post*, October 24, 1910.

12. *New York Times*, June 9, 1918.

13. *Baseball Digest*, November 1948, p. 53.

14. *Baseball Magazine*, March 1949, p. 332.

15. Billy Evans, "Glad Pinelli Is Gone," *Kansas City Star*, April 9, 1921, p. 8.

16. *Washington Post*, June 10, 1923.

17. *Pittsburgh Gazette Times*.

18. *New York Times*, August 6, 1926.

19. *New York Times*, May 1, 1932.

20. Francis J. Powers, "The Art of Nipping Base-Nappers," *Baseball Digest*, May 1945.

21. *New York World-Telegram*, July 1, 1936.

22. *Sporting News*, September 16, 1937, p. 4.

23. *New York Times*.

24. *Sporting News*, October 14, 1937, p. 7.

25. Edward T. Murphy, "Crosetti and His Pet Trick," *Baseball Magazine*, September 1938, p. 471.

26. *New York Times*, May 29, 1938.

27. *New York Times*, May 18, 1941.

28. *New York Times*, June 3, 1941.

29. *New York Times*.

30. *Sporting News*.

31. *New York Times*, May 16, 1942.

32. *New York Times*, June 24, 1942.

33. *Sporting News*, May 19, 1948, p. 2.

34. *Sporting News*, August 11, 1948, p. 7.

35. *New York Times*, August 26, 1948.

36. *Sporting News*, September 8, 1948, p. 17.

37. Shirley Povich, "This Morning," *Washington Post*, July 20, 1950, p. 19.

38. *Sporting News*, May 7, 1952, p. 6.

39. *New York Herald Tribune*.

40. *New York Times*, October 4, 1953.

41. *Sporting News*, October 14, 1953, p. 21.

42. Harold Kaese, *A Rooter's Guide to the Red Sox* (Boston: Self-published, 1974).

43. *New York Times*, October 5, 1957.

44. *Sporting News*, August 23, 1961, p. 6.

45. *Sporting News*, August 11, 1962, p. 32.

46. *Sporting News*, August 24, 1968, p. 8.

47. *New York Times*, August 7, 1970.

48. Ron Luciano, *The Umpire Strikes Back* (New York: Bantam, 1982).

49. *Boston Globe*, August 9, 1984.

50. *Boston Globe*, April 11, 1986.

51. *Boston Globe*, October 9, 1986.

52. *Boston Globe*, May 22, 1989.

18. UNSUBSTANTIATED POSSIBILITIES

1. *New York Clipper*, September 6, 1879, p. 187.

2. *Buffalo Courier*, September 1, 1881; *Chicago Tribune*, September 11, 1881.

3. *Chicago Tribune*, April 26, 1891.

4. *Chicago Times*.

5. *Washington Post*, April 26, 1891.

6. *Washington Post*, January 30, 1910, p. M8.

7. *Spartanburg Herald-Journal* (South Carolina), July 14, 1968.

8. *Waukesha Daily Freeman* (Wisconsin), November 5, 1923.

9. *Baseball Digest*, January–February 1955, p. 70.

10. *Baseball Digest*, April 1954, p. 32.

11. Bruce Nash and Allan Zullo, *The Baseball Hall of Shame's Warped Record Book* (New York: Collier, 1991).

12. *Baseball Digest*, November 1948, p. 54.

13. *Sporting News*, August 11, 1948, p. 7.

14. *Baseball Digest*, October 1951, p. 78.

15. Dick Bartell, with Norman Macht, *Rowdy Richard* (Berkeley, CA: North Atlantic Books, 1993), 95.

16. *Sporting News*, April 26, 1945, p. 10.

17. *Sporting News*, May 24, 1945, p. 12.

18. Bartell, with Macht, *Rowdy Richard*, p. 95.

19. Dan Schlossberg, *The Baseball Catalog*, Millennium ed. (Middle Village, NY: Jonathan David Publishers, 2000).

20. *Baseball Digest*, July 1951, p. 71.

21. *Baseball Digest*, July 1946, p. 39.

22. Paul Dickson, *The New Dickson Baseball Dictionary* (San Diego, CA: Harcourt Brace & Company, 1999), 244.

23. *Washington Post*, January 13, 1962, p. A10.

24. David Pietrusza, Matthew Silverman, and Michael Gershman, eds., *Baseball: The Biographical Encyclopedia* (Kingston, NY: Total Sports Illustrated, 2000), 730.

25. Bill James, *The New Bill James Historical Baseball Abstract* (New York: Free Press, 2001), 636.

19. ODDS AND ENDS

1. *Brooklyn Daily Eagle*, May 20, 1873.

2. *Brooklyn Daily Eagle*, May 20, 1873.

3. *New York Clipper*, July 11, 1874, p. 115.

4. *New York Clipper*, November 2, 1878.

5. *Hartford Post*, September 11, 1874.

6. *Sporting News*, March 10, 1888.

7. *St. Louis Republican*, July 25, 1875.

8. *Cincinnati Enquirer*.

9. *New York Clipper*, October 30, 1875.

10. *Cincinnati Enquirer*, April 24, 1877.

11. *New York Clipper*, October 11, 1879, p. 229.

12. *Sporting Life*, May 20, 1883.

13. *Sporting Life*, May 6, 1885.

14. *Sporting Life*, October 28, 1885.

15. *Sporting News*, June 11, 1887, p. 4.

16. *Chicago Times*.

17. *Sporting News*, April 21, 1900.

18. *Washington Post*, June 29, 1902, p. 9.

19. *Chicago Tribune*.

20. *New York Times*, March 22, 1910.

21. *Washington Post*, April 5, 1912.

22. *Detroit News*, June 19, 1913.

23. *St. Louis Globe-Democrat*, August 8, 1915.

24. *Street & Smith's Official 1971 Baseball Yearbook* (New York: Condé Nast Publications, 1971).

25. *Washington Star*, July 14, 1918.

26. *St. Louis Times*, June 13, 1919, p. 14.

27. *Sporting News*.

28. *Cleveland Plain Dealer*.

29. *New York Times*, April 16, 1931.

30. *New York Times*, January 19, 1942.

31. *New York Times*, April 7, 1933.

32. *New York Times*, May 18, 1939.

33. Mark Armour, ed., *Rain Check: Baseball in the Pacific Northwest* (Cleveland, OH: Society for American Baseball Research, 2006), 73.

34. *Boston Herald*, July 23, 1985, p. B3.

35. *New York Times*, March 23, 1948.

36. Shirley Povich, "This Morning," *Washington Post*, July 20, 1950, p. 19.

37. *Portland Press-Herald* (Maine), March 29, 1948.

38. *Sporting News*, April 7, 1948, p. 14.

39. *Sporting News*, September 10, 1952, p. 12.

40. *New York Times*, June 14, 1948.

41. Povich, "This Morning," *Washington Post*, July 20, 1950, p. 19.

42. *New York Times*, July 7, 1950.

43. *Sporting News*, June 20, 1951, p. 37.

44. *Street & Smith's Official 1953 Baseball Yearbook* (New York: Condé Nast Publications, 1953).

45. Hank Aaron, with Lonnie Wheeler, *I Had a Hammer* (New York: HarperCollins, 1991), 90.

46. *Baseball Digest*, August 1955, p. 40.

47. *Chicago American*.

48. *Sporting News*, September 9, 1972.

49. *Sports Illustrated*, August 28, 1972, p. 12.

50. *Boston Herald*, July 8, 1985, p. 50.

51. *Riverside Press-Enterprise*, October 1, 1992.

52. Paul Dickson, *New Dickson Baseball Dictionary* (San Diego, CA: Harcourt Brace & Company, 1999), 244–45.

53. David Brown, "Rangers Pull Hidden-Ball Trick without Even Trying on Wandering Astros Rookie Max Stassi," *Yahoo! Sports Online*, September 20, 2013. Available online at http://sports.yahoo.com/blogs/big-league-stew/rangers-pull-hidden-ball-trick-without-even-trying-143722744.html (accessed October 14, 2014).

Appendix A

SUCCESSFUL EXECUTIONS OF THE HIDDEN-BALL TRICK (264): AN INCOMPLETE LISTING

Note: This section was compiled with major assistance from Retrosheet and notable contributions by, alphabetically, David Arcidiacono, Greg Beston, Charlie Bevis, Cliff Blau, Steve Boren, Jim Charlton, Clem Comly, Dan Desrochers, John Gecik, Mike Grahek, Billy Hitchcock, Dick Hunt, Herm Krabbenhoft, Dave Lamoureaux, John Lewis, Joe McGillen, Peter Morris, Rod Nelson, Bill Nowlin, Marc Okkonen, Tom Ruane, Joseph St. George, David Smith, Lyle Spatz, Steve Steinberg, Dick Thompson, Rich Thurston, Bob Timmermann, Wayne Townsend, Frank Vaccaro, and David Vincent, among others.

Date	In.	LG	Perpetrator	P	Club	Victim	Club	Notes
05/01/1876	3	NL	Jack Burdock to Everett Mills	2B 1B	HAR	Joe Borden	BOS	
05/08/1876	8	NL	Mike McGeary	2B	SL	John Peters	CHI	
05/25/1876	1	NL	Bill Hague	3B	LOU	George Zettlein	PHI	
05/25/1876	7	NL	Tom Carey to Bob Ferguson	SS 3B	HAR	Cap Anson	CHI	
06/29/1876	7	NL	Cherokee Fisher to Charlie Gould	SS 1B	CIN	Jack Remsen	HAR	
08/09/1876	5	NL	Jack Burdock	2B	HAR	William Coon	PHI	
09/05/1876		NL	Davy Force	SS	PHI	Ross Barnes	CHI	
06/28/1877	7	NL	Bill Craver	SS	LOU	Tim Murnane	BOS	

Date	In.	LG	Perpetrator	P	Club	Victim	Club	Notes
05/20/1881	9	NL	Ed Williamson to Joe Quest	3B 2B	CHI	Jack Burdock	BOS	
05/23/1884		AA	Jim Field	1B	COL	C. Comiskey	SL	
06/17/1884		NL	Dan Brouthers	1B	BUF	Billy Sunday	CHI	
07/04/1884 (2)		AA	Pete Browning	3B	LOU	Adonis Terry	BKN	Hecker aids
07/10/1884		UA	John Irwin	3B	BOS	C. Householder	CHI	
09/27/1884		NL	Dan Brouthers	1B	BUF	Buck Ewing	NY	
06/23/1886	9	NL	Dan Brouthers	1B	DET	Ed Andrews	PHI	ends game
05/17/1887	2	AA	Joe Werrick	3B	LOU	Chris Fulmer	BAL	
06/17/1888	9	AA	Jack Farrell	2B	BAL	Bob Caruthers	BKN	ends game
05/04/1889	3	NL	John M. Ward to Roger Connor	SS 1B	NY	Sam Thompson	PHI	
05/26/1889	9	AA	Bill Shindle to Reddy Mack	3B 2B	BAL	Curt Welch	PHI	
07/02/1889	9	NL	Patsy Tebeau	3B	CLE	Walt Wilmot	WAS	
08/09/1890	3	AA	Charlie Reilly	3B	COL	Dave McKeough	ROC	
09/18/1892 (2)	4	NL	Sy Sutcliffe	1B	BAL	Chief Zimmer	CLE	
05/22/1893		NL	Jake Beckley	1B	PIT	Kid Gleason	SL	
05/30/1893 (1)	3	NL	Jake Beckley	1B	PIT	Joe Kelley	BAL	
06/05/1893	7	NL	Perry Werden	1B	SL	John M. Ward	NY	
06/07/1893	7	NL	Perry Werden	1B	SL	Tommy Burns	BKN	
09/28/1893	9	NL	Jake Beckley	1B	PIT	John M. Ward	NY	Kelly coach
06/19/1894	8	NL	Piggy Ward	2B	WAS	T. Corcoran	BKN	
07/04/1894 (1)		NL	Ed Cartwright	1B	WAS	Joe Quinn	SL	
04/28/1896	2	NL	Ed Cartwright	1B	WAS	Willie Keeler	BAL	
08/19/1896 (1)	1	NL	Gene DeMontreville	SS	WAS	Cupid Childs	CLE	
08/27/1896 (1)		NL	Jim Rogers	1B	LOU	Fielder Jones	BKN	
04/22/1897		NL	Perry Werden	1B	LOU	Chief Zimmer	CLE	

Date	In.	LG	Perpetrator	P	Club	Victim	Club	Notes
05/26/1897		NL	Jim Rogers to Perry Werden	2B 1B	LOU	Herman Long	BOS	Opening Day
05/27/1897	2	NL	Jim Rogers to Perry Werden	2B 1B	LOU	John O'Brien	WAS	
06/02/1897	7	NL	Ed Cartwright	1B	WAS	Tim Donahue	CHI	
07/09/1900	5	NL	Bob Wood	3B	CIN	Elmer Flick	PHI	C. Peitz aids
05/08/1901	9	NL	John Ganzel	1B	NY	Harry Wolverton	PHI	at 3B; ends game
09/24/1901	2	AL	Bill Coughlin	3B	WAS	Jack Cronin	DET	
04/17/1902		NL	Jake Beckley	1B	CIN	Frank Chance	CHI	Opening Day
05/02/1902		AL	Candy LaChance	1B	BOS	Billy Gilbert	BAL	
05/11/1902	5	NL	Hal O'Hagan	1B	CHI	Doc Newton	BKN	
05/13/1902	7	NL	Charlie Dexter	3B	CHI	Bill Dahlen	BKN	
05/15/1902	1	AL	Bill Coughlin	2B	WAS	Kip Selbach	BAL	
06/03/1902	4	AL	Bill Coughlin	SS	WAS	Ducky Holmes	DET	
06/25/1902	1	AL	Bill Coughlin	SS	WAS	Patsy Dougherty	BOS	
06/25/1902	8	NL	Rudy Hulswitt	SS	PHI	Steve Brodie	NY	
05/30/1903 (1)	6	NL	Dutch Jordan	3B	BKN	Bill Hallman	PHI	
06/03/1904	9	NL	Fred Jacklitsch	1B	BKN	Ed Phelps	PIT	
06/13/1904	8	AL	Wid Conroy	SS	NY	Doc White	CHI	
06/24/1904	10	AL	Bill Coughlin	3B	WAS	D. McGuire	NY	
08/26/1904	2	AL	Hunter Hill to Mal Kittridge	3B C	WAS	Charlie Carr	CLE	
04/22/1905	6	AL	Germany Schaefer	2B	DET	Lee Tannehill	CHI	
04/29/1905	3	AL	Hunter Hill	3B	WAS	Freddy Parent	BOS	
05/06/1905	7	NL	Fred Abbott	1B	PHI	Fred Mitchell	BKN	
05/12/1905	2	AL	Bill Coughlin	3B	DET	Hobe Ferris	BOS	Cy Young coach
07/23/1905	1	AL	George Davis	SS	CHI	Topsy Hartsel	PHI	
08/03/1905	9	NL	Shad Barry	1B	CIN	Charlie Malay	BKN	
05/12/1906	1	NL	Shad Barry to Tommy Corcoran	1B SS	CIN	R. Bresnahan	NY	
05/18/1906	8	NL	Honus Wagner	SS	PIT	Bill Dahlen	NY	

Date	In.	LG	Perpetrator	P	Club	Victim	Club	Notes
09/03/1906 (2)	1	AL	Bill Coughlin	3B	DET	George Stone	SL	
04/13/1907	6	AL	Lave Cross to Nig Perrine	3B SS	WAS	Wid Conroy	NY	
08/19/1907	12	AL	Charley O'Leary	3B	DET	John Knight	BOS	
09/22/1907 (2)	7	NL	Fred Tenney	1B	BOS	Joe Tinker	CHI	ends game
10/09/1907	1	—	Germany Schaefer to Bill Coughlin	2B 3B	DET	Jimmy Slagle	CHI-N	World Series Game 2
05/13/1908	3	AL	Bill Coughlin	3B	DET	A. McConnell	BOS	
05/24/1908	9	NL	Miller Huggins	2B	CIN	Tim Jordan	BKN	
08/29/1908	2	AL	Harry Lord	3B	BOS	Tom Jones	SL	
04/15/1909	3	NL	Miller Huggins to Dick Hoblitzel	2B 1B	CIN	Fred Clarke	PIT	opener
07/22/1909	8	NL	Johnny Evers to Frank Chance	2B 1B	CHI	Josh Devore	NY	PR
07/31/1909	4	NL	Miller Huggins	3B	CIN	Wally Clement	BKN	
05/18/1910	6	AL	George Stovall	1B	CLE	Gabby Street	WAS	
05/19/1910	10	AL	George Stovall	1B	CLE	Hal Chase	NY	
06/28/1910	4	NL	Joe Ward	1B	PHI	Josh Devore	NY	
07/13/1910	9	AL	Hal Chase	1B	NY	George Stovall	CLE	revenge
08/06/1910	5	AL	George Moriarty to Jim Delahanty	3B 2B	DET	Birdie Cree	NY	
09/22/1910 (1)	5	NL	Fred Merkle	1B	NY	Johnny Evers	CHI	
06/01/1911 (2)	1	NL	Miller Huggins	2B	SL	Bob Bescher	CIN	
06/30/1911	9	NL	Miller Huggins	2B	SL	Max Carey	PIT	
07/09/1911	2	AL	Charley O'Leary	2B	DET	Jack Lelivelt	WAS	
09/01/1911	9	AL	Ivy Olson	SS	CLE	Felix Chouinard	CHI	PR
04/14/1912	8	NL	Arnold Hauser	SS	SL	Jimmy Sheckard	CHI	
05/11/1912	5	AL	George Stovall	1B	SL	Les Nunamaker	BOS	
06/15/1912	6	AL	Del Pratt to George Stovall	2B 1B	SL	Bert Daniels	NY	
06/17/1912 (1)		NL	Ed McDonald to Johnny Kling	3B C	BOS	A. Marsans	CIN	

Date	In.	LG	Perpetrator	P	Club	Victim	Club	Notes
07/03/1912 (1)	2	AL	Chick Gandil	1B	WAS	Jack Martin	NY	
07/14/1912 (1)	6	NL	Wally Smith	3B	SL	Fred Snodgrass	NY	
08/29/1912	7	NL	Ed McDonald	3B	BOS	Doc Miller	PHI	
09/02/1912 (2)	7	NL	Dick Egan	2B	CIN	Bob Harmon	SL	PR
09/03/1912	7	AL	George McBride	SS	WAS	Eddie Murphy	PHI	
09/25/1912 (1)	4	AL	Del Pratt to Jimmy Austin	2B 3B	SL	Rollie Zeider	CHI	
09/30/1912	6	NL	Miller Huggins	2B	SL	Hank Severeid	CIN	
04/13/1913		AL	George Stovall	1B	SL	Frank Lange	CHI	
05/14/1913		AL	Ivy Olson	3B	CLE	Birdie Cree	NY	
05/28/1913	3	AL	George Stovall	1B	SL	Donie Bush	DET	
05/31/1913 (2)	1	NL	Lee Magee to Ed Konetchy	2B 1B	SL	Johnny Bates	CIN	
07/13/1913	9	AL	Del Pratt to Bunny Brief	2B 1B	SL	Ezra Midkiff	NY	
07/28/1913	9	NL	Art Phelan	3B	CHI	Wilson Collins	BOS	PR; ends game
05/26/1914	2	AL	Buzzy Wares	SS	SL	Amos Strunk	PHI	
05/26/1914	5	AL	Nap Lajoie	2B	CLE	Del Gainer	BOS	
05/26/1914	7	NL	Miller Huggins to Dots Miller	2B 1B	SL	Jack Martin	BOS	
05/30/1914 (2)	11	FL	Otto Knabe	2B	BAL	Tex McDonald	PIT	
06/09/1914	8	NL	Honus Wagner	SS	PIT	Beals Becker	PHI	
06/23/1914	8	AL	Ivy Olson	3B	CLE	Bobby Veach	DET	
07/04/1914 (1)	8	FL	Eddie Holly	SS	PIT	Harvey Russell	BAL	
07/10/1914	9	AL	Billy Purtell to Marty Kavanaugh	3B 2B	DET	Eddie Collins	PHI	
07/14/1914 (1)	4	FL	Harry Swacina	1B	BAL	Everett Booe	BUF	
09/09/1914 (1)	1	NL	Rabbit Maranville to Red Smith	SS 3B	BOS	Jack Martin	PHI	Martin's 2nd in 1914
05/01/1915	7	NL	Miller Huggins	2B	SL	Tommy Leach	CIN	
05/10/1915	2	NL	Bob Fisher	SS	CHI	Doug Baird	PIT	

Date	In.	LG	Perpetrator	P	Club	Victim	Club	Notes
06/17/1915	9	NL	Alex McCarthy	SS	PIT	Dave Robertson	NY	
08/29/1915	8	AL	Del Pratt	2B	SL	Horace Milan	WAS	debut; PR
08/09/1916 (2)	2	NL	Bruno Betzel	2B	SL	Fred Merkle	NY	
07/03/1918	9	NL	Bob Fisher	2B	SL	Dode Paskert	CHI	
07/04/1918 (2)	6	AL	Ty Cobb	1B	DET	Joe Benz	CHI	
07/26/1918	4	AL	Jimmy Austin	SS	SL	Wildfire Schulte	WAS	
09/02/1918 (2)		AL	Babe Pinelli	3B	CHI	George Harper	DET	
06/18/1919	9	AL	Jimmy Austin	3B	SL	Wally Schang	BOS	ends game
07/25/1919	1	AL	Fred McMullin	3B	CHI	Joe Gedeon	SL	
09/11/1919 (2)	3	NL	Gene Paulette to Lena Blackburne	2B 3B	PHI	Billy Southworth	PIT	
06/19/1920	6	AL	Babe Pinelli	3B	DET	Stuffy McInnis	BOS	
06/22/1920	1	AL	Babe Pinelli	3B	DET	Sam Rice	WAS	
08/08/1920	5	AL	Ralph Young	2B	DET	Ping Bodie	NY	Pinelli aids
09/18/1920	4	AL	Bucky Harris	2B	WAS	Doc Johnston	CLE	
07/04/1921 (2)		AL	Jimmy Austin	SS	SL	Joe Sargent	DET	
07/09/1921	9	AL	Jimmy Austin	SS	SL	Patsy Gharrity	WAS	ends game
08/02/1921	5	AL	Bobby Jones	3B	DET	Bing Miller	WAS	
04/22/1922	7	NL	Jack Fournier	1B	SL	Max Carey	PIT	
04/24/1922	1	AL	Joe Judge	1B	WAS	Shano Collins	BOS	
06/24/1922 (2)	1	AL	George Burns	1B	BOS	Chick Fewster	NY	
07/11/1922	2	AL	Joe Judge	1B	WAS	Johnny Mostil	CHI	
08/20/1922 (2)	4	NL	Babe Pinelli to Ike Caveney	3B SS	CIN	Ray Schmandt	BKN	
09/21/1922	8	AL	Bobby Jones to Johnny Bassler	3B C	DET	Everett Scott	NY	
05/26/1923	5	AL	Johnny Mitchell	SS	BOS	Bucky Harris	WAS	
05/17/1924	7	AL	Danny Clark	3B	BOS	Roy Elsh	CHI	

Date	In.	LG	Perpetrator	P	Club	Victim	Club	Notes
06/30/1926	4	AL	Marty McManus	3B	SL	H. Heilmann	DET	Ty Cobb coach
07/20/1926	4	NL	Frank Emmer to Babe Pinelli	SS 3B	CIN	Johnny Butler	BKN	
05/17/1927	2	NL	Chuck Dressen	3B	CIN	George Harper	NY	
04/23/1928	5	AL	Willie Kamm	3B	CHI	Jackie Tavener	DET	
07/27/1928	8	AL	Willie Kamm	3B	CHI	M. Cochrane	PHI	
09/13/1928	7	AL	Lu Blue	1B	SL	Art Shires	CHI	
04/21/1929	2	AL	Frank O'Rourke	3B	SL	N. Richardson	DET	
04/30/1929	7	AL	Willie Kamm	3B	CHI	C. Jamieson	CLE	triple play
07/18/1929	9	NL	Billy Rhiel to Dave Bancroft	2B SS	BKN	R. Stephenson	CHI	
09/20/1930	1	NL	Leo Durocher to Tony Cuccinello	SS 3B	CIN	Freddy Leach	NY	
06/25/1931	9	AL	Willie Kamm	3B	CLE	Jack Rothrock	BOS	
07/15/1931	9	NL	Joe Stripp to Tony Cuccinello	3B 2B	CIN	R. Maranville	BOS	
09/06/1931 (2)	6	NL	Leo Durocher to Tony Cuccinello	SS 2B	CIN	Chick Hafey	SL	triple play
06/15/1933	5	NL	Billy Jurges	SS	CHI	Hal Smith	PIT	pro-tested
08/21/1933	6	AL	Marty McManus	3B	BOS	Earl Averill	CLE	
07/15/1934 (1)	7	NL	Joe Stripp	3B	BKN	Bill DeLancey	SL	
08/22/1935	5	AL	Oscar Melillo	2B	BOS	Billy Rogell	DET	
05/09/1936	8	NL	Johnny Mize	1B	SL	Frank Demaree	CHI	
06/19/1936	8	AL	Frank Crosetti	SS	NY	Goose Goslin	DET	
05/29/1937 (1)	8	AL	Frank Crosetti	SS	NY	Billy Werber	PHI	
07/16/1937	3	AL	Frank Crosetti	SS	NY	B. Poffenberger	DET	
08/29/1937	5	AL	Frank Crosetti	SS	NY	Gee Walker	DET	
07/04/1938 (1)	5	AL	Frank Crosetti	SS	NY	George Case	WAS	
07/02/1939 (1)	6	AL	Frank Crosetti	SS	NY	Joe Cronin	BOS	
04/24/1940	5	AL	Frank Crosetti	SS	NY	Al Brancato	PHI	
07/28/1940	3	NL	Bobby Bragan	SS	PHI	Billy Werber	CIN	

Date	In.	LG	Perpetrator	P	Club	Victim	Club	Notes
06/01/1941 (2)	10	AL	Mike Tresh to Joe Kuhel	C 1B	CHI	Doc Cramer	WAS	
06/03/1941	8	NL	Bobby Bragan	SS	PHI	Augie Galan	CHI	
06/24/1941	2	AL	Lou Boudreau	SS	CLE	S. Newsome	BOS	
08/13/1941	4	NL	Bobby Bragan	SS	PHI	Dixie Walker	BKN	
05/31/1942 (2)	5	AL	Johnny Pesky	SS	BOS	Bill Zuber	WAS	
07/04/1942 (2)	8	AL	Johnny Pesky	SS	BOS	Tommy Henrich	NY	
08/22/1942	9	AL	Lou Boudreau	SS	CLE	Don Kolloway	CHI	
06/02/1943 (2)	8	AL	Bobby Doerr	2B	BOS	D. Galehouse	SL	
04/17/1945	6	AL	Tony Cuccinello	3B	CHI	Lou Boudreau	CLE	opener
05/13/1945 (1)	6	AL	Roy Schalk	2B	CHI	Harlond Clift	WAS	
05/23/1945	6	NL	Bill Schuster	SS	CHI	Jimmie Foxx	PHI	
09/02/1946 (1)	1	NL	Bill Rigney	3B	NY	Billy Herman	BOS	
07/06/1947 (1)	1	AL	Johnny Pesky	SS	BOS	Buddy Lewis	WAS	
05/12/1948	5	NL	Pee Wee Reese	SS	BKN	J. Vander Meer	CIN	
07/25/1948 (2)	2	NL	Connie Ryan	2B	BOS	Del Rice	SL	
07/27/1948	2	NL	Gene Mauch	2B	CHI	Dick Sisler	PHI	
07/01/1950	7	AL	Billy Hitchcock	2B	PHI	Eddie Yost	WAS	
07/18/1950	7	NL	Connie Ryan	2B	CIN	Monte Kennedy	NY	
09/08/1950	5	AL	Billy Hitchcock	2B	PHI	Mickey Grasso	WAS	
05/06/1951 (1)	10	NL	Connie Ryan	2B	CIN	W. Lockman	NY	
08/07/1951 (1)	8	NL	Earl Torgeson	1B	BOS	Willie Jones	PHI	
06/15/1952 (2)	6	AL	Billy Hitchcock	3B	PHI	Darrell Johnson	SL	
07/14/1952	8	AL	Ferris Fain	1B	PHI	Ray Coleman	CHI	
07/20/1952 (2)	3	AL	Billy Hitchcock	3B	PHI	Fred Hatfield	DET	
08/31/1952	7	AL	Neil Berry	SS	DET	Vic Wertz	SL	
04/30/1953	4	NL	Del Crandall to Joe Adcock	C 1B	MIL	Sal Yvars	NY	

Date	In.	LG	Perpetrator	P	Club	Victim	Club	Notes
06/21/1953	7	AL	Billy Hunter	SS	SL	Jimmy Piersall	BOS	
06/24/1955	9	AL	Chico Carrasquel	SS	CHI	Sammy White	BOS	
05/13/1956	1	AL	Earl Torgeson	1B	DET	Minnie Minoso	CHI	
06/05/1958	9	NL	Orlando Cepeda	1B	SF	Wes Covington	MIL	
07/29/1959	6	AL	Harmon Killebrew	3B	WAS	Harry Chiti	KC	
08/11/1959	1	NL	Joe Adcock	1B	MIL	Vada Pinson	CIN	Pinson's birthday
08/31/1960 (2)	9	NL	Joe Adcock	1B	MIL	George Altman	CHI	ends game
06/23/1961	8	NL	Joe Adcock	1B	MIL	Billy Williams	CHI	
06/30/1961	7	NL	Tony Taylor to Pancho Herrera	2B 1B	PHI	Willie Davis	LA	
07/16/1961	7	AL	Billy Moran	2B	LA	Gene Green	WAS	
08/14/1961	5	AL	Danny O'Connell	3B	WAS	Leon Wagner	LA	
08/16/1961	9	AL	Billy Martin	2B	MIN	Gene Stephens	KC	
07/01/1962 (1)		AL	Nellie Fox	2B	CHI	Al Luplow	CLE	
07/27/1963	2	NL	Frank Thomas	1B	NY	Jimmy Wynn	HOU	
09/20/1963 (1)	11	AL	Pedro Gonzalez	2B	NY	Ken Harrelson	KC	
07/17/1966 (2)	5	AL	Norm Cash	1B	DET	Chico Salmon	CLE	
09/04/1966	8	NL	Jim Ray Hart to Hal Lanier	3B 2B	SF	Orlando Cepeda	SL	
09/12/1966	6	NL	Bud Harrelson to Ron Hunt	SS 2B	NY	Lou Johnson	LA	
06/16/1967	2	NL	Chico Ruiz	2B	CIN	John Roseboro	LA	
05/08/1968	9	AL	Don Mincher	1B	CAL	Sandy Alomar	CHI	
06/05/1968	7	NL	Julio Gotay	2B	HOU	Julian Javier	SL	
09/17/1968	7	AL	Gene Michael	SS	NY	Tom Matchick	DET	
09/18/1968	5	AL	Joe Foy	3B	BOS	M. Rettenmund	BAL	
06/21/1969 (1)	11	AL	George Thomas	1B	BOS	Jerry Kenney	NY	
06/21/1969	5	AL	Tim Cullen	2B	WAS	Willie Horton	DET	
06/28/1969	6	AL	Gene Michael	SS	NY	Zoilo Versalles	CLE	
04/26/1970	2	NL	Bobby Wine	SS	MON	Willie Mays	SF	
06/13/1970	6	AL	Gene Michael	SS	NY	Joe Keough	KC	

Date	In.	LG	Perpetrator	P	Club	Victim	Club	Notes
07/27/1970	9	AL	Gene Michael	SS	NY	Jarvis Tatum	CAL	
06/09/1972	6	AL	Toby Harrah	SS	TEX	Paul Blair	BAL	
06/06/1973	5	AL	Gene Michael	SS	NY	Vic Harris	TEX	
06/14/1974	3	AL	Dave Nelson	2B	TEX	Bob Coluccio	MIL	
08/01/1975	6	AL	Jerry Terrell	1B	MIN	Nyls Nyman	CHI	
06/22/1976	2	AL	Jack Brohamer	2B	CHI	Hal McRae	KC	
08/29/1976	3	NL	Bob Watson	1B	HOU	Jerry Mumphrey	SL	
04/17/1977	8	NL	Bob Watson	1B	HOU	Pat Rockett	ATL	
07/09/1977	3	AL	Jim Spencer	1B	CHI	Ron LeFlore	DET	
05/06/1978	1	AL	Willie Randolph	2B	NY	Bump Wills	TEX	
08/27/1978	1	AL	John Mayberry	1B	TOR	Hosken Powell	MIN	
06/29/1980	8	NL	Rich Murray to Johnny LeMaster	1B SS	SF	Dusty Baker	LA	
07/03/1980 (2)	7	NL	Garry Templeton to Ken Oberkfell	SS 2B	SL	Bake McBride	PHI	
10/04/1980 (1)	7	AL	Lou Whitaker	2B	DET	Willie Randolph	NY	
04/10/1981	6	AL	Brian Doyle	2B	OAK	Glenn Adams	MIN	
04/14/1981	8	AL	Rod Carew	1B	CAL	Mike Heath	OAK	
06/12/1982	4	NL	Phil Garner	2B	HOU	Ruppert Jones	SD	
06/21/1982	2	AL	Mike Hargrove to Alan Bannister	1B 2B	CLE	Al Bumbry	BAL	
07/08/1982	7	AL	Bruce Bochte	1B	SEA	Rich Dauer	BAL	
09/27/1982 (2)	2	AL	Mike Squires to Vance Law	1B SS	CHI	Todd Cruz	SEA	
08/17/1984	7	AL	Jackie Gutierrez	SS	BOS	Tim Teufel	MIN	
07/07/1985	2	AL	Marty Barrett	2B	BOS	Bobby Grich	CAL	
07/21/1985	6	AL	Marty Barrett to Glenn Hoffman	2B SS	BOS	Doug DeCinces	CAL	
09/26/1985	7	AL	Kent Hrbek	1B	MIN	Bill Stein	TEX	
06/17/1986	3	AL	Dave Bergman	1B	DET	Alan Wiggins	BAL	
06/30/1986	8	AL	Steve Lombardozzi	2B	MIN	Mike Stanley	TEX	
04/08/1988	9	NL	Steve Jeltz	SS	PHI	Gary Carter	NY	ends game, Carter's birthday
05/08/1988	8	AL	Brad Wellman	2B	KC	Dale Sveum	MIL	

Date	In.	LG	Perpetrator	P	Club	Victim	Club	Notes
09/05/1988	2	AL	Marty Barrett to Jody Reed	2B SS	BOS	Jim Traber	BAL	
10/02/1988	6	AL	George Brett	1B	KC	Mike Diaz	CHI	
06/23/1989 (2)	9	AL	Greg Brock	1B	MIL	Ozzie Guillen	CHI	
08/05/1989	7	AL	Dave Bergman	1B	DET	Ozzie Guillen	CHI	
08/11/1989	9	NL	Jeff Treadway	2B	ATL	Marvell Wynne	SD	
05/18/1990	2	NL	Delino DeShields	2B	MON	Terry Kennedy	SF	
04/27/1991	6	NL	Jeff Treadway	2B	ATL	Eric Yelding	HOU	
05/13/1991	4	AL	Steve Lyons	2B	BOS	Ozzie Guillen	CHI	
07/08/1992 (2)	3	NL	Delino DeShields	2B	MON	Jose Offerman	LA	
06/28/1994	6	NL	Matt Williams	3B	SF	R. Bournigal	LA	
06/28/1995	1	NL	Vinny Castilla	3B	COL	Darren Lewis	SF	
05/30/1996	4	NL	Eric Karros	1B	LA	Glenn Murray	PHI	
08/19/1997 (1)	3	AL	Robin Ventura to Ray Durham	3B 2B	CHI	Jose Cruz Jr.	TOR	
09/19/1997 (2)	1	AL	Matt Williams	3B	CLE	Jed Hansen	KC	
04/25/1998	3	AL	Rafael Palmeiro	1B	BAL	R. Henderson	OAK	
06/26/1999	4	NL	J. T. Snow	1B	SF	Carlos Perez	LA	
09/15/2004 (1)	4	NL	Mike Lowell	3B	FLA	Brian Schneider	MON	
08/10/2005	8	NL	Mike Lowell	3B	FLA	Luis Terrero	ARI	
06/08/2007	3	—	Julio Lugo	SS	BOS	A. Callaspo	ARI	interleague
08/10/2013	4	—	James Loney to Yunel Escobar to Evan Longoria	1B SS 3B	TB	Juan Uribe	LA (N)	interleague
09/19/2013	1	NL	Todd Helton	1B	COL	Matt Carpenter	SL	

Appendix B

UNSUBSTANTIATED POSSIBILITIES (38)

Date	In.	LG	Perpetrator	P	Club	Victim	Club	Notes
08/1879		NL	Ed Cogswell	1B	BOS	Al Hall	TRO	
08/1881		NL	Dan Brouthers	1B	BUF	Billy Taylor	CLE	
07/08/1887	7	AA	Jim Toy	SS	CLE	Ed Seward	PHI	
04/25/1891		NL		1B	PIT	Bill Dahlen	CHI	
04/25/1891		AA	Bill Hallman	2B	PHI	Gil Hatfield	WAS	
1905–1909		NL	Del Howard					
08/19/1907	7	AL			CHI	Sam Lanford	WAS	Lanford's debut
1911–1913		NL	Mickey Doolan	SS	PHI			
1916		NL		SS	SL	Casey Stengel	BKN	
1916		NL	Larry Doyle	2B	NY	Rabbit Maranville	BOS	
1920		AL	Babe Pinelli	3B	DET	Ossie Vitt	BOS	
1921–1924		NL	Rabbit Maranville	PIT		Hy Myers		
1922–1936		NL	Travis Jackson	SS	NY			
1923–1926		AL	Willie Kamm	3B	CHI			Mor'ty ump
1926–1929		AL	Jimmy Dykes	2B	PHI	Bill Regan	BOS	
1931–1940		NL	Tony Cuccinello			Ernie Lombardi		
1933–1937		NL				Leo Durocher	SL	
09/11/1936	2	AL	Billy Rogell	SS	DET	Pat Malone	NY	
1942		AL	Lou Boudreau to Ray Mack	SS 2B	CLE			

Date	In.	LG	Perpetrator	P	Club	Victim	Club	Notes
05/30/1951 (1)		AL	Phil Rizzuto	SS	NY	Walt Dropo	BOS	
1951		AL	Billy Hitchcock		PHI			
1955–1969		NL	Ken Boyer			Willie Mays		
1956–1963		AL	Nellie Fox	2B	CHI	Billy Gardner		
1960–1966		AL			NY	Ken Hamlin		
1961		AL	Danny O'Connell		WAS	Norm Cash	DET	
1973–1975			Cookie Rojas					
1968–1982		AL	Jim Spencer	1B				On *TWIB*
1968–1982			John Mayberry	1B				4x in all
1972–1982		AL	John Mayberry	1B		Bobby Grich		
1977–1978		AL	Mike Hargrove	1B	TEX	Andre Thornton	CLE	
1977–1988		AL	Eddie Murray		BAL			
06/29/1978	6	NL	Pat Rockett	SS	ATL	Johnny Oates	LA	
1981–1983		NL	Dave Bergman	1B	SF	Alan Wiggins	SD	
1985–2000			Ozzie Guillen					2x/2 days
1987–1997			Matt Williams					
1988–1992		NL	Mark Grace	1B	CHI	Mike Scioscia	LA	
1991–1998		AL	Mo Vaughn	1B				
1994		NL				Orlando Miller	HOU	2x/game

BIBLIOGRAPHY

BOOKS

Aaron, Hank, with Lonnie Wheeler. *I Had a Hammer*. New York: HarperCollins, 1991.

Armour, Mark, ed. *Rain Check: Baseball in the Pacific Northwest*. Cleveland, OH: Society for American Baseball Research, 2006.

Bartell, Dick, with Norman Macht. *Rowdy Richard*. Berkeley, CA: North Atlantic Books, 1993.

Blake, Mike. *Baseball Chronicles*. Cincinnati, OH: Betterway Books, 1994.

Commissioner of Baseball. *2004 Official Rules of Major League Baseball*. Chicago: Triumph Books, 2003.

Dickson, Paul. *New Dickson Baseball Dictionary*. San Diego, CA: Harcourt Brace & Company, 1999.

Gillette, Gary, and Pete Palmer, eds. *The ESPN Baseball Encyclopedia*. New York: Sterling Publishing, 2008.

Gutman, Dan. *It Ain't Cheatin' If You Don't Get Caught*. New York: Penguin, 1990.

James, Bill. *The New Bill James Historical Baseball Abstract*. New York: Free Press, 2001.

Jones, David, ed. *Deadball Stars of the American League*. Dulles, VA: Potomac Books, 2006.

Kaese, Harold. *A Rooter's Guide to the Red Sox*. Boston: Self-published, 1974.

Luciano, Ron. *The Umpire Strikes Back*. New York: Bantam, 1982.

Maranville, Walter "Rabbit." *Run, Rabbit, Run*. Cleveland, OH: Society for American Baseball Research, 1991.

Mead, William B. *Even the Browns*. Mineola, NY: Dover Publications, 2010.

Nash, Bruce, and Allan Zullo. *The Baseball Hall of Shame 2*. New York: Pocket Books, 1986.

———. *The Baseball Hall of Shame 4*. New York: Pocket Books, 1991.

———. *The Baseball Hall of Shame's Warped Record Book*. New York: Collier, 1991.

Neft, David S., and Richard M. Cohen. *The World Series*. New York: St. Martin's, 1990.

Pietrusza, David, Matthew Silverman, and Michael Gershman, eds. *Baseball: The Biographical Encyclopedia*. Kingston, NY: Total Sports Illustrated, 2000.

Schlossberg, Dan. *The Baseball Catalog*, Millennium ed. Middle Village, NY: Jonathan David Publishers, 2000.

Shatzkin, Mike, ed. *The Ballplayers: Baseball's Ultimate Biographical Reference*. New York: Arbor House, 1990.

Smith, Ira L. *Baseball's Famous First Basemen*. New York: A. S. Barnes and Company, 1956.

Street & Smith's Official 1953 Baseball Yearbook. New York: Condé Nast Publications, 1953.

Street & Smith's Official 1971 Baseball Yearbook. New York: Condé Nast Publications, 1971.

NEWSPAPERS, MAGAZINES, AND JOURNALS

Atlanta Constitution
Baltimore Evening Sun
Baseball Digest
Baseball Magazine
Boston Daily Advertiser
Boston Globe
Boston Herald
Boston Morning Journal
Boston Post
Bridgeport Post (Connecticut)
Brooklyn Daily Eagle
Buffalo Courier
Chicago American
Chicago Daily News
Chicago Daily Tribune
Chicago Evening American
Chicago Sun-Times
Chicago Sunday Tribune
Chicago Times
Chicago Tribune
Cincinnati Commercial Tribune
Cincinnati Enquirer
Cleveland Plain Dealer
Commercial Gazette
Detroit Free Press
Detroit Journal
Detroit News
Detroit Times
Elyria Chronicle Telegram (Ohio)
Frederick Post (Maryland)
Hartford Daily Courant
Hartford Post
Hartford Times
Helena Independent (Montana)
Kansas City Star
Los Angeles Times
Louisville Courier-Journal
Louisville Journal
Milwaukee Journal
National Pastime
New York Clipper
New York Daily News
New York Evening Journal
New York Evening Telegram
New York Evening World
New York Herald Tribune
New York Mirror
New York Sun
New York Telegram
New York Times
New York World-Telegram
New York World-Telegram-Star
Ohio State Journal
Palm Beach Post

Philadelphia Bulletin
Philadelphia Inquirer
Philadelphia Press
Pittsburgh Gazette Times
Pittsburgh Post-Gazette
Portland Press-Herald (Maine)
Riverside Press-Enterprise
San Francisco Chronicle
San Francisco Examiner
Spartanburg Herald-Journal (South Carolina)
Sport
Sporting Life
Sporting News
Sports Collectors Digest
Sports Illustrated
St. Louis Globe-Democrat
St. Louis Post-Dispatch
St. Louis Republican
St. Louis Star
St. Louis Times
Toledo Blade
USA Today Baseball Weekly
Washington Post
Washington Star
Waukesha Daily Freeman (Wisconsin)

ELECTRONIC SOURCES

ESPN www.ESPNLosAngeles.com
Major League Baseball www.MLB.com
Retrosheet www.Retrosheet.org
Yahoo! Sports online http://sports.yahoo.com/

OTHER SOURCES

Boyer, Clete. Presentation at Utica–Cooperstown SABR Chapter meeting, August 5, 2001.
Bragan, Bobby. Telephone interview, January 28, 2008.
Brancato, Al. Speech at the Historical Society of Pennsylvania, February 24, 1990.
Crosetti, Frank. Correspondence with author, 2001.
Giles, Warren G. July 21, 1953, letter from the National League president to National
    League umpires.
Hitchcock, Billy. Correspondence with author, February 2001.
Lewis, Buddy. Correspondence with author, April 2001.
Werber, Billy. Telephone interview, October 8, 2002.

INDEX

ABOUT THE AUTHOR

Bill Deane has been an active member of the Society for American Baseball Research (SABR) since 1982, and served as senior research associate at the National Baseball Hall of Fame from 1986 through 1994. He has authored eight books—including *Baseball Myths: Debating, Debunking, and Disproving Tales from the Diamond* (Scarecrow Press, 2013)—and hundreds of book chapters and articles about baseball. He served as managing editor of *Total Baseball* and has performed as a paid consultant for such authors as Roger Kahn and Bill James, and such organizations as Curtis Management Group and Topps Baseball Cards. In 1989, Deane won the SABR-Macmillan Baseball Research Award for his book *Award Voting*. In 2001, he became the youngest honoree ever of the SABR Salute for research that "has contributed significantly to baseball knowledge." And in 2003, Deane won his regional SABR chapter's Cliff Kachline Award. He resides in Cooperstown, New York.